BUDDHIST ETHICS AND THE BODHISATTVA PATH

Bloomsbury Introductions to World Philosophies

Series Editor:
Monika Kirloskar-Steinbach

Assistant Series Editor:
Leah Kalmanson

Regional Editors:
Nader El-Bizri, James Madaio, Ann A. Pang-White, Takeshi Morisato, Pascah Mungwini, Mickaella Perina, Omar Rivera and Georgina Stewart

Bloomsbury Introductions to World Philosophies delivers primers reflecting exciting new developments in the trajectory of world philosophies. Instead of privileging a single philosophical approach as the basis of comparison, the series provides a platform for diverse philosophical perspectives to accommodate the different dimensions of cross-cultural philosophizing. While introducing thinkers, texts and themes emanating from different world philosophies, each book, in an imaginative and path-breaking way, makes clear how it departs from a conventional treatment of the subject matter.

Titles in the Series:

A Practical Guide to World Philosophies, by Monika Kirloskar-Steinbach and Leah Kalmanson
Daya Krishna and Twentieth-Century Indian Philosophy, by Daniel Raveh
Māori Philosophy, by Georgina Tuari Stewart
Philosophy of Science and The Kyoto School, by Dean Anthony Brink
Tanabe Hajime and the Kyoto School, by Takeshi Morisato
African Philosophy, by Pascah Mungwini
The Zen Buddhist Philosophy of D. T. Suzuki, by Rossa Ó Muireartaigh
Sikh Philosophy, by Arvind-Pal Singh Mandair
The Philosophy of the Brahma-sūtra, by Aleksandar Uskokov
The Philosophy of the Yogasūtra, by Karen O'Brien-Kop
The Life and Thought of H. Odera Oruka, by Gail M. Presbey
Mexican Philosophy for the 21st Century, by Carlos Alberto Sánchez

BUDDHIST ETHICS AND THE BODHISATTVA PATH

Śāntideva on Virtue and Well-Being

Stephen E. Harris

BLOOMSBURY ACADEMIC
LONDON • NEW YORK • OXFORD • NEW DELHI • SYDNEY

BLOOMSBURY ACADEMIC
Bloomsbury Publishing Plc
50 Bedford Square, London, WC1B 3DP, UK
1385 Broadway, New York, NY 10018, USA
29 Earlsfort Terrace, Dublin 2, Ireland

BLOOMSBURY, BLOOMSBURY ACADEMIC and the Diana logo are trademarks of Bloomsbury Publishing Plc

First published in Great Britain 2024

Series design by Louise Dugdale
Cover image © Katrinaku / iStock

A catalogue record for this book is available from the British Library.

A catalog record for this book is available from the Library of Congress.

ISBN: HB: 978-1-3503-7954-1
PB: 978-1-3503-7953-4
ePDF: 978-1-3503-7955-8
eBook: 978-1-3503-7956-5

Series: Bloomsbury Introductions to World Philosophies

Typeset by RefineCatch Limited, Bungay, Suffolk

For William F. Harris and Richard P. Hayes.

CONTENTS

SERIES EDITOR PREFACE

The introductions we include in the World Philosophies series take a single thinker, theme or text and provide a close reading of them. What defines the series is that these are likely to be people or traditions that you have not yet encountered in your study of philosophy. By choosing to include them you broaden your understanding of ideas about the self, knowledge and the world around us. Each book presents unexplored pathways into the study of world philosophies. Instead of privileging a single philosophical approach as the basis of comparison, each book accommodates the many different dimensions of cross-cultural philosophizing. While the choice of terms used by the individual volumes may indeed carry a local inflection, they encourage critical thinking about philosophical plurality. Each book strikes a balance between locality and globality.

In *Buddhist Ethics and the Bodhisattva Path: Śāntideva on Virtue and Well-Being*, Stephen Harris offers a rich and fascinating study of core themes found in the *Guide to the Practices of Awakening (Bodhicaryāvatāra)* composed by the eighth century Mahāyana monk, Śāntideva. Harris foregrounds Śāntideva's attempt to balance the Buddhist view on metaphysical selflessness with morally conducive ways of motivation that can enable one to pursue a multi-life project dedicated to moral perfection. He analyzes how Śāntideva bases his project on understanding the qualities of generosity (*dāna*), patience (*kṣānti*), compassion (*karuṇā*) and wisdom (*prajñā*) and provides therapeutic tools to work toward their perfection so that their implementation can effectively eradicate the suffering of all beings.

ACKNOWLEDGMENTS

The ideas for this book began forming during my dissertation research at the University of New Mexico. I owe an enormous debt of gratitude to the entire philosophy faculty for years of training and support. Particular thanks go to my dissertation committee members: John Taber, Iain Thomson, and Anne Baril, as well as my external member, Damien Keown. Thanks as well to Roy Perrett, by whom I was introduced to Śāntideva as a philosophical interlocutor while a student at the University of Hawaiʻi. Thanks also to Arindam Chakrabarti for philosophical guidance during those years.

I am thankful for good philosophical conversation and support from my colleagues at Leiden University's Institute for Philosophy. Particular thanks go to my friends in the intercultural philosophy group: Ahab Bdaiwi, Douglas Berger, Michael Eze, and Jingjing Li. I also benefited from discussing Śāntideva's ideas with my students when teaching Buddhist Ethics courses for the university. Thanks in particular to the students in my Spring 2020 seminar on Śāntideva's *Guide*. This book was completed during a teaching sabbatical funded by Leiden University, for which I am enormously grateful.

Amod Lele and Perry Schmidt-Leukel both read the entire manuscript, offering many perceptive comments and saving me from numerous errors. Jay Garfield, at several points, offered insightful criticism which greatly improved the result. Other philosophical friends and interlocutors who have contributed ideas in conversation or writing to the development of the book include (but are certainly not limited to!): William Barnes, Henk Blezer, Nicolas Bommarito, André van der Braak, Adam Buben, Barbara Clayton, Daniele Cuneo, Gordon Davis, Amy Donahue, Douglas Duckworth, William Edelglass, Christopher Framarin, Charles Goodman, Laura Guerrero, Maria Heim, Stephen Jenkins, Malcolm Keating, Joseph Markowski, Emily McRae, Ethan Mills, Reiko Ohnuma, Krupa Patel, Chiara Robbiano, Shalini Sinha, Phillip Schoenberg, and Mark Siderits. Thanks also go to the Buddhist-Platonist research group, of which I have been fortunate to be a part. I am grateful to Amber Carpenter and Pierre-Julien Harter for facilitating this group, and to all the members for their comments on my work.

My thanks go as well to Monika Kirloskar-Steinbach, the series editor for Bloomsbury Introductions to World Philosophies, as well as senior Bloomsbury editor Colleen Coalter. Both were a pleasure to work with, and I am grateful for their many valuable suggestions during the editing process. My thanks also to the entire editorial and production staff at Bloomsbury Academic, and to three anonymous reviewers for their helpful critiques.

Most of all, I am grateful to Richard Hayes. Richard chaired my dissertation on Śāntideva that formed an origin point for many of the ideas expressed in this book. Along the way, he offered years of wise advice, encouragement, and good humor. Somehow, to my great fortune, his mentorship transformed seamlessly into friendship as I graduated and began my career. I am thankful that he allowed me to co-dedicate this book to him.

INTRODUCTION

1. The aims of the book

Among the most significant contributions the Indian Buddhist tradition makes to the study of philosophy is its nuanced moral psychology of pathological emotions (*kleśas*), which cause or constitute suffering, and the virtuous mental states (*kuśala-dharmas*) which eliminate them.[1] This book provides an introduction to Buddhist moral psychology and virtue theory through a close reading of one of its most influential proponents, the eighth-century CE Mahāyāna monastic, Śāntideva.[2] Śāntideva's most influential text, the *Guide to the Practices of Awakening* (*Bodhicaryāvatāra*; hereafter, *Guide* or BCA), had great influence on premodern Indian Buddhism, and in contemporary times has attained the status of a religious and philosophical classic. The chapters which follow provide studies of central virtues as presented by Śāntideva in the *Guide*, showing how each contributes to his account of well-being. This will also require exploring other reoccurring themes of Śāntideva's moral thought, including the impoverished nature of ordinary conceptions of happiness, the dysfunctionality of self-centered desire, and the ethical entailments of accepting a Buddhist ontology of dependently arisen impermanent selfless entities.

A complementary goal of this book is to analyze a theme central to Śāntideva's moral thought: his account of the relation between altruism and self-interest.[3] As I introduce in detail in the following section, Śāntideva argues that the only route to deep and lasting happiness is to dedicate oneself with intensely focused commitment to the happiness of others. In Buddhist terminology, he holds that liberation from the sufferings of saṃsāra requires embracing and progressing on the bodhisattva path.[4] A bodhisattva is the being (*sattva*) who strives for full Buddhist awakening (*bodhi*) for the sake of eliminating the suffering of all sentient life. This requires committing to a multi-lifetime process of developing virtuous character, during which the bodhisattva will undergo numerous hardships for the sake of others. It is a study of four of these virtues, the qualities of generosity (*dāna*), patience (*kṣānti*), compassion (*karuṇā*), and wisdom (*prajñā*), which is the central task of this book. We will see that these virtues have a dual role: they enable the bodhisattva to effectively remove others' suffering, while also benefiting the bodhisattva themself, in part by eliminating the propensities for the arising of their own pathological emotions.

The remaining sections of this introduction offer background that will be helpful for readers unfamiliar with Śāntideva, or the Buddhist philosophical tradition. In the section which follows, I introduce Śāntideva's claim that altruistic commitment and the development of the bodhisattva's virtues are the only reliable means to achieving one's own happiness. The next section explains who Śāntideva was, and introduces the *Guide* as well as his other text, the *Training Anthology*. I then offer a brief introduction to the relationship between Mahāyāna and early Buddhism and give a short explanation of some central Buddhist concepts which are presupposed by Śāntideva. There are a number of excellent introductions to Indian Buddhism, so I keep these explanations to a minimum.[5] Next, I comment on the universal applicability of Śāntideva's moral reasoning. I then discuss the role of karmic causality, Buddhist cosmology, and rebirth in Śāntideva's writing, and explain why his incorporation of these concepts into his moral theory should not impede cross-cultural engagement with his thought.

2. Altruism and self-interest in Śāntideva's ethics

A striking feature of many Indian Mahāyāna Buddhist ethical texts is their integration of a radically altruistic conception of moral perfection with the position that this moral development benefits the aspirant.[6] Few Buddhists illustrate this theme as forcefully as the eighth-century monk, Śāntideva, for whom the relation between altruism and self-interest is a repeating theme:

> All those who suffer in the world do so because they desire their own happiness. All those who are happy in the world are this way because they desire the happiness of others. (BCA 8:129)[7]

This verse, coming toward the end of Śāntideva's masterwork, forcefully states two of its central themes. First, suffering arises because of desire, and therefore restraining desire is a requirement for attaining happiness. Śāntideva here affirms the central early Buddhist soteriological prescription presented most influentially as the second noble truth: the cause of suffering is craving. Revealing of his Mahāyānist commitments, Śāntideva integrates this claim with a second: it is selfish desires which are destructive of one's well-being.[8] To attain happiness, therefore, desire need not be eliminated, but must be reformed into altruism, the wish for the happiness of the world.

Śāntideva's emphasis on the self-benefiting nature of altruism and the bodhisattva's virtues is one of the most prominent themes in the *Guide* (BCA 1:8; 6:133; 7:27–30; 7:44; 8:107–8; 8:126–36). Progressing on the bodhisattva path entails undergoing numerous difficult trainings, as well as remaining in the realm of rebirth for eons.[9] For this reason, many Buddhists hold that the bodhisattva path is supererogatory, a worthy goal but far beyond the ability of ordinary persons, who should instead follow the early Buddhist path and aim at liberation for themselves. By contrast, as we will see, Śāntideva holds that the only rational way of life is to adopt the bodhisattva path and commit to eliminating the suffering of all.[10] Remarkably, he claims that this *benefits* the bodhisattva himself. One of his most explicit statements of this position is given toward the *Guide*'s beginning:

> *Bodhicitta* should never be abandoned by those desiring to escape from the many sufferings of existence, by those desiring to eliminate the evil predicament of sentient beings, and by those desiring to experience many kinds of enjoyments. (BCA 1:8)

Bodhicitta, literally the thought or aspiration (*citta*) for awakening (*bodhi*), is the bodhisattva's root motivation to attain buddhahood in order to benefit all sentient beings.[11] The passage introduces three motivations to develop it and thereby take up the bodhisattva path. Strikingly, the term Śāntideva uses to refer to all three is *kāma*, which is naturally translated as "desire," suggesting the theme of refining motivation which reoccurs throughout the *Guide*. The third line claims that developing *bodhicitta* allows the bodhisattva to work most effectively to remove the evil predicament (*vyasana*) of sentient beings, that is to liberate them from saṃsāra. This makes sense, given that she trains to develop virtues such as generosity and patience which will enable her to help others. The other two benefits of *bodhicitta* are initially rather puzzling. In the first line, Śāntideva claims that those wanting to escape from the suffering (*duḥkha*) of existence (*bhava*) should develop it. This is surprising, since the bodhisattva, motivated by *bodhicitta*, delays liberation from rebirth in order to progress on the bodhisattva path. It would seem that the early Buddhist goal of individual liberation would be the natural endpoint for one whose deepest motivation is to quickly escape from saṃsāra. The final line refers to experiencing many enjoyments (*saukhya*). The reference here is to the ordinary happiness experienced by persons in saṃsāra, such as pleasant rebirths and material prosperity. Śāntideva is claiming that even ordinary goods can only truly be enjoyed by one who has transformed their motivation from self-interest to compassion for others and dedicated themselves to developing the qualities of buddhahood.

The verse therefore claims that developing *bodhicitta* and progressing on the bodhisattva path both prepares the bodhisattva to benefit others, while also benefiting the bodhisattva herself. As I will show in the chapters to come, fully eliminating the bodhisattva's vulnerability to suffering and enabling her to interact fruitfully with material goods are both results of developing the virtues of the bodhisattva path. Moreover, the verse suggests another of the repeating themes of Śāntideva's *Guide*: that of the gradated path. Śāntideva accepts that persons may enter into bodhisattva training with various motivations; there is no bar to pursuing buddhahood at least initially for egoistic reasons. The path, although long and challenging, has been constructed so that benefits accrue at every stage of its training (see BCA 7:20–30). It is not, in other words, demanding, in the sense that the bodhisattva is never asked to sacrifice her own well-being while progressing toward buddhahood.

Śāntideva's strongest representation of the self-benefiting properties of altruistic commitment and the bodhisattva's virtues is given in the *Guide*'s eighth chapter, in a pair of verses which use Buddhist cosmological imagery to portray the strength and depth of the bodhisattva's compassion:

> The bodhisattvas with cultivated (*bhāvita*) minds and equal concern for the suffering of others dive into the Avīci hell like swans into a pool of lotuses. (BCA 8:107)
>
> When sentient beings are liberated, they become oceans of joy (*prāmodya*). They alone find fulfillment. Why would they seek insipid liberation? (BCA 8:108)

The reference to the hell realms may initially suggest that the passage expresses religious aspirations with limited philosophical interest. Śāntideva, however, is using this cosmological language to present philosophical positions central to his moral thought. Buddhists hold that beings are reborn in hell realms because of past negative actions, where they suffer until their negative karma is exhausted.[12] Śāntideva depicts the bodhisattva, by contrast, as voluntarily visiting hell, thereby illustrating the depth of her compassion. Moreover, the bodhisattva making this incredible choice is described as "cultivated" (*bhāvita*), indicating her development of virtuous character, which protects her from suffering, even in this terrible place. Instead, she is portrayed as attaining fulfillment (*paryāptaṁ*) and erupting into joy when she succeeds at liberating sentient beings from suffering.

In the cosmological imagery of the bodhisattva's descent into hell, therefore, we should recognize Śāntideva as making two cross-culturally important philosophical claims, each of which is central to his conception of well-being. First, the high-level bodhisattva can flourish in any circumstance whatsoever.[13] Like the ancient Greek school of Stoicism, Śāntideva holds that the fully virtuous person is impervious to misfortune.[14] Second, we find Śāntideva repeating the claim made in the verses cited above, in which the bodhisattva's flourishing is linked to his dedication to benefit others. In all these verses, Śāntideva forges an extremely close connection between altruism and personal happiness. As this study progresses, we will see that Śāntideva differs from many ethicists in holding that the virtuous individual experiences absolutely no tension between self-interest and altruistic commitment. In this book I want to make philosophical sense of these two claims, both of which are central to Śāntideva's ethics: that fully virtuous persons are immune to suffering, and that radical altruistic dedication to others also benefits oneself. As we will see in the chapters that follow, this should not only be of interest to students of Buddhism, since Śāntideva provides cross-culturally accessible arguments for many of his central ethical positions.

I will argue that Śāntideva's views on the self-benefiting properties of *bodhicitta* and the bodhisattva path are most centrally explained by his understanding of the relation between virtue and well-being. Like many ancient Greek thinkers, he believes that virtue is the primary constituent of human happiness.[15] According to Śāntideva, suffering is primarily constituted by habitually reoccurring unstable mental states, caused by delusion about reality, which in Sanskrit are called *kleśas*, and which I will usually translate as "pathological emotions," or "psychopathologies."[16] The most pernicious of the pathological emotions are delusion (*avidyā*), craving (*tṛṣṇā*), and anger (*krodha*), and these are eliminated by their opposites, the virtuous mental states of wisdom (*prajñā*), generosity (*dāna*), compassion (*karuṇā*), and patience (*kṣānti*).[17] The primary purpose of this book is to illustrate the role of virtuous character and virtuous mental states in Śāntideva's conception of well-being, through providing studies of these four virtues. This will answer the two questions just introduced: it will illustrate how the highly developed bodhisattva's altruistic motivations and virtuous character benefit her, where these benefits include protection from all forms of suffering.

My exploration of Śāntideva's account of virtue will take place over seven chapters. In the first, I introduce the main features of Śāntideva's virtue theory, including his understanding of the perfections (*pāramitas*), the habitually reoccurring mental states which constitute the bodhisattva's virtuous experience, as well as their opposites, the pathological emotions, which constitute suffering. I also address an objection against taking Buddhist accounts of virtue as an important aspect of their moral theory: the concern that Buddhist metaphysical commitments to selflessness and radical impermanence entail they cannot be understood as developing a rich account of virtuous character. In response, I argue that the Abhidharma Buddhist account of reliably repeating casually connected mental states provides a sufficient metaphysical basis for theorizing conventionally existing virtuous habitual dispositions, for authors such as Śāntideva. The chapter also introduces the phenomenological aspect of Śāntideva's account of virtuous response and summarizes the techniques he uses to develop the bodhisattva's character, which include argumentation, imaginative visualization, and ritual.

The next three chapters provide studies of three of the four virtues which are the central focus of this book. The second chapter reconstructs Śāntideva's account of generosity, which he characterizes as the elimination of craving from all possessions, conceiving of them instead as offered to all beings. Generosity benefits the bodhisattva by preventing the pernicious effects of craving, and by enabling him to interact with material possessions without fear of loss. My third chapter turns to the perfection of patience, which according to Śāntideva is a calm state of mind that enables the bodhisattva to remain tranquil in times of difficulty. It benefits the bodhisattva by eliminating anger, which Śāntideva argues always damages its possessor, as well as by enabling the bodhisattva to endure any amount of physical pain without mental suffering. We will find the elimination of craving reoccur as a theme in this chapter also, given Śāntideva's claim that anger can only be fully overcome when selfish desires have been transformed into *bodhicitta*. The fourth chapter turns to Śāntideva's account of compassion, which he understands as the aspiration for others to be happy and free from suffering. Compassion benefits the bodhisattva by weakening the deepest form of craving, self-grasping (*ātmaparigraha*), the spontaneous wish to prioritize one's own benefit that arises from the delusive belief in an enduring self. In so doing, it eliminates the mental suffering of fear. Compassion also eradicates the pathological social emotions of envy, competitiveness, and arrogant pride, and thereby harmonizes the bodhisattva's relationships.

My fifth chapter analyzes the role that various kinds of virtuous joy play in the *Guide*. These mental states are not themselves perfections, but are valuable in promoting the development of virtue, or in accompanying virtuous mental states. Śāntideva is often trenchant in his critique of the pernicious nature of sense pleasures, which stimulate craving and anger, and this chapter provides an important corrective against a too austere reading of the *Guide*. It also shows that virtuous joy, for Śāntideva, is a matter of moral importance; in fact, many of the perfections cannot be stably experienced unless the mind is happy. The sixth chapter offers a partial reading of Śāntideva's difficult chapter on wisdom, which he understands as the realization of the lack of intrinsic existence (*svabhāva*) of all phenomena. My focus in this chapter is in showing how wisdom transforms the bodhisattva's experience of conventionally real entities, resulting in the elimination of the pathological emotions, and thereby completing the work of the other perfections. I close my study with a brief treatment of the last chapter of the *Guide*, in which the bodhisattva dedicates the karmic merit she has created to all beings. In addition to directing karmic causality, I argue that the mental offerings depicted in this chapter continue the work of the main part of the text, in developing the virtuous dispositions of compassion, generosity, and *bodhicitta*.

Each of these chapters analyze some aspect of Śāntideva's position that the virtuous character of the bodhisattva, which facilitates helping others, is also deeply conducive to his own happiness. As we will see, restraining selfish desire and cultivating altruistic motivation reoccur as central components of Śāntideva's characterization of each of these virtues. Most of the chapters are also intended to act as relatively self-standing studies of the virtue in question. Topics treated in the chapters differ, given that Śāntideva's own interests vary depending on the perfection he is characterizing; however, at least some attention will always be given to defining the relevant virtue, to illustrating the trainings Śāntideva provides to develop it, and to showing how it weakens or eliminates one or more of the pathological emotions.

3. Śāntideva and his works

Very little is known about Śāntideva's life. He is generally accepted to have lived between the late seventh and mid-eighth centuries CE. Traditional Tibetan biographies claim that he spent much of his career at the Indian monastic university of Nālandā. Almost all commentators agree that he was a proponent of the Mahāyāna Madhyamaka school of philosophy, whose central metaphysical commitment is the tenet of universal emptiness (*śūnyatā*) of intrinsic existence (*svabhāva*) of all entities. His two extant texts, the *Guide to the Practices of Awakening* (*Bodhicaryāvatāra*) and the *Training Anthology* (*Śikṣāsamuccaya*) are training manuals for the development of the virtues of the bodhisattva, the being who takes a vow to achieve full buddhahood in order to liberate all sentient beings. The influence of the shorter text, the *Guide*, is attested to by the existence of numerous Indian and Tibetan commentaries (Williams 1998, 4–5). Recently, it has undergone a resurgence of popularity, with several influential contemporary practitioners of Tibetan Buddhism, including the 14th Dalai Lama and Pema Chödrön, writing commentaries on it (Dalai Lama XIV 1994 and 1997, Chödrön 2007). The last several decades have also seen an increase in academic attention to the *Guide*; it is often characterized as the most significant text for the study of Indian Buddhist ethics (Goodman 2009, Garfield 2012). By contrast, until recently the *Training Anthology* received relatively little academic attention, and almost no philosophical study. A new translation of this text by Charles Goodman (2016a) as well as several recent important studies (Mahoney 2002, Clayton 2006, Harrison 2007, Lele 2007, Mrozik 2007) have increased its academic visibility.

The canonical version of the *Guide* is composed of ten chapters that total 913 verses. This recension has been the subject of almost all extant commentaries and has been translated into English recently a number of times (Śāntideva 1970, 1979, 1995, 1997, 2001, 2006, 2015, 2019).[18] A shorter version of the *Guide*, composed of nine chapters and 701.5 verses, is preserved in Tibetan translation; no complete critical edition and translation of this version has been published. Akira Saito's analysis of differences between the two versions suggests that parts of the longer text are later additions, and are perhaps not original to Śāntideva; in particular, the eighth and ninth chapters have been dramatically increased in length in the longer canonical version (Saito 1993).[19] My method in this study is to take the longer version, as it has come down to us, as my object of analysis; I do not appeal to the history of its formation in my interpretation of the text.

Śāntideva describes the *Guide* as an introduction (*avatāra*) to the training discipline (*saṁvara*) of the bodhisattvas (BCA 1:1). The first four chapters focus on *bodhicitta*, the motivation to attain full awakening for the sake of all beings. The first chapter explains *bodhicitta*'s benefits; the second and third present the Mahāyāna ritual of unexcelled worship (*anuttarapūja*), at the end of which the bodhisattva takes their vow (BCA 3:22–3:23). The fourth offers trainings to develop non-negligence (*apramāda*), a mental state which protects the nascent bodhisattva's commitment to attain buddhahood. The next five chapters focus on developing the perfections (*pāramitās*), the central virtues of the bodhisattva path. Chapter five cultivates mindfulness (*smṛti*) and introspection (*saṃprajanya*), two virtuous qualities of awareness which Śāntideva takes to constitute the essence of the perfection of ethical discipline (*śīla*).[20] The next four chapters each focus on a single perfection: patience (*kṣānti*: chapter six); effort (*vīrya*: chapter seven); meditative concentration (*dhyāna*: chapter eight);[21] and wisdom (*prajñā*: chapter nine). The text concludes with a short dedication during which all progress made toward awakening is offered to sentient beings. The text contains no chapter on the perfection of generosity (*dāna*), a surprising omission for which there is no obvious explanation. There are, however, several verses on generosity scattered throughout the text (see especially 3:11, 5:9–10, 7:25–6).

Like the *Guide*, Śāntideva's other text, the *Training Anthology*, provides exercises to develop the virtuous qualities of the bodhisattva. The text differs from the *Guide*, however, in presenting its account of the bodhisattva path in a sparse frame of twenty-seven root verses. These verses are then amplified by numerous quotations from Mahāyāna sutras, which make up most of the text's length. These quotations are themselves occasionally supplemented by additional commentary in Śāntideva's own voice.[22]

Śāntideva's account of the self-benefiting properties of altruistic commitment and virtue is most systematically developed in the *Guide* and my study focuses primarily on this text. However, I also draw upon the *Training Anthology* at two places. The first is my analysis of Śāntideva's account of generosity in my second chapter. Although there are several important verses on generosity in the *Guide*, it lacks a chapter of its own or systematic development in that text. In contrast, the *Training Anthology* provides a chapter-length treatment of giving, including numerous relevant Mahāyāna sutra quotations. I therefore draw upon its longer and more systematic treatment in reconstructing Śāntideva's account of giving and its self-beneficial properties. Second, in my third chapter, focused on Śāntideva's account of patience, I consider a meditational attainment called "All Things are Overcome by Happiness" (*sarva-dharma-sukha-ākrānta*), in which the bodhisattva becomes impervious to physical pain. This meditative state is described in the *Training Anthology* but not in the *Guide*. As does Śāntideva's Sanskrit commenter, Prajñākaramati, I argue that this meditational attainment should be understood as the final outcome of the trainings provided to withstand physical pain that are given in the *Guide*.

At several places in my study, I also draw upon Śāntideva's most influential Indian commentator, Prajñākaramati (*c.* tenth century CE), as an aid in understanding his insights. Prajñākaramati's *Pañjikā* is the only commentary to the *Guide* still extant in Sanskrit, and has had immense influence on the way the text has been understood in India and Tibet. It is natural, therefore, to incorporate his explanations in developing a stronger understanding of Śāntideva's moral thought.[23]

4. *Early Buddhism and the Mahāyāna movement*

Although we are not clear about what his exact dates were, the historical Buddha probably founded the religion of Buddhism somewhere in the fifth century BCE. The goal of Buddhist practice, as illustrated in the earliest texts that are available to us, is to liberate oneself from the round of rebirth that is saṃsāra, and the various kinds of suffering experienced within it. The Buddhist path is represented in these texts, as well as throughout the entire tradition, by the four noble truths. The first truth, that of suffering (Pali: *dukkha* / Sanskrit: *duḥkha*), is the claim that the experience of non-liberated beings is pervaded by both obvious and subtle forms of suffering, which include physical and emotional pain, and continued rebirth in saṃsāra.[24] The second truth claims that the cause of our suffering is craving (*taṇhā/tṛṣṇā*). This craving itself arises because of delusion (*avijjā/avidyā*), referring to both a mistaken intellectual belief that phenomena are permanent, independent, and able to provide lasting satisfaction, as well as the cognitive processes by which these non-existent attributes are superimposed upon transitory and dependent entities. The third noble truth, nirvāṇa (Pali: *nibbāna*), represents the cessation of craving and delusion which cause suffering and rebirth. The final noble truth of path (*magga/mārga*) is composed of the Buddhist teachings and training practices by which liberation from suffering is attained. All these early Buddhist insights are adopted by Mahāyāna Buddhists like Śāntideva.

Already in the early Buddhist canon, there are references to the historical Buddha being, in his past lives, a bodhisattva, that is a being (*sattva*) aiming toward enlightenment (*bodhi*). The contrast here is to the *arhat*, or worthy one, the spiritual ideal emphasized in early Buddhist texts, who eliminates her own suffering and escapes rebirth. The bodhisattva, by contrast, aims at a higher state of awakening whereby she can teach beings effectively and lead them to liberation. Although the historical Buddha was said to be a bodhisattva in his past lives, early Buddhist texts provide little if any encouragement for ordinary persons to aspire to this goal.

Recent scholarship has shown that for much of its history in India, the Mahāyāna movement was a doctrinal development existing within early Buddhist communities, rather than a separately existing school.[25] A key piece of evidence for this view is that the Mahāyāna schools have no ordination lineages of their own. Mahāyāna monks like Nāgārjuna, then, must have been ordained in the lineages of the early Buddhist schools. What this strongly suggests is that early Mahāyāna monks lived and practiced alongside their mainstream Buddhist counterparts. What distinguished monks who came to identify with the Mahāyāna movement was the gradual acceptance of a new group of Mahāyāna scriptures (*sūtras*) and certain key doctrines emphasized within them. One such tenet is the Mahāyāna doctrine of emptiness (*śūnyatā*), an expansion of the early Buddhist doctrine of metaphysical selflessness (*anātman*). For Madhyamaka Buddhists like Śāntideva, this means that all entities are empty (*śūnya*) of intrinsic existence (*svabhāva*).[26] In brief, this means that they exist relationally, as causally dependent on other entities for their reality, and conceptually dependent on human concepts and practices for their identity. Such relational entities are said to be conventionally existent; ultimately, however, the Mādhyamika holds that they are empty of intrinsic existence.[27]

The doctrinal development in the Mahāyāna movement that is most central to my study is the greater emphasis placed on the role of the bodhisattva, the saint who develops *bodhicitta*, the aspiration to attain full buddhahood in order to liberate all sentient beings. In many non-Mahāyāna early Buddhist texts, there is not yet a clear distinction between the awakening of an *arhat* whose focus is on his own liberation, and that of a fully awakened buddha who has completed the bodhisattva path.[28] As both Mahāyāna and early Buddhist traditions continued to develop, however, the awakening of a buddha became distinguished from that of an *arhat* in that a buddha destroys the defilements (*āśravas*) of delusion (*avidyā*). As a result, buddhas and high-level bodhisattvas gain supernormal powers, including a limited omniscience that allows them to perceive the karmic propensities of all beings, and thereby work most effectively for their benefit. Likewise, there is more emphasis in Mahāyāna texts like Śāntideva's *Guide* on other-regarding virtues like compassion (*karuṇā*) and generosity (*dāna*). Of course, it is also only the bodhisattva who develops the root bodhisattva virtue of *bodhicitta*. As time progresses, Mahāyāna texts such as the *Lotus Sutra* begin to denigrate the early Buddhist emphasis on liberation for oneself, referencing this motivation as *hīnayāna*, a derogatory term that means inferior.[29] The *Lotus Sutra* also claims that there is only one path to liberation, that of the bodhisattva as portrayed by Mahāyāna Buddhism, and one possible spiritual attainment, that of full buddhahood attained by following the bodhisattva path.

As we will see in many of the chapters to follow, Śāntideva's relation to early Buddhist teachings is complex. Early Buddhist insights into dependent origination, suffering, and metaphysical selflessness are incorporated into many of his arguments regarding well-being, the value of the bodhisattva path, the impoverished nature of desire and so on. Nevertheless, Śāntideva is sharply critical of the early Buddhist goal of liberation for oneself. He refers to the aspiration for individual liberation from suffering derogatorily as *arasika*, meaning insipid, or literally "without taste."[30] Furthermore, he offers arguments that prioritizing one's own happiness is irrational, implying that all beings should commit to the bodhisattva path.[31] In addition, he argues that the early Buddhist path cannot wholly eliminate craving, and therefore has less benefit for its practitioners than the bodhisattva path.[32]

5. *The universality of Śāntideva's moral claims*

Śāntideva's arguments for the value of bodhisattva virtues and the superiority of the bodhisattva path, in contrast to the *arhat* ideal of early Buddhism, point to a more general issue related to his moral thought. As we will see in the chapters to come, most of Śāntideva's arguments in the *Guide* are universal, meant to convince all persons, regardless of religious commitment, of the truth of his moral claims.[33] In my third chapter, for instance, we will examine his arguments for the harmfulness of anger; and in my fourth chapter, we turn to his argument for the irrationality of selfish behavior.[34] These arguments appeal to premises that Śāntideva thinks any reasonable person should accept; for instance, he uses introspective description to convince the interlocuter that anger mentally disturbs the mind (BCA 6:3), appeals to rational consistency in arguing for the impermissibility of selfishness (BCA 8:90–103), and claims that anger is irrational in that it arises based upon the false belief that harm is caused by autonomous agents (BCA 6:22–31). Śāntideva, therefore, is not usually presenting positions which he takes to apply only to those who have joined the bodhisattva path, although his arguments suggest that persons outside the path should adopt it. This invites the question of why he thinks these universal claims are consistent with his acceptance of the Madhyamaka doctrine of emptiness. As a Mādhyamika, he cannot appeal to a moral realist position, in which the mind-independent reality of intrinsically good and bad moral properties accounts for the truth of ethical claims (Finnigan and Tanaka 2015, 322–3).

This question largely parallels frequently raised concerns about emptiness in relation to Madhyamaka metaphysics and epistemology (Tillemans 2010/11). The Mādhyamika claims that the emptiness of all phenomena is consistent with the conventional existence of persons, material objects, dependable causal relationships, reliable epistemic functioning of conventional means of knowledge and so on. The basic Madhyamaka position, developed by Nāgārjuna and Candrakīrti, is that emptiness is not equivalent to non-existence; rather to be empty is to exist relationally, in dependence on causal conditions, one's parts, and conceptual labeling. There is a rich literature by both classical commentators and contemporary scholars regarding the adequacy of this response.[35]

Madhyamaka ethics rests on parallel claims about the compatibility of a metaphysics of emptiness and conventionally real moral properties. To accept that virtuous and afflictive mental states are empty does not entail they do not exist, nor that they do not possess positive or negative value, but rather that they are dependently arisen.[36] Śāntideva claims that there is no reasonable possibility of disagreeing about the badness of suffering, for example, regardless of its merely conventional status. Moreover, its empty nature does nothing to weaken the fact that we should eliminate it.[37] Claims like this, and about the beneficial value of the virtuous mental states, provide the basis on which he builds his moral thought. I return to this issue at the conclusion of my sixth chapter, where I consider Śāntideva's response to nihilistic concerns about the necessity of eliminating empty suffering.

There remain important metaethical questions about the compatibility of a metaphysics of emptiness and Śāntideva's account of virtue and well-being which I will not discuss in depth. Whether an appeal to the conventional existence of moral properties can provide sufficient justification for moral claims, for instance, deserves careful attention.[38] Śāntideva's *Guide* does not consider metaethical questions systematically, however, and my study is intended primarily as an analysis of his thought in this text. Moreover, normative argumentation in any tradition is often conducted without explicit discussion of the metaethical questions that such reasoning raises. Therefore, for the most part, I will not engage in metaethical analysis in this study.[39] My hope is that the explication of Śāntideva's account of well-being and virtue given in the chapters to follow will act as a resource for future discussions that take these topics as their focus.

6. *Karmic causation and the hell realms*

One of the initial challenges to working philosophically with Indian Buddhist moral texts from a cross-cultural standpoint is their frequent appeal to karmic causality, thereby claiming that morally good intentions and actions produce beneficial circumstances and good rebirths in the future, while morally bad intentions and actions do the opposite.[40] We find that Śāntideva refers to karmic causality frequently in the *Guide*; in particular he often references rebirth in a hell realm as a consequence of being dominated by the pathological emotions and performing harmful actions under their influence. Usually, these appeals are incorporated into a training to develop virtue; for instance, contemplating bad future rebirths is used as a tool for maintaining mindful awareness (BCA 5:7–8; 5:20; 5:27–9); and rebirth in hell is said to result from anger, thereby strengthening the bodhisattva's motivation to prevent it (BCA 6:73–4). Given the frequency with which Śāntideva and other Buddhist authors appeal to non-natural karmic causation, however, we may initially wonder to what extent their ethical thought is relevant outside a Buddhist context, where presuppositions about the functioning of karmic causality will usually not be shared.

One of my aims in this study is to show that much of Śāntideva's moral thought is cross-culturally accessible and that therefore his appeals to karmic causation and rebirth should not prevent cross-cultural engagement with his insights. It is helpful to keep in mind that the root meaning of karma is action, and therefore to talk of karmic consequence is simply to talk of the consequences of intentional actions. In addition, the Buddhist term "karma" has a broader semantic range than the corresponding English term, "action." According to

Buddhists, not only physical and verbal actions have karmic effects, but also mental responses, such as the wish to harm others, or to remove suffering and so on. Śāntideva's basic claim when discussing karmic consequences, therefore, is that what we do with our body, speech, and mind has consequences for ourselves and for others. Throughout the text, he argues that the consequences of virtuous mental responses and actions are positive, while the effects of the psychopathologies are harmful.

Moreover, as I will show in detail in the chapters to come, many of the positive and negative consequences of the virtuous mental states and the pathological emotions described by Śāntideva do not depend on karmic causation operating outside ordinary physical or psychological regularities.[41] He frequently references the harmful psychological and social effects of pathological emotions. For example, all the pathological emotions disrupt and destabilize the mind (BCA 4:26–9). Anger is painful, impedes sleep, and damages our social relationships (BCA 6:3). Likewise, craving is insatiable, for upon attaining its object, it transforms into paranoid fear and possessive clinging (BCA 8:5–7). These claims require phenomenological introspection, matched with careful attention to social experience, to assess their validity; none of them depend on a belief in non-natural karmic causality and rebirth.

Non-natural karmic causality *is* of deep importance to Śāntideva's moral thought, however, and I will refer to it frequently in reconstructing his arguments. Nevertheless, we will see that the core conceptions of each of the perfections and the pathological emotions can be articulated without reference to it. Very often the role of karmic causation in the *Guide* is to extend and magnify positions which have already been established through argumentation or phenomenological description. For instance, Śāntideva takes anger to be the mental state which wishes to hurt sentient beings. It is harmful in that it disrupts the mind, mentally hurts, artificially narrows our focus and distorts our thinking, inspires harmful actions, ruins social relationships—and it causes negative rebirths in a future life (see BCA chapter 6 and the third chapter of this study). The karmic consequence of negative rebirth in this case vastly magnifies the badness of anger, but the core conception of what the pathological emotion is and why it is harmful is articulated through psychological introspection and social observation in a way that is cross-culturally accessible.

Moreover, Buddhists hold that there are strong connections between psychological states and cosmology, and this suggests that there are multiple layers of meaning contained in Śāntideva's references to karmic causality and rebirth in hell realms. In Buddhist cosmology, the mind of a being born in hell is dominated by anger and suffering. Descriptions of the hell realms, therefore, have a phenomenological function, in illustrating the nature of human minds that are overwhelmed by anger and suffering.[42] In so doing they provide evidence for Śāntideva's claims about the harmfulness of the pathological emotions. I am not suggesting that Śāntideva did not consider the hell realms to be literal places of rebirth; nevertheless, we should recognize that his cosmological descriptions also have phenomenological content which is cross-culturally and philosophically relevant when assessing the reasonableness of his positions. I return to this point in my first chapter, when I introduce the pathological emotions in more detail.

This study will therefore show that the naturalistic elements of Śāntideva's defense of his conception of well-being are much stronger than might initially be thought. Nevertheless, I will not present a naturalized version of Śāntideva's thought in what follows.[43] This is because appeals to karmic causality and its results in future lives provide important premises he incorporates repeatedly into his arguments. We will understand his reasoning better if we attend to the role they play in supporting his conclusions. Moreover, Śāntideva is doing good philosophy in his own cultural context when he appeals to karmic causation, given that belief in karma is a shared presupposition among most of his potential readers. Considering both naturalistic and non-natural lines of argumentation presented in the *Guide* helps us better evaluate his skill as a philosopher. Nevertheless, given that my own interests are primarily the cross-culturally accessible elements of Śāntideva's account of virtue, I will tend to emphasize appeals to non-natural aspects of karmic causation less frequently than the psychological and social effects of the virtues and the pathological emotions.

7. *Multi-life commitment and liberation*

This book is intended as a study of the virtuous mental states and character dispositions that the bodhisattva develops as he progresses toward buddhahood. Before turning to Śāntideva's account of virtue, however, there are two issues relevant to his conception of the bodhisattva path which it will be helpful to briefly consider. The first is that unlike many proponents of virtue theory, such as Aristotle,

Aquinas, and Mencius, Śāntideva conceives of the training program of the bodhisattva as a multi-life project. As a result of good karma accumulated in one life, Śāntideva holds that the bodhisattva creates the conditions for taking an auspicious rebirth in which he will encounter appropriate Buddhist teachers and be able to retake his vow. Eventually, the bodhisattva develops the supernormal power to remember his past lives, thereby linking these conventional identities into a singular, trans-lifetime project of attaining buddhahood (see BCA 10:51).[44]

Most of the arguments and meditations presented in the *Guide* are developed to be accessible to practitioners of various levels of skill, including those just beginning or even outside the bodhisattva path. For this reason, I will not need to consider in depth the multi-life dimension of the bodhisattva path. Nevertheless, we can recognize that, as with his appeals to cosmology, Śāntideva's references to the bodhisattva's commitment to take repeated rebirths have psychological and phenomenological dimensions. To use the most obvious example, compassion for Śāntideva is not merely a very strong wish to help a few beings. It is the radical aspiration to remove the suffering of all beings whatsoever, and to remain in saṃsāra for infinite rebirths in order to do so. Noticing Śāntideva's appeal to trans-lifetime commitment helps us understand the depth, breadth, and intensity of his conception of compassion.

Similarly, the multi-life dimension of Śāntideva's account of the bodhisattva path helps us understand his enormously optimistic conception of human potential. For instance, Śāntideva claims that a virtuous person who has developed patience is wholly invulnerable to irritation of any kind; he remains tranquil while experiencing all kinds of verbal abuse, or intense physical pain. We might think that attaining such a condition is not possible, and Śāntideva would probably agree if training were limited to one lifetime. His claim instead is that perfect virtue is developed gradually, over eons of dedicated practice. Throughout this study we will see that the core conception of virtue Śāntideva provides is often intuitive, in that we can imagine human exemplars developing it in a single lifetime. Nevertheless, the fully developed virtues as articulated in the *Guide* are often radical in intensity and breadth: the mindful bodhisattva is never distracted; the generous bodhisattva gives up all items wholly without regret and so on. This is a challenging aspect of Śāntideva's thought, but it is an important and distinctive feature of his account of virtue, and I will draw attention to it throughout this study.

The second and related issue that it is helpful to introduce now is the question of Śāntideva's conception of liberation. Given that the development of the perfections constitutes progress on the bodhisattva path, it is natural to suppose that the experience of a fully awakened buddha who has completed the path would be characterized by the perfect functioning of each of the virtuous mental states described in the *Guide*: he would be unfailingly generous, wholly free from craving, unphased by situations of adversity, fluidly and continually mindful and so on. This is indeed the conception of liberation which I believe most clearly emerges from the *Guide*. Nevertheless, there is an influential Mahāyāna Buddhist position that is in tension with this interpretation. This is the claim that fully awakened buddhas have no mental experience whatsoever; rather, they respond automatically, due to their past aspirations, in their continuing interventions to benefit beings. Certain passages in the work of the great Madhyamaka philosopher Candrakīrti seem to suggest this conception of liberation, for instance (Dunne 1996). Somewhat surprisingly, there are a handful of verses in the *Guide* which suggest that Śāntideva may have held it as well. He characterizes the awakened mind as having no intentional object (BCA 9:34), and then follows this claim with a discussion of how a buddha without awareness can be soteriologically efficacious on behalf of sentient beings (BCA 9:35–8). These verses claim that just as certain insentient objects, like a magic tree or gem which fulfills wishes, can benefit beings without conscious thought, the fully awakened Buddha is able to benefit them without any explicit mental intention to do so (BCA 9:35).

There is at least the appearance of a tension between these passages, and Śāntideva's careful attention to the bodhisattva's mental experience throughout almost all of the rest of the *Guide*. Moreover, as I show later in this study, Śāntideva also argues that a mind developed in wisdom can continue to experience conventional reality, including suffering sentient beings, in a purified mode of perception. This seems in tension with his claim in BCA 9:34 that liberated minds take no objects of awareness. One way to resolve this issue is to take a metaphorical interpretation of the mindlessness passages in the *Guide*; we can understand Śāntideva, for instance, as arguing that upon developing full buddhahood, dispositions to respond virtuously in all situations will have been perfected, and therefore the Buddha will intervene on sentient beings' behalf spontaneously, without the need for explicit decision-making or any deliberative conceptual thought.[45] The point of the analogy with the wish-fulfilling tree and gem, in this interpretation, is that deliberate *intention* is lacking in awakened buddhas; the verses need not be read as a denial of all mental experience.

This is a complex issue, and I cannot treat it adequately here. As I have said already, most of the meditations and arguments in the *Guide* are intended to train beings who are still developing toward buddhahood, rather than to characterize the nature of awakening itself. Given that my focus in this study is on Śāntideva's conception of virtue as presented in the *Guide*, this means that I do not need to attempt to resolve this interpretive question about the nature of his conception of awakened experience. If it turns out that the best reading of Śāntideva is one in which a fully awakened buddha has no awareness whatsoever, then what I am offering in this study is an analysis of his conception of the experience and character of highly realized (but not yet awakened) bodhisattvas. In this regard, the *Guide* would be analogous to the treatments of virtue left us by many of the other great traditions. To use a prominent example, Confucius on numerous occasions characterizes himself as one who continues to develop in learning and virtue (*Analects* 2:4).

8. *Notes on the translation*

Unless otherwise indicated, all translations of Śāntideva's *Guide* and *Training Anthology* are my own. I base my translation of the *Guide* on the edition of the Sanskrit version of the canonical text edited by P. L. Vaidya (1960). I benefited immensely from consulting four existing translations of the *Guide*, all from the Sanskrit: Crosby and Skilton (Śāntideva 1995), Wallace and Wallace (Śāntideva 1997), Gomez (Śāntideva 2015), and Steinkellner and Peck-Kubaczek (Śāntideva 2019). My translation is also partly based on a rough translation of much of the *Guide*, completed during dissertation research guided by Dr. Richard Hayes, and is enormously in his debt. Readers are also directed toward influential translations of the Tibetan version of the text, by Batchelor (Śāntideva 1979) and Padmakara Translation Group (Śāntideva 2006).[46]

I base my translation of the excerpts from the *Training Anthology* on the Sanskrit edition by P. L. Vaidya (1961). Citations, however, follow the pagination of the earlier edition published by Cecil Bendall, which are reproduced as well in Vaidya's edition. I have benefited greatly from consulting Charles Goodman's recent translation (2016a), and warmly recommend it for a fuller study of this text.

Suggestions for further study

Good general introductions to Indian Buddhism include Gethin 1998 and Westerhoff 2018. Williams 2009 introduces the Mahāyāna Buddhist tradition. Article-length introductions to Śāntideva include Goodman 2016b, Heim 2020 chapter three, and Harris 2022. Harris 2021 provides an overview of Śāntideva's *Guide* and a short introduction to his moral thought. An excellent collection of essays on Śāntideva's *Guide*, written from a variety of academic perspectives, is Gold and Duckworth 2019. Gowans 2014 offers a helpful introduction to Buddhist ethics, with good treatments of Buddhist accounts of virtue and moral psychology. Other useful studies of Buddhist ethics include Keown 1992, Harvey 2000, and Garfield 2021. Recent English-language translations of Śāntideva's *Guide* include Śāntideva 1995, 1997, 2006, 2015, and 2019. Pelden 2010 is an English-language translation of an influential early-twentieth-century Tibetan commentary on the *Guide*. Schmidt-Leukel 2019 offers a commentary on the *Guide* that examines resonances between Śāntideva's thought and Christian theology.

Chapter 1

SELFLESS CHARACTER: VIRTUE WITHOUT A SELF

1.1. Introduction

The characterization of the bodhisattva that emerges from the writings of the eighth-century Mahāyāna Buddhist, Śāntideva, provides a striking cross-culturally accessible depiction of human excellence. The bodhisattva is limitless in her compassion, serenely mindful and introspective, relentlessly generous and enthusiastic, all the while experiencing with penetrating insight the empty nature of phenomena. Her virtuous character enables skillful response to challenging circumstances, is deeply conducive to human flourishing, and is admired, as Śāntideva puts it, among gods and humans (BCA 1:23).[1] The high-level bodhisattva should take her place alongside the cross-cultural collection of human exemplars left us by the various global traditions: Aristotle's man of practical wisdom who responds with courage on the battlefield, and temperance at the banquet; the *junzi* of Confucius and Mencius who expresses benevolence through mastery of ritualized action; the man of faith, hope, and charity depicted by Aquinas and so on.

Nevertheless, many of these theorists of human excellence ground their accounts of character in robust metaphysical positions about human nature. Aristotle, for instance, conceives of virtue as excellence resulting from the development of human potentials inhering in the metaphysical structure of the soul. Likewise, for Mencius, virtue is cultivated from innate moral tendencies which partially constitute human nature. Similarly, authors with theistic beliefs are likely to ground their accounts of virtue in facts about divinely created beings and so on. All such approaches at least appear to contrast strongly with Śāntideva and much of the Buddhist tradition, whose core tenets include metaphysical selflessness and the radical momentariness of all phenomena. Virtuous dispositions, for Buddhist thinkers, cannot be conceived of as developments of the metaphysical structure of the person, given that no enduring unified self exists. Likewise, virtuous character traits must be stable over long periods of time, and it may be initially unclear how this is compatible with a Buddhist metaphysics of momentariness.

This opening chapter of my study will complete three preliminary tasks preparatory to my analysis of specific virtues in Śāntideva's account of the bodhisattva path which occupies the rest of the book. In the immediately following section, I respond to the above concerns by arguing that the Buddhist account of momentary virtuous mental states repeating in reliable patterns provides a sufficient metaphysical basis for Buddhist accounts of conventionally existing virtuous dispositions. I also show that conceiving of Śāntideva as a theorist of virtue is not in tension with two recent understandings of his ethics: the phenomenological interpretation of Jay Garfield, and the consequentialist interpretation of Charles Goodman. The next section of this chapter begins to lay the groundwork for the rest of this book by introducing the basic virtue terminology Śāntideva uses in the *Guide*, with particular focus on the perfections (*pāramitas*) and their opposites, the pathological emotions (*kleśas*). This section introduces a key thesis of my study: the claim that virtue is a central component of Śāntideva's conception of well-being, given that the virtues benefit their possessor, in part by protecting him from the suffering of the pathological emotions. The chapter's final part summarizes the techniques Śāntideva uses to cultivate virtue throughout his *Guide*, the most prominent of which is the application of the perfections as antidotes to destroy the pathological emotions.

1.2. *Śāntideva's virtue theory*

Early Buddhist moral psychology places great importance on developing virtuous mental states which stabilize the mind and constitute progress toward liberation. The early Buddhist canon provides numerous overlapping lists of these qualities, including the four Brahmavihāras of love, compassion, rejoicing, and equilibrium; the five powers of faith, effort, mindfulness, concentration, and wisdom; the seven factors of awakening: mindfulness, investigation of phenomena, effort, joy, tranquility, concentration, and equanimity and so on.[2] An important role that these virtuous mental factors play is to eliminate the afflictive mental factors which cause suffering and bind sentient beings to saṃsāra: wisdom eliminates delusion, love and compassion act as antidotes to anger and so on. During the period of Abhidharma thought, these early lists are systematized and classified into virtuous (*kuśala*) mental states which are conducive to liberation, and pathological emotions (*kleśa* or *upakleśa*) which cause suffering and bondage to the cycle of rebirth.[3] Śāntideva presupposes and develops this basic psychological framework in his *Guide*, employing a common Mahāyāna list of virtuous qualities called "the perfections" (*pāramitas*) which I introduce in the next section.

The terminology developed by these Buddhist theorists of virtue refers primarily to the mental states themselves, rather than habitual dispositions, as in a virtue theory like that of Aristotle. Compassion (*karuṇā*), for instance, refers to the present wish to remove suffering; wisdom (*prajñā*) to an occurrent moment of insight and so on. This attention to the mind and mental experience has made some scholars suggest that we should conceive of Buddhist texts as providing a phenomenology of experience, rather than a virtue theory. Jay Garfield, for instance, has argued that Śāntideva's *Guide* is better understood as providing a moral phenomenology, given that its primary emphasis is on transforming the way the individual experiences the world by eliminating egoistic self-centeredness, and purifying mental experience of aggression and harmful attachment (Garfield 2010, Garfield 2019a, 192–6, and Garfield 2021, chapter three).[4]

Garfield is right to emphasize Śāntideva's interest in purifying mental experience of egoicity, thereby transforming the bodhisattva's perception of the world. Nevertheless, there is no conflict between recognizing phenomenological elements in Śāntideva's moral thought and acknowledging that an important part of his project is developing virtuous character.[5] A virtue is an excellent trait of character, meaning that it is a reliable disposition to respond excellently in all relevant situations. Moreover, for many accounts of virtue, excellent responses which are theorized will include not only actions, but also mental and perceptual elements. The virtuous person does the right thing, for the right reasons, but she also feels the proper amount of emotion; notices morally relevant situational features; makes accurate and unbiased judgments and so on. An honest person, for instance, will not steal, but also reliably judges that stealing is wrong, feels distress at the thought of stealing, and makes subtle distinctions about what should count as stealing, rather than borrowing. The kinds of excellent responses to be emphasized will depend on the specifics of the virtue theory in question, but perceptual and experiential aspects will be stressed by many sophisticated accounts of virtue.[6]

Moreover, in the *Guide* Śāntideva is not just interested in characterizing phenomenal experience; the text develops a careful study of the excellent character of the bodhisattva, who is patient in all relevant circumstances, unfailingly generous, reliably enthusiastic, continually mindful and so on. Also, as we will see in the chapters to follow, the regulation of desire, and in particular the refinement of selfish motivation into altruistic commitment, is one of Śāntideva's perennial concerns. Śāntideva gives trainings throughout the *Guide* to develop these aspects of the bodhisattva's virtuous character.[7] What Garfield persuasively shows is that many of the kinds of virtuous responses that Śāntideva emphasizes are perceptual and internal; the bodhisattva reliably experiences the world as it is, as impermanent, selfless, and empty of intrinsic existence, and does so free of craving and animosity and so on. Throughout this study, I will focus both on Śāntideva's characterizations of occurrent virtuous mental states, and the virtuous character the bodhisattva develops as he trains to continually respond to the world in these ways. Significantly, the virtue terms Śāntideva uses, like *dāna* (giving/generosity) and *kṣānti* (patient/patience), can function in both ways, as indicating occurrent mental states or character traits.

Another reason that might be given for suggesting that Buddhist ethics cannot be understood as providing a virtue theory is its metaphysics of impermanence. Virtuous mental states for all Buddhists are momentary; according to Abhidharma thinkers, they last for only a fraction of a second. This contrasts with Aristotle and many other ancient Greek virtue theorists, who focus explicitly on enduring habitual dispositions to feel the right amount of emotion and act excellently in the relevant situation. Such habitual dispositions will not be part of the final ontology of Buddhists, however, and this may seem to entail that they cannot give an account of virtuous character.

A virtue theory, however, does not need to commit to an ontology of enduring substantially real character traits to develop an account of excellent habitual response. Abhidharma philosophers provide the theoretical background to develop an account of virtue compatible with radical momentariness. In such a framework, momentary virtuous mental states reoccur in reliable patterns, according to causal regularities. Particularly relevant here is what Abhidharma thinkers call the "immediately preceding condition" (*samanantara-pratyaya*), a mental state which can cause an immediately successive qualitatively similar mental state.[8] For instance, if a bodhisattva patiently endures verbal abuse by foolish people for several minutes, this means that thousands of qualitatively similar causally connected instants of the mental state of patience have arisen and dissolved in a continuous stream.

Moreover, according to Buddhist psychology, the occurrence of virtuous or afflictive mental states strengthens the tendency for them to reoccur in similar circumstances. Bodhisattvas therefore can train to develop the ability to be patient over long periods of time, reliably, in all relevant situations. When speaking with Abhidharmic precision, this means that streams of qualitatively similar mental states arise in quick succession. In the ordinary language of conventional reality, however, Buddhists can simply describe this as a bodhisattva possessing the character trait of patience. We will find that Śāntideva often uses virtue terms in this way. At other times his focus is more explicitly phenomenological, in characterizing the nature of a particular mental state, or its overall impact on a bodhisattva's experience.

Another important difference between Buddhist treatments of virtue and other virtue theories is that many non-Buddhist systems conceive of virtue as the development of human nature. Mencius, for instance, claims that virtuous character is a refinement and expansion of innate moral feelings (Van Norden 2019), while Aristotle conceives of it as the actualization of the potentialities of the person, representing the fulfillment of a distinctive human function (Snow 2020, 74–81). The Buddhist rejection of an enduring self (or for Madhyamaka Buddhists, their claim that all phenomena are empty of intrinsic existence) entails that they cannot ground virtuous character in metaphysical facts about human nature in this way.[9] Some contemporary philosophers, therefore, have suggested that virtue is not an adequate concept to capture the central insights of Śāntideva and other Buddhist moral philosophers (Siderits 2007, 292; see discussion in Gowans 2014, 114–19).

Although this is an important difference between Buddhist and other global systems of virtue, it does not prevent theorizing Buddhist accounts of virtuous character. First, virtue theorists need not presuppose any specific metaphysical commitments to explain the regularities and reliability of virtuous response. Appealing to the metaphysical structure of a person conceived of as a unified entity is only one way of doing so. Contemporary empirically minded accounts, by contrast, may emphasize brain states as the causal realizers of the virtuous response in question. Likewise, Buddhists can appeal to the account introduced above, in which causal connections and karmic influence results in patterns of impermanent virtuous mental states reliably occurring and replicating in quick succession.

Second, a virtue theory does not need to explain the value of the virtues in terms of the development of a metaphysically robust human nature. Although Buddhists reject an intrinsically existing human nature, all Buddhists, including Madhyamaka philosophers, can conceive of virtue as the development of conventionally existing human nature.[10] This strategy is central to Śāntideva's moral thought, since he shares the common Mahāyāna position that conventional human nature is contaminated by dispositions to experience pathological emotions such as craving and anger. As I explain in the following section, Śāntideva believes that these pathological emotions are largely constitutive of suffering. An important function of virtue, in his account, is to eliminate the dispositions for their reoccurrence. Moreover, the bodhisattva's virtues represent the perfection of his conventional nature, enabling him to engage with the world with maximal effectiveness to achieve his goal of eliminating the suffering of all beings. The excellence of the virtues for Śāntideva, therefore, is grounded in their role in promoting well-being and eliminating suffering, both one's own and that of others.

There are, however, two contrasting ways contemporary commentators have interpreted the conceptual relationship between virtue and well-being in Buddhist ethics. One possibility is to understand virtue as possessing only instrumental value, in being a means to eliminate suffering (Siderits 2007; Todd 2013, 30–2). In this interpretation, the virtues are conceived of as conceptually distinct from well-being and are seen as valuable in reliably promoting it; the compassionate bodhisattva is more effective at lessening suffering and so on. The role of virtue on an instrumental account is analogous to using an aspirin to eliminate the pain of a headache, in that the means and the end are conceptually independent of each other. Moreover, the means in both cases has no value of itself but possesses instrumental value in reliably lessening pain.

This is not the most plausible way to understand the relation between virtue and well-being in Śāntideva's moral thought, however. We can understand why by recognizing that according to Śāntideva, developing virtuous character results in an almost total positive transformation of the experience of the bodhisattva. For instance, motivationally, the bodhisattva's deluded self-interested desires are replaced with altruistic concern for others. Affectively, she takes pleasure in virtuous activity, becomes indifferent to sense pleasures, and ceases to feel unstable aversion to physical pain. Emotionally, harmful mental states like craving, anger, and jealousy are replaced by positive emotions like compassion, patience, and generosity. The holistic quality of her mental experience is transformed from an erratic uncontrollable mind to a tranquil and stable one in which mental and physical responses are carefully controlled. The chapters of my study to follow will show how these and other characteristics are either constituted by or result from the development of the virtues of the bodhisattva path.

Attending to the depth and breadth of the transformation of experience resulting from the bodhisattva's development of virtuous character suggests that it is more plausible to understand Śāntideva as holding that virtue has intrinsic value, in at least partly constituting well-being. It is implausible to interpret the bodhisattva's virtues as having only instrumental beneficial value since they cannot be conceived of as conceptually independent of the bodhisattva's flourishing. A hedonic interpretation of Buddhism, such as that suggested by Siderits (2007) claims that Buddhist virtue is valuable in instrumentally promoting pleasure and eliminating pain. But as we will see in my third and fifth chapters, Śāntideva holds that the value of both pleasure and pain depends on its relation to virtue; when it stimulates or accompanies virtuous mental states, it is positive, but when it stimulates or accompanies pathological emotions, it is negative. Likewise, we cannot claim that Śāntideva accepts a desire theory of well-being, with virtue conceived of as instrumental to getting what we want, because Śāntideva believes that the fulfillment of non-virtuous goals, such as acquiring material possessions and increasing reputation, does not increase well-being.[11] We do not need to repeat this argument by considering every possible non-virtue-centric conception of well-being. Given that the development of virtuous character constitutes positive transformation of virtually every aspect of the bodhisattva's experience, it follows that he holds virtue has intrinsic value, in being at least partly constitutive of well-being.[12]

It might be objected, however, that Śāntideva's acceptance of the Madhyamaka doctrine that all phenomena are empty of intrinsic existence entails that nothing, including the virtues, can have intrinsic value. But, as Shelly Kagan argues, we can distinguish between intrinsic value, in the sense of value which depends on the object's non-relational properties, and intrinsic value in the sense of having value "as an end," that is in being valuable for its own sake, rather than being merely instrumental to some more basic form of value (Kagan 1998, 278–9). Only the first kind of intrinsic value is in obvious tension with a Madhyamaka metaphysics of emptiness. It is the second, however, that I am arguing best characterizes Śāntideva's conception of virtue.

Throughout this book, I follow the common practice in philosophical writing of using the phrase "intrinsic value" to refer to the property of having value as an end. For Śāntideva, all such value is, like everything else, only conventionally real, in that it is empty of intrinsic existence.[13]

Another concern sometimes raised against the project of developing a Buddhist virtue theory is the possibility that some other frame of ethical analysis will more accurately capture Buddhist moral commitments. Charles Goodman, in particular, has argued that Śāntideva is best understood as a consequentialist, committed to the impersonal maximization of happiness. In response, several scholars have argued that Śāntideva's theory of right action is underdetermined (Harris 2015a), or that it is better understood as analogous to another contemporary ethical theory, such as particularism (Barnhart 2012) or deontology (Davis 2013a). In this book, however, I am not taking a position as to what theory of right action Śāntideva holds. I am neutral, therefore, regarding Goodman's claim that Śāntideva is a consequentialist. My analysis focuses instead on Śāntideva's conceptions of virtue and well-being, concepts which will be relevant for any attempt to analyze the structure of Śāntideva's ethical thought. Goodman, in fact, agrees that Śāntideva holds virtue is at least partly constitutive of well-being (Goodman 2009, 110–15).[14]

Helpful in articulating how I conceive of the contribution of this book to the field of moral philosophy is Julia Driver's distinction between virtue ethics and virtue theory. For Driver, a virtue theory is any systematic account of the virtues and their role in moral life. Significantly, any moral theory may develop a virtue theory; for instance, a universal consequentialist might hold that virtues are those qualities that help the agent maximize good consequences, and a deontologist can theorize the importance of virtue in performing one's duty or following the relevant rules. In contrast to a virtue theory, Driver defines virtue ethics as "the project of basing ethics on virtue evaluation" (1998, 113 n. 1). Virtue ethicists, in Driver's sense, conceive of virtue as the foundational unit in moral theory, and see themselves as developing an ethical theory structurally distinct from consequentialism and deontology. They might, for instance, provide a virtue-based theory of right action, where the morally obligatory action is defined in relation to how a virtuous person would act in the relevant situation.[15][16]

In arguing that virtue is a central component of Śāntideva's conception of well-being, this book will demonstrate its importance to Śāntideva's moral thought. Nevertheless, if we take offering a virtue-based theory of right action as a requirement to qualify as a virtue ethics, then in Driver's terminology, my book is a study of Śāntideva's virtue theory. I am neutral as to whether he should be classified as a virtue ethicist, given that I do not argue that virtue is the *central concept* in his moral thought; nor is my interpretation in opposition to consequentialist and deontological readings of his thought. This book's arguments, however, may be helpful to scholars who wish to defend a stronger, virtue-ethical reading of Śāntideva.[17]

1.3. The perfections and the pathological emotions

In the last section, I summarized the basic account of virtue shared by early Buddhist and Mahāyāna traditions, in which habitually recurring harmful mental states cause or constitute suffering, while reliably recurring virtuous mental states remove them. Śāntideva, like most Mahāyāna authors, calls the contaminated mental states the *kleśas*, which I will usually translate as "pathological emotions" or "psychopathologies." The three primary pathological emotions are delusion, anger, and craving, but Śāntideva also frequently references envy and pride, and various kinds of mental distraction. Śāntideva adapts a common Mahāyāna schema, called "the perfections," to structure his presentation of the bodhisattva's virtues. A primary way the perfections and related virtuous mental states like compassion benefit their possessor is by acting as antidotes to the pathological emotions: patience eliminates anger, wisdom eliminates delusion and so on. In this section, I introduce the perfections and the pathological emotions. The following section introduces the techniques Śāntideva uses in the *Guide* to develop the perfections and eliminate the pathological emotions.

1.3.1. The pathological emotions

A shared tenet of all Indian Buddhists is that suffering arises because of the pathological emotions, the deepest of which is delusion, the superimposition of permanence, unity, and intrinsic existence upon fragmentary, impartial, and selfless phenomena. Delusion is not merely an intellectual lack of knowledge but is an active misperception of the world, out of which all other pathological emotions arise. Delusion conceptually synthesizes collections of radically momentary physical and mental events into temporally extended persons, which are reified as independently existing enduring selves. Other collections of momentary events are synthesized and reified into spatially extended objects with which supposedly enduring persons interact. All other pathological emotions arise from this basic series of cognitive errors. Ordinary persons seek the well-being of their own falsely conceived selves, experience anger when it is threatened, magnify the significance of events that affect it and so on. Likewise, they crave reified external objects, become angry when they are lost, or fearful of losing them while they are possessed. These three central pathological emotions of delusion, craving, and anger give rise to a host of further afflictive responses, various kinds of aggressive feelings, stinginess, laziness, and a sluggish or over-excited mind.[18] Śāntideva frequently refers to envy and arrogant pride in the *Guide*, both of which result from falsely reifying experiential elements into enduring selves of which we can be overly proud, in the case of oneself, or of whose achievements and possessions we can be envious, in the case of others.

Śāntideva holds that the pathological emotions are the ultimate sources of suffering. Although his treatment is not systematic, we can identify four reoccurring and overlapping ways in which they harm their possessor. First and most basically, they destabilize the mind, causing a lack of mental, verbal, and physical control.[19] A mind affected by craving, for instance, recklessly pursues sense pleasures (BCA 8:71–85), while an angry mind retaliates without restraint against its enemies (BCA chapter six). This results in harmful mental, physical, and verbal actions, which injure others while strengthening the propensity for the pathological emotion to recur.

References to the destabilization of the mind by the pathological emotions appear frequently throughout the *Guide*, but are most deeply emphasized in chapter four, which is devoted to developing non-negligence (*apramāda*), a virtue which protects the bodhisattva's commitment to the bodhisattva path. The pathological emotions are targeted as the chief obstacles which threaten to undermine the bodhisattva's progress:

> Somehow or other, I have obtained a favorable situation that is difficult to gain. Even knowing this, I am led to those same hells once more.
>
> Here, as if bewitched by spells, I have no will of my own. I do not know by whom I am deluded, or who dwells in me.

> Enemies such as craving and anger are deprived of hands, legs, and so on. They are neither courageous nor wise. How have they made me their slave? (BCA 4:26–8)

Śāntideva refers specifically to the root pathological emotions of craving (*tṛṣṇā*) and anger (*dveṣa*) in verse 28, but uses the Sanskrit term *ādi* to indicate the rest of the pathological emotions. Chief among the unnamed afflictions is delusion, the superimposition of permanence, unity, and intrinsic existence upon fragmental, transitory, and empty phenomena. Verses 26 and 27 describe one of the ways the pathological emotions cause suffering. A mind dominated by them has lost its will (*cetanā*), meaning that it is out of control, subject to violent emotional swings between craving, anger, envy and so on. As verse 28 puts it, the individual has become a slave to their power. This verse also refers to pathological emotions as "enemies," identifying them as the deepest threats to the bodhisattva's well-being. A few verses later, Śāntideva is even more explicit, characterizing the pathological emotions as the cause of all suffering in saṃsāra (BCA 4:34).

Being under the control of the pathological emotions is itself a kind of suffering. But this basic destabilization of the mind also causes additional sources of disvalue, since it gives rise to other pathological emotions, as well as harmful physical and mental actions. This results in one of the most frequently stressed sources of suffering caused by the pathological emotions: negative karmic effects, and in particular rebirth in hell. This danger is already referred to in verse 4:26 quoted above and reoccurs in the immediately following verses:

> Even if all gods and humans were my enemies, they could not lead me to the fires of the Avīci hell.
>
> But my mighty enemies, the pathological emotions, throw me there instantly, into that place where even Mt. Meru is turned into ashes.
>
> The long life of all other enemies is not like that of my foes, the pathological emotions, which is without beginning or end and is great in duration. (BCA 4:30–2)

In Buddhist psychology, the pathological emotions are considered karmic acts which deposit karmic propensities (*vāsanā*) which will ripen into unfavorable conditions in the future. Verses 30 and 31 refer to these karmic consequences, which can include negative rebirths such as in a hell realm. Negative karma and unfortunate rebirths are stressed frequently throughout many of the *Guide*'s chapters.[20]

The hells, for Śāntideva and other Buddhist authors, are literal places of rebirth, and the possibility of being reborn in a hell realm is one of the terrors of saṃsāra. However, as we saw in the introduction, cosmological realms and psychological states are intricately linked in many Buddhist texts. Animal rebirth is said to be dominated by delusion and rebirth as a *preta*, a kind of insatiable ghost, is a manifestation of craving. Beings in the hell realms are overwhelmed by intense anger and mental pain, analogous to human suffering in terrible times. References to the tortures of unfortunate births, therefore, illustrate what the mind is like under the influence of the pathological emotions, even during a human life. Hell-imagery describes the pain and confusion of a mind consumed by anger; *preta* rebirth draws attention to the painfulness of insatiable craving and so on. Likewise, the basic conception of saṃsāra as cycling through the various possible realms of rebirth represents the psychological confusion and helplessness of a mind dominated by the pathological emotions.[21] Śāntideva's cosmological descriptions, therefore, provide cross-culturally accessible evidence for his understanding of well-being, when we recognize that they also function as phenomenological descriptions of the badness of mental experience infected by pathological emotions.

A third source of disvalue which overlaps with both of the above is the psychological suffering which is either constituted by or results from the pathological emotions. This aspect of suffering is clearly present in Śāntideva's characterization of anger, which is described as a dart embedded in the mind (BCA 6:3). The most frequently reoccurring reference to emotional disturbance caused by the pathological emotions, however, is fear, particularly in relation to death and the unfortunate rebirths which may follow. Passages referencing fear occur in multiple places in the *Guide* (e.g., BCA 2:28–46; 7:4–14); their purpose is to stimulate a strong motivation for engaging in the bodhisattva path. Yet they also illustrate the reoccurring mental unease, punctuated by moments of absolute terror, experienced by ordinary persons who must die repeatedly, under the influence of the pathological emotions. The verses quoted below, describing the fear (*bhaya/trāsa*) experienced at the time of death, are some of the most graphic in all Mahāyāna literature:

> I have not contemplated my own transience. Because of anger and courtesy of delusion, I have done many harmful acts. (BCA 2:39)[22]
>
> Day and night, life decays incessantly and is never replenished. Shall I therefore not die? (BCA 2:40)
>
> Even though lying on a bed in the midst of relatives, I alone must bear the sensation of being cut off from myself. (BCA 2:41)
>
> When I am seized by death's messengers, what use are relatives and friends? At that time, karmic merit alone offers protection, but I have not acquired it. (BCA 2:42)
>
> While being dragged to have a limb amputated, a person is completely overcome. Parched with thirst, with haggard eyes, he sees the world differently. (BCA 2:44)
>
> How much more for the man overpowered by the terrifying messengers of death, as he is tormented by fever, covered in voided excrement? (BCA 2:45).

Notice the explicit reference to the root pathological emotions of delusion and anger in verse 2:39. The passage is intended to stimulate deeper commitment to the bodhisattva path by indicating that good karmic acts and the development of virtue alone can save the individual from taking a negative rebirth (2:42). Yet it also describes the terror accompanying repeated death under the influence of the pathological emotions, and thereby gives insight into the mental suffering which they cause (Garfield 2010). Śāntideva is aware that humans have deeply engrained psychological blocks that prevent acknowledging the reality of our future death. For this reason, he offers the example of amputation as a contrast (2:44). The image of having a leg or arm cut off as punishment for a crime or as treatment for an infection creates a visceral reaction. Reading the lines or hearing the words forces the reader to imagine the event, giving them a sense of the terrible fear and pain that would accompany it. Śāntideva can then point out that the suffering of death will be much greater than this, since not just a limb but one's entire body, as well as friends and possessions, will be lost (2:45). We should note in the second line the language Śāntideva uses to help us feel some sense of the terrible suffering resulting from the separation from everything at the time of death. One is tormented by fever, so terrified that one defecates in petrifaction. All this results from the pathological emotions of craving and anger, which cause clinging to possessions and continued existence, and emotional pain when these items are lost.

A distinct kind of disvalue caused by the pathological emotions is the disruption of social relationships. This is one result of anger, which destabilizes family and friendships, infecting interactions with fear and aggression (BCA 6:4–5). In addition, Śāntideva characterizes the pathological social emotions of envy, competitiveness, and arrogant pride as causing perennial strife in society (BCA 8:5–25). We will return to Śāntideva's depictions of these pathological emotions in my third and fourth chapters.

Although these four sources of disvalue caused by the pathological emotions are distinguishable, they are closely related and often overlap in the text. The lack of control and instability of the mind is itself a kind of painful experience, but it also results in negative actions which lead to rebirth in the hells and disrupt social relationships. Likewise, the intensive suffering of the hell realms illustrates the psychological pain of the pathological emotions, since the hells are where anger and pain are most deeply experienced. Similarly, psychological suffering is caused by socially dysfunctional relationships. We will look at Śāntideva's characterizations of the suffering caused by specific pathological emotions in more detail in the chapters to come.

In the last section, I claimed that the value of Śāntideva's conception of virtue results in part from its elimination of the pathological emotions. We can ask, therefore, which of these forms of suffering are intrinsically bad, according to Śāntideva, and whether some may be only instrumentally bad. Śāntideva does not explicitly distinguish between intrinsic and instrumental value in his writings. Nevertheless, his repeated characterizations of the experience of the pathological emotions, and the accompanying lack of mental control and psychological pain, as the deepest source of suffering, suggest that he would hold they have intrinsic disvalue, were he to apply this distinction.[23] This would apply not just to the pathological emotions, but also to the mental pain (*daurmanasya*) which frequently accompanies them.[24] The other items of physical pain, social dysfunction, and even taking negative rebirths are harder to classify. As my study progresses, however, we will see that Śāntideva argues that physical pain does not decrease the well-being of a fully virtuous person. Moreover, he holds that even rebirth in a hell realm does not harm the high-level bodhisattva.[25] Likewise, he will identify the pathological emotions of craving, arrogant pride, and envy as both the underlying causes of dysfunctional social relationships and the actual suffering that is experienced in these interactions. Moreover, social isolation of itself, according to his analysis, does not harm the bodhisattva.[26] Therefore, although Śāntideva often characterizes these items as kinds of suffering caused by the pathological emotions, it seems that they possess only instrumental disvalue, in the role they play in stimulating further instances of psychopathologies, as well as fear and mental pain.[27]

We can conclude, therefore, that it is the pathological emotions, and the mental pain and loss of mental control which they cause, which constitutes suffering for Śāntideva. My argument for this position will continue to be developed in the chapters which follow, in which we will find Śāntideva reasoning that apparently bad items, like the loss of material goods and even rebirth in a hell realm, are not instances of suffering for a fully virtuous person. It will be reinforced as well through examining his repeated descriptions of the emotional anguish constituted by the pathological emotions.

We now turn to introducing Śāntideva's account of the perfections which, as we will see, benefit the bodhisattva by eliminating the pathological emotions.

1.3.2. The perfections

In the *Guide*, Śāntideva employs an adapted version of an influential Mahāyāna list of virtues, called the perfections (*pāramitās*), consisting of generosity (*dāna*), ethical restraint (*sīla*), patience (*kṣānti*), effort (*vīrya*), meditative concentration (*samādhi/dhyāna*), and wisdom (*prajñā*).[28] The *Guide* has separate chapters focused on developing patience, effort, concentration, and wisdom. There is no chapter titled "ethical restraint," but chapter five is often identified as covering this topic.[29] This is because the chapter develops two virtuous factors of awareness: mindfulness (*smṛti*) and introspection (*saṃprajanya*). As we will see below, these virtuous mental states play an important role in preventing and eliminating pathological emotions, and this in turn ensures no harmful physical or verbal actions will be performed, and that therefore ethical commitments are not broken. The *Guide* also does not have a chapter on generosity, an omission for which there is no obvious explanation. In my second chapter, I reconstruct Śāntideva's account of generosity by analyzing scattered verses throughout the

Guide, in conjunction with passages from the generosity chapter in Śāntideva's other text, the *Training Anthology*. A central function of the Mahāyāna perfections is the elimination of the pathological emotions, and as with early Buddhists accounts of virtue, this protects their possessor's well-being.[30] However, the perfections are also the qualities which will allow the bodhisattva to work effectively to benefit others. This dual role results in the self and other benefiting structure of Śāntideva's virtue theory. I will examine how it manifests in relation to specific virtues in the chapters to come.

Each of the perfections arise in dependence on wisdom, the correct understanding and experience of oneself and the world as impermanent, selfless, dependently originated, and empty of intrinsic existence. By eliminating the pathological emotions, they restore accurate perception of the world. In particular, they eliminate the deep psychological tendency to conceive of oneself as the central figure in the universe, which arises from delusive reification of the self. By purifying egocentric bias in this way, the perfections facilitate equal concern for self and others. I will explore aspects of this cognitive shift from deluded to accurate perception of the world in each of the chapters to follow.

The convergence of altruism and self-interest that we find in Śāntideva's *Guide*, therefore, depends on this dual role played by the perfections and the other virtuous mental states, and can now be summarized quite simply.[31] As we have seen, Śāntideva holds that the pathological emotions constitute suffering. The virtues eliminate the pathological emotions. Therefore, developing virtue benefits the bodhisattva as he progresses on the path. These same virtues also enable the bodhisattva to work most effectively for the well-being of sentient beings. This is because they remove the pathological emotions which impede concern for others, but also because specific virtues prepare the bodhisattva for engaging effectively in altruistic behavior. Perfecting giving allows the bodhisattva to benefit those in need; compassion motivates deep commitment to removing suffering and so on. Developing the virtues, therefore, is in the bodhisattva's own interest, and prepares him to benefit others most effectively.

In the previous section, I argued that the perfections were at least partially constitutive of well-being, given that they holistically transform their possessor's experience for the better to the point where it is not possible to characterize well-being independently of them. In this section, I have argued that their central beneficial role is eliminating the pathological emotions. We might wonder, therefore, whether the value of the perfections might be instrumental after all, given that their role is to eliminate the pathological emotions.

We misunderstand the perfections, however, if we think of them as wholly reducible to the removal of the pathological emotions, even though this is their most immediate and visible function. The experience of the virtuous high-level bodhisattva is not some kind of value-neutral blankness; rather, the perfections themselves exemplify positive states of being. Each of my chapters will provide a partial argument for this position by characterizing aspects of the quality of the virtuous bodhisattva's experience. Nicolas Bommarito (2014) effectively makes this point in his analysis of patience in Mahāyāna moral thought. As Bommarito convincingly argues, the mental state of patience, as understood by Śāntideva and other Mahāyāna authors, is partly constituted by insight into the dependently originated nature of phenomena, resulting in an accurate appraisal of the significance of harmful events in relation to one's overall goals. Patience, therefore, refers to a certain way of experiencing the world that is qualitatively richer, and therefore more valuable than the experience of an angry mind, or even of a mind temporarily tranquilized through medication. Bommarito draws the plausible conclusion that patience itself has intrinsic value for Mahāyāna authors like Śāntideva (278 –9). Similar conclusions can be drawn in relation to each of the virtuous mental states characterized by Śāntideva. To use another intuitive example, the generous bodhisattva's mind is alive with the joy of giving, in a way that is qualitatively richer than the indifference to wealth shown by a rich bachelor dispersing possessions to others to amuse himself.[32] We will gain a better appreciation of the positive value of the perfections as my study progresses.

1.3.3. Well-being and material goods

As we have seen, the primary forms of suffering for Śāntideva are the pathological emotions. Likewise, the perfections which eliminate the pathological emotions and stabilize the mind benefit their possessor. We will later see that Śāntideva also emphasizes beneficial kinds of pleasure and joy which accompany virtuous mental states and activity.[33] Śāntideva's conception of well-being, therefore, has much in common with the theories of well-being developed in ancient Greece, which take virtue as the primary constituent of human flourishing. Like the Stoics, this allows Śāntideva to claim that the virtuous individual can flourish in conditions of apparent hardship, a point to which we will return in my third chapter.

A corollary of his claim that virtue is the primary element of well-being is Śāntideva's radical deemphasis of the value of material possessions, bodily health, and most kinds of pleasure. The disadvantages of saṃsāric success and the dangers of sensory pleasure are one of the most frequently repeating themes of the text. Śāntideva claims that possessions and sensual pleasures are not worth seeking because they are impermanent (BCA 6:55–9; 8:5; 8:20) and will increase emotional suffering at the time of death (BCA 8:17). Pursuing material success also motivates negative actions (BCA 6:60) and can put one's health or safety at risk (BCA 6:92; 8:40, 8:73–9). Pursuit of possessions hinders the development of virtue (BCA 6:92; 8:79; 8:81); moreover, possessions cause emotional anguish when they are lost (BCA 6:93; 8:18) and cannot provide deep satisfaction even while they are retained (BCA 7:64; 8:80). This is all in line with early Buddhist conceptions of subtle forms of suffering which contaminate pleasure (Harris 2014a, Sumanacara 2019). Śāntideva's position, therefore, provides a sharp contrast to much contemporary philosophical work which grants positive well-being value to material goods and ordinary relationships.[34]

We will return to various aspects of Śāntideva's account of suffering and well-being in the chapters that follow. Now, there are two additional points that it will be helpful to introduce. First, we should be attentive to the way that Śāntideva's descriptions of suffering play differing roles at various places in the text. In the second chapter, meditations on the dangers of saṃsāra stimulate fear (*bhaya*) which motivates deep commitment to the bodhisattva path (BCA 2:27–65). In the fifth chapter, the terrors of karmic retribution are described to motivate developing mindfulness and introspection (BCA 5:1–8; BCA 5:29). In the sixth chapter, Śāntideva's depictions of the suffering that anger causes acts as a premise in his argument that anger is irrational (BCA 6:1–6). In the eighth chapter, his depictions of societal disfunction allow him to articulate the benefits of compassion, which eliminates mental aversion to envious and arrogant behavior (BCA 8:5–25). Śāntideva's *Guide* does not have a section explicitly dedicated to characterizing suffering; instead, we find him integrating descriptions of it throughout the text, to motivate engaging in the path, to illustrate the benefits of developing virtue, and to describe the badness of the pathological emotions.

Second, although the drawbacks and dangers of saṃsāric success and sensual pleasure are a reoccurring theme of the text, we should not conclude that Śāntideva holds possessions or pleasure of themselves are intrinsically harmful. These items are dangerous because they stimulate the pathological emotions, and as we will see in the chapters to come, an important function of the virtues is to enable the bodhisattva to interact with them safely, without harmful mental response. As I show in my second chapter, for instance, developing generosity enables the bodhisattva to interact with material objects without craving. Likewise, in my fourth chapter, I show how developing compassion enables the bodhisattva to conduct harmonious social relationships, and to develop an influential reputation without becoming arrogant. Śāntideva believes that material success is neutral, in terms of happiness, but becomes instrumentally harmful when it stimulates pathological emotions, and is of instrumental value when it helps the bodhisattva to lessen suffering. We can recognize, therefore, that an important feature of his account of well-being is its deemphasis on the value of material success, in relation to many other ethical theories.

1.4. *Perfecting selfless persons*

1.4.1. *Introspection, mindfulness, and the perfections*

The last section introduced the dual role that the bodhisattva's virtues play in Śāntideva's moral thought, as protecting the bodhisattva's well-being by eliminating the pathological emotions, while also developing his ability to benefit others. Most of the chapters which follow will provide studies of specific virtues that illustrate this self and other benefiting aspect of Śāntideva's moral thought. In the remaining sections of the current chapter, I summarize the techniques he uses to reliably generate virtuous mental states, and apply them as antidotes against the pathological emotions. The procedure of application itself is presented in the *Guide*'s fifth chapter, which is devoted to characterizing and developing two virtuous qualities of attention: mindfulness (*smṛti*) and introspection (*saṃprajanya*).

Śāntideva's strategy for purifying the mind of pathological emotions is rooted in early Buddhist soteriology and can be understood as analogous to the sixth limb of the eightfold path, right effort. Traditionally, right effort is said to consist of four activities: preventing pathological emotions from arising; eliminating arisen pathological emotions; causing virtuous mental states to arise; and developing arisen virtuous mental states (Williams and Tribe 2000, 54). Śāntideva adopts this general strategy but does not explicitly reference right effort in the *Guide*.[35] Instead, he focuses on two virtuous qualities of awareness, mindfulness (*smṛti*) and introspection (*saṃprajanya*), which jointly allow the bodhisattva to become aware of arising pathological emotions, and to eliminate them through applying the relevant virtue as an antidote.[36]

This process is laid out in the *Guide*'s fifth chapter, which is named after introspection (*saṃprajanya*), one of these virtuous qualities of attention. This chapter immediately follows Śāntideva's characterizations of the pathological emotions as sources of suffering, which we examined in the last section. Chapter five is itself followed by chapters devoted to developing the virtues of patience (*kṣānti:* chapter six), energetic effort (*vīrya*: chapter seven), concentration (*dhyāna*: chapter eight), and wisdom (*prajñā*: chapter nine). Śāntideva's general strategy for developing the bodhisattva's character, therefore, is as follows. First, in chapter four, the pathological emotions are identified as the root causes of suffering, and as impediments to effectively working to benefit others. Therefore, a primary objective of the *Guide* will be to eliminate them. Second, in chapter five, a procedure is introduced in which mindfulness and introspection focus the mind on virtuous objects of attention and alert the bodhisattva when pathological emotions distract and destabilize it. The next four chapters contain training exercises to stimulate the relevant perfection to act as antidote to the arisen pathological emotion: patience, in the case of anger; effort, in the case of laziness; concentration, in the case of mental instability; and wisdom, in the case of delusion. Over time, this weakens the propensities for the pathological emotions to arise, and strengthens virtuous dispositions.[37]

What are the two virtuous factors of mindfulness and introspection and how do they aid in eliminating the pathological emotions? Unfortunately, Śāntideva does not define mindfulness in chapter five, or anywhere in the *Guide*. We can begin to understand how he conceives of it, however, by considering how he introduces it at the beginning of the chapter:[38]

> Unrestrained elephants in heat do not cause as much carnage in this world as the unleashed elephant of the mind does in Avīci and the other hells. (BCA 5:2)
>
> But if the elephant that is the mind is bound in every direction by the rope of mindfulness, then all danger is gone and complete prosperity arrives. (BCA 5:3)

The characterization of the mind as a sexually aroused elephant on the rampage should recall verses 4:26–7 quoted above, which present the mind afflicted by the pathological emotions as out of control, impelled to create negative karma by performing harmful actions. The description of mindfulness as a rope which restrains the mind suggests that Śāntideva understands it to be a kind of awareness which stabilizes the mind by focusing upon virtuous objects of contemplation. This is confirmed in verse 5:40:

> Similarly, the mad elephant of the mind is to be observed with all one's effort, so that, tethered to the great pillar of reflecting on the Dharma, it does not break free. (BCA 5:40)[39]

Smṛti, the term translated as mindfulness, literally means memory, and the reference in the verse to "reflecting on the Dharma" (*dharma-cintā*) suggests that mindfulness is not limited to occurrent objects of awareness but can also recall ethical commitments, such as the bodhisattva's vow to help sentient beings. The mindful bodhisattva will keep in mind his commitment to benefit beings, therefore, even when they are hostile toward him. When lethargic in his practice, he will be mindful of the precious opportunity human life provides to develop virtue (BCA 7:12–15). When encountering potential objects of craving, such as attractive companions, the mindful bodhisattva focuses on unpleasant bodily features by imagining the bones beneath the skin (BCA 8:43) or recalling the fact that all human bodies will inevitably decay (BCA 8:31–2). I will examine some of these strategies in the chapters to follow.

The work of introspection, as developed by Śāntideva in chapter five, is to support mindful awareness by monitoring the quality of attention and alerting the bodhisattva of arising pathological emotions. Śāntideva describes its role in verse 5:41:

> The mind is to be watched in this way: "Where is mine engaged?" so that it does not release the axis of concentration even for a second. (BCA 5:41)

He defines introspection at the end of chapter five as follows:

> This alone is the concise definition of introspection: the repeated examination of the condition of one's body and mind. (BCA 5:108)

Introspection, then, is a kind of meta-awareness which tracks the quality of mindful attention, and the overall condition of the bodhisattva's mind and body. When there is a lapse in virtuous physical or mental activity, through improper bodily etiquette (BCA 5:91–6), or through the arising of a pathological emotion (BCA 5:48–53), introspection sounds the alarm, alerting the bodhisattva to the arisen danger. The bodhisattva is then instructed to freeze all physical and/or mental activity until the situation has been rectified. Śāntideva repeatedly uses the technique of imagining one's mind as being a block of insentient wood as a way of enabling the bodhisattva to temporarily stun the progress of the pathological emotion:

> When one sees one's mind is attracted or repelled, then one should neither act nor speak; one should remain still like a block of wood. (BCA 5:48)

> When the mind is arrogant, derisive, filled with conceit and pride, very sarcastic, cruel, or deceptive; when it appears to be elevating itself, but is actually disparaging others, or when it shows contempt or is enraged, then one should remain still like a block of wood. (BCA 5:49–50)

> When my mind seeks wealth, honor, fame, or followers and attention, then I should remain still like a block of wood. (BCA 5:51)

As the above verses describe, whenever one of the pathological emotions or any kind of harmful intention begins to form, disrupting mindfulness, the bodhisattva is alerted by introspection, freezes all mental and physical activity, and turns his attention to eliminating it. The final step of the procedure is made explicit in verse 5:54:

> Thus, having seen that the mind is afflicted or embarking on fruitless activities, the warrior should always firmly restrain it by applying an antidote. (BCA 5:54)

After the bodhisattva freezes all activity, his mindful and introspective awareness of the pathological emotion in question facilitates the selection of the appropriate antidote (*pratipakṣa*) that will eliminate it. Frequently these antidotes are the virtuous mental states themselves; patience and compassion are antidotes to anger; generosity is the antidote to craving and so on.[40] The relevant psychological principle, shared widely in Buddhist psychology, is that certain mental states are incompatible and cannot coexist in the same mind. If one is angry and can generate patience, then anger will be eliminated and so on. A primary role of each perfection, therefore, is to act as the antidote to the relevant pathological emotion. In the chapters to follow, we will see instances of this strategy at work in Śāntideva's development of generosity, patience, compassion, and wisdom.

In summary, the *Guide*'s chapters four and five can be read together as articulating Śāntideva's general psycho-therapeutic strategy, both for protecting and enhancing the bodhisattva's own well-being, and for preparing him to effectively work to benefit others. First, the pathological emotions are identified as the root sources of suffering, as well as impediments to working effectively for others' benefit. Second, the qualities of mindfulness and introspection are deployed to maintain awareness on virtuous objections of attention (via mindfulness) and to alert the mind when a pathological emotion disrupts mindful focus (via introspection). Third, the bodhisattva freezes all activity and prepares to address this existential threat to his own and others' well-being. This is done in step four, in which the appropriate antidote is generated by means of training exercises which are contained in the later chapters of the *Guide* as well as in the *Training Anthology*. If anger infects the mind, for example, introspection recognizes this and the bodhisattva generates patience by contemplating one of the many arguments contained in the *Guide*'s sixth chapter. In these later chapters, Śāntideva does not explicitly repeat the procedure of freezing the mind, nor does he usually reemphasize the role of mindfulness and introspection. Nevertheless, this general method is presupposed throughout the remainder of the text.

This is the most basic procedure used by Śāntideva to shape the bodhisattva's character, the virtuous conventional self, which is free of the pathological emotions, highly resistant to physical pain, and eternally dedicated to benefiting others. As the virtuous mental states are repeatedly generated to eliminate the pathological emotions, they begin to naturally reoccur, constituting virtuous character. This weakens the tendency for anger, craving, and the other pathological emotions to arise. Ultimately, wisdom must be used to eliminate all possibility of the pathological emotions reoccurring, a practice that I address in the sixth chapter of this study.

1.4.2. Argument, imagination, and ritual

In the last subsection, I summarized the way the perfections and other virtuous mental states are used as antidotes to eliminate pathological emotions. In this subsection, I introduce techniques Śāntideva uses to generate these virtuous mental states themselves. The techniques described below are mutually supportive, and will sometimes overlap, but it will be helpful to introduce them now as an aid to recognizing them in the chapters to follow.

Perhaps the most prominent technique Śāntideva uses to develop virtue and eradicate the pathological emotions in the *Guide* is argumentation. Reasoning is an effective means to eliminate psychopathology because, as explained above, they are generated from erroneous conceptualizations of the world. Reasoning oneself out of these errors weakens or eliminates the resulting pathological emotions. For instance, Śāntideva argues that anger toward beings who harm us is irrational, given that they are driven by pathological emotions, and therefore cannot control their behavior (BCA 6:35–8). This forms part of his strategy to develop patience and eliminate anger. Likewise, he argues that accepting the non-existence of an enduring unified self entails that selfish behavior is irrational (BCA 8:101–3) as a way of developing compassion and eliminating self-centered craving. He also frequently argues that eliminating pathological emotions benefits oneself; anger, for instance, causes mental unrest and social disharmony (BCA 6:3–5), and arrogant pride and envy contaminate relationships with loved ones (BCA 8:5–25). In each case, Śāntideva's arguments are not merely intended to cause intellectual acceptance of a conclusion but are tools to craft virtuous character by developing virtue and weakening the propensity for the pathological emotions to arise. We will look at all these arguments in more detail in the chapters to come.

Śāntideva's use of argumentation to attack the pathological emotions suggests that discussions over whether the *Guide* should be understood as a meditation manual or an argumentative philosophical text miss the mark. Like many of the ancient Greek schools, Śāntideva conceives of philosophical argumentation as a way of developing virtuous character. Many passages, therefore, are simultaneously arguments and contemplative practices, with the premises intended to be reflected on repeatedly as a way of strengthening the disposition for virtuous mental states to reoccur. Likewise, the premises and conclusions of these arguments can be recalled in daily life when encountering situations which stimulate the pathological emotions.[41] Moreover, many passages in the *Guide* that do not take the form of an explicit argument still implicitly argue for the accuracy of elements of Śāntideva's worldview. For instance, Śāntideva presents meditations on decomposing bodies in the charnel ground as an imaginative exercise to eliminate lust (BCA 8:30–70). These passages are not presented as part of a syllogism; nevertheless, they reinforce his claims about the impoverishment of ordinary saṃsāric goals, and the greater value of the bodhisattva path. Meditative exercises, in drawing attention to underappreciated features of human experience, frequently provide phenomenological support for Śāntideva's positions as a complement and reinforcement to explicit argumentation. I will alternate between describing passages in the *Guide* as "arguments" and "meditations" or "contemplations" depending on how overtly Śāntideva presents premises and conclusions, but we should keep in mind that most of the text does argumentative work supporting features of Śāntideva's conception of suffering, well-being, and moral responsibility.

Imaginative visualization, such as that used in these charnel ground meditations, is itself a reoccurring strategy employed by Śāntideva to develop virtue and eliminate pathological emotions. A beautiful example of this technique is given in the second chapter, in which the bodhisattva mentally conjures offerings for buddhas and bodhisattvas as a way of developing faith and reverence toward them (BCA 2:2–22). Additional examples come in the eighth chapter, in which the bodhisattva imagines the filth and feces inside the body as a tool to eliminate lust (BCA 8:56–69). Also in the eighth chapter, Śāntideva presents a sequence of meditations in which the bodhisattva imaginatively exchanges perspectives with others as a way of developing empathy and compassion toward them (BCA 8:140–54). We will examine all these examples in more detail in future chapters.

A particularly important use of imagination reoccurring in the *Guide* is imaginative disidentification with the pathological emotions, by which the bodhisattva conceives of anger, craving and so on as external to her conventionally constructed identity. We have already examined one of the clearest examples of this technique, in the verses quoted above in which Śāntideva characterizes the pathological emotions as external invaders attempting to enter the mind (BCA 4:28–47). According to basic Buddhist ontology of persons, both the pathological emotions and the perfections, as elements in the conditioned factors aggregate (*samskāra skandha*), partially constitute the conventional self.[42] It is therefore a strategic choice on Śāntideva's part to conceive of the perfections as part of the ongoing stream of mental events which constitute the bodhisattva's identity, while conceptually externalizing the pathological emotions. Doing so disrupts their embeddedness in habitual narratives of self-construction, and thereby weakens their force. Externalizing the pathological emotions in this way is not a metaphysical mistake; since the boundaries of the person are only conceptually constructed, Śāntideva has some flexibility to strategically redraw them for his purposes. His use of this technique has resonances with certain approaches to identity developed in contemporary Euro-American philosophy. These include Harry Frankfurt's emphasis on identification with first-order motivations as part of his compatibilist account of free will (Frankfurt 1971 and 1977), and the narrative account of personal identity developed by Marya Schechtman, who claims that experiences are integrated into a coherent narrative in the process of constructing and maintaining personal identity (Schechtman 2007).[43] To put this in the language of Madhyamaka Buddhism, through disidentification, the skilled bodhisattva interrupts habitual processes of self-appropriation (*upādāna*) of pathological emotions as a way of weakening their force (see Ganeri 2007, chapter 7).

A final technique that Śāntideva uses in the *Guide* for developing virtue and eliminating pathological emotions is ritual activity. As Eric Huntington has argued, the first three chapters of the *Guide* present Śāntideva's version of the ritual of unexcelled worship (*anuttarapūjā*), a ceremony appearing in multiple Mahāyāna texts (Huntington 2019). This ritual is composed out of eight parts: praise, worship, going for refuge, confession of misdeeds, rejoicing in merits, request for the buddhas to teach, supplication for them to remain, and dedication of merit (135).[44] Śāntideva presents the praise of *bodhicitta* in the *Guide*'s first chapter, then describes the remaining limbs in chapters two and three. During the ritual, various positive mental states are generated, including generosity through repeated imaginative acts of making offerings (BCA 2:1–22), *bodhicitta* through reciting the bodhisattva vow (BCA 3:22–3) and aversion to saṃsāra (*saṃvega*) during a ritual confession of past misdeeds (BCA 2:27–53). Moreover, Huntington makes the interesting suggestion that the final limb of the ritual, the dedication of merit, is presented again in the tenth chapter at the close of the *Guide* (Huntington 135–6). We can take this to suggest that the ritual, which is initiated in the first verses of the text, does not end in chapter three, but is rather concluded only at the text's completion. This in turn entails that every other element of the text, including its extended arguments and visualizations, takes place in the ritual space of the ceremony of unexcelled worship.[45]

We should keep in mind that these techniques not only support each other, but are often integrated, with a particular training exercise incorporating more than one element. For instance, many of the passages in the *Guide*'s first three chapters, which present the first seven limbs of the ritual of unexcelled worship, also do argumentative work (for instance, through drawing attention to the dangers of saṃsāra), and therefore provide good reasons for taking up the bodhisattva path. Likewise, we have already remarked on Śāntideva's use of imagination in the conjuring of mental offerings, which is itself an important part of the ritual. We will see examples of all these techniques in the chapters to come.

Suggestions for further study

Bodhi 2011 offers helpful background on early Buddhist understandings of mindfulness. A good complement to his approach is the philosophically sensitive treatment of mindfulness and its importance to Śāntideva provided in Garfield 2012. Goodman 2009 gives a systematic and influential argument that Śāntideva is best understood as a consequentialist. A good treatment of the role of the ritual of unexcelled worship in the *Guide* is Huntington 2019. Jenkins 2015b offers an analysis of the self and other benefiting structure of Buddhist ethics, drawing on both early Buddhist and Mahāyāna sources. Mackenzie 2018 gives a brief introduction to Śāntideva's virtue theory, as well as an argument that he should be understood as a virtue ethicist. Also helpful for background on Buddhist virtue theory is Wright 2009 and Snow 2020. Burley 2017 provides a nuanced discussion of the advantages and disadvantages of reading cosmological descriptions in Buddhist texts like Śāntideva's *Guide* as psychological descriptions of afflictive mental states.

Questions for reflection

1. Contrast the phenomenological interpretation of Śāntideva's *Guide* with an approach that emphasizes his commitment to developing virtuous character. Do you think these approaches are complementary, or are they in opposition to each other?
2. What are the pathological emotions and why are they harmful, according to Śāntideva? What is the relationship between pathological emotions such as craving and anger, and virtuous mental states such as compassion and patience?
3. In his *Guide*, Śāntideva frequently references fear of rebirth in cosmological realms such as hell as a reason for virtuous behavior.

Are these passages important for a philosophical reading of the text? Why or why not?

4. Describe the methods used by Śāntideva to cultivate virtue. How do these methods interact? Which do you think would be most effective?

Chapter 2

GIVING AS ABANDONING

2.1. Introduction

One of the surprises of Śāntideva's *Guide* is the absence of a chapter on generosity (*dāna*).[1] This is remarkable since the text is structured as a presentation of the perfections (*pāramitās*), the six virtues the bodhisattva develops on his way to full awakening, the first of which is traditionally held to be generosity. Four of the six perfections are given their own chapters in the text: patience (*kṣānti*: chapter 6), effort (*vīrya*: chapter 7), concentration (*dhyāna*: chapter 8), and wisdom (*prajñā*: chapter 9). The fifth chapter, focused on the mental disciplines of mindfulness (*smṛti*) and introspection (*saṃprajanya*), acts as the chapter on the perfection of ethical restraint (*śīla*).[2] This leaves generosity alone without explicit systematic treatment.

The importance of generosity in Śāntideva's articulation of the bodhisattva path is better appreciated when we turn to his less studied text, the *Training Anthology* (*Śikṣāsamuccaya*: hereafter SS), in which it is an object of extended attention. Doing so helps us see that giving is, after all, a deep theme in the *Guide*. Essential characteristics of Śāntideva's conception of perfect generosity are presented in short sets of verses throughout its chapters, and when we examine these alongside the longer treatment provided in the *Training Anthology*, their meaning becomes clearer. The account of generosity that emerges when the texts are read together is powerful but also somewhat startling: generosity is radical and total, yet also essentially mental and private; it is impartial and in a certain sense altruistic, and yet giving can be perfect without benefiting any specific being other than its possessor.

Perhaps the most distinctive feature of Śāntideva's account of generosity is his identification of giving (*dāna*) with abandoning (*tyāga* or *utsarga*), or, as it is sometimes translated, renouncing. Giving, as we will see, primarily means leaving behind one's sense of ownership toward all property, and the bodhisattva does this by offering everything to all beings. Conceiving of generosity in this way lets Śāntideva tightly interweave the early Buddhist aspiration for liberation for oneself, with the Mahāyāna goal of remaining in saṃsāra to benefit all sentient beings. In so doing, he fuses altruism and the pursuit of self-interest in a philosophically intriguing fashion.

In the following section, I examine the brief scattered treatments of giving that Śāntideva provides in the *Guide*. In the next section, I amplify this account by engaging with the longer treatment provided in the *Training Anthology*. In the final section I analyze how early Buddhist and Mahāyāna commitments, as well as altruistic and self-interested elements, are interwoven into Śāntideva's account of giving.

2.2. Generosity in the Guide

*2.2.1. Giving and the ritual of unexcelled worship (*anuttarapūjā*)*

A prominent example of giving in the *Guide* makes up a section of an eight-part ceremony called the "ritual of unexcelled worship" (*anuttarapūjā*) which spans the second and third chapters.[3] Toward the end of the ritual, the aspirant takes the bodhisattva vow to remain in saṃsāra for all time to work for the benefit of sentient beings (BCA 3:22–3). The ritual begins with an extended practice of making mental offerings to the buddhas and bodhisattvas which is meant to establish confidence (*śraddhā*) and *prasāda*, an affective state which combines an attitude of confidence, joy, and reverence to Buddhist teachers and teachings (Lele 2007, 140–1).[4] It is tempting to think of these mental offerings as only a simulation of real generosity; however, as we will see, Śāntideva takes the visualizations themselves to be acts of generosity, regardless of whether anything physically changes hands. Śāntideva's description of these mental offerings also suggests another important feature of his account of giving: when successful, giving constitutes a positive state of mind for the giver. All acts of generosity are intended for the self-benefit of the giver as much or even more than for that of the recipient.[5]

Two sets of verses from this section are particularly important for my study. The first portrays the bodhisattva as mentally taking possession of what he intends to offer:

> I will take the grains of the fields—wild and cultivated. And I will take any other treasure I may find in the immeasurable ends of space, that I may use to adorn the venerable buddhas. All these treasures that have no owner I make my own in thought, and I offer them to the bulls among the sages, together with their sons. May they, who deserve the best offerings and are endowed with the greatest pity, accept this offering of mine, out of compassion for me. (BCA 2:5–6, translation by Gomez)[6]

Notice the fluid conception of ownership portrayed in these verses, a flexibility that reoccurs in many of Śāntideva's characterizations of giving. The aspiring bodhisattva has nothing, but mentally makes his own (*ādāya*) unclaimed precious things so that he can offer them. Ownership is provisional and strategic; we "possess" what we do not have merely to give it away. As we will see, this is the inverse of the usual strategy found in the *Guide* and *Training Anthology*, in which the bodhisattva removes their sense of ownership from what remains in their physical possession.

A second set of verses within the ritual suggests the radical and total nature of generosity:

> I also offer (*dadāmi*) myself without constraint to the victorious conquerors and their sons. "Take me as your property, oh sublime beings. Devoutly I become your slave. Therefore, having become your property, I will, without hesitation or fear, dedicate myself to the well-being and benefit of living beings. In this way I free myself from my past faults and do not commit any further evil." (BCA 2:8–9, translation by Gomez, my insertion of parenthesis)[7]

This pair of verses offers a tranquil representation of what in Mahāyāna Buddhist imagery is more frequently expressed through the blood and gore of the stories of the bodhisattva's gift of his body: perfect giving is total and wholly without regret.[8] In these verses, the bodhisattva makes himself a slave of others, a theme which we will find reoccur in the *Training Anthology*, in which the bodhisattva gives up his entire person. It is this complete self-abandonment which enables full dedication to the well-being of others.

Another relevant set of passages in the ritual of unexcelled worship is the group of compassionate aspirations that surround the taking of the bodhisattva vow.[9] These are some of the most beautiful verses in the *Guide*, and perhaps all Mahāyāna literature:

> I am a protector for the defenseless; a leader for the caravan of travelers; I will act as a boat, a bridge or a vehicle for those desiring to obtain the further shore.
>
> Let me be a lamp for those seeking light; a refuge for those seeking rest; a servant for all those beings seeking a servant.
>
> For all beings, let me be a wish-fulfilling gem; a vase of wealth; an efficacious spell; a great medicinal herb; a wish-fulfilling tree; a desire-granting cow. (BCA 3:17–19)

These verses are most obviously manifestations of compassion, the aspiration to free all sentient beings from suffering. They also contain an element of generosity, however, since the bodhisattva gives *himself* in service to all beings. A surprising feature of many of Śāntideva's characterizations of giving is that the other-regarding aspects of generosity partially recede into the background; as we will see below, perfect generosity does not necessary immediately benefit anyone. Nevertheless, Śāntideva's conception of generosity takes its place alongside a larger system of virtues and ethical commitments whose overriding aim is always the equal benefit of all.

2.2.2. *Three passages on generosity in the* Guide

Although there is no chapter or extended theoretical treatment of generosity in the *Guide*, there are three short sets of verses, interspaced throughout the text, which develop important aspects of Śāntideva's account of giving. The first is a single verse which comes in the third chapter, appearing shortly before the bodhisattva takes his vow:

> Abandoning everything is nirvāṇa, and my mind longs for nirvāṇa.
> If I am to abandon everything it is best to give it to sentient beings. (BCA 3:11)

An intimate connection between giving (*dāna*) and abandoning (*tyāga*) is announced in this verse; it is in abandoning everything that the bodhisattva gives it to sentient beings. Just as intriguingly, the verse also identifies abandoning with nirvāṇa. This claim is repeated in the *Training Anthology*, except that giving is equated with awakening (*bodhi*) (Goodman 2016a, 37). Taken together, the passages suggest a three-way identification: abandoning (*tyāga*) = giving (*dāna*) = liberation (*nirvāṇa*).

The identification of abandoning with nirvāṇa is relatively natural; nirvāṇa is the cessation of the pathological emotions, and these arise in relation to possessions, because of attachment to them, or aversion to losing them, jealously of another person possessing them and so on. One first abandons possessions by becoming a monastic, and then abandons pathological emotions through meditational cultivation.[10] This is done by abandoning our metaphysically inaccurate sense of self. We will see this theme developed in the *Training Anthology*, where abandoning is explained to be the elimination of the sense of ownership (*mamatvam*) toward objects and one's own person.

The identification between giving and abandoning is less intuitive, and I will explore it in greater depth in my analysis of generosity in the *Training Anthology*.[11] In the present verse, however, we can already notice Śāntideva's manipulation of the semantic overlap between the Sanskrit terms *tyāga* (abandoning) and *dāna* (giving). They can act as synonyms; both can mean giving, what is given, as well as abandoning/renouncing. Nevertheless, the most common meaning of *tyāga* is abandoning or renouncing, and it is generally this meaning which is most prominent in Śāntideva's use of it in both his texts. Likewise, the most common meaning of *dāna* is giving. Śāntideva can lean on this overlap in meanings to offer the creative partial identification of giving and abandonment which we see at play in this verse. Giving up everything, in the sense of abandoning it for the sake of nirvāṇa, is what we do when we give it to sentient beings. In this verse, we find the hint of a two-part structure that emerges more explicitly in the *Training Anthology*. When we give, first we abandon everything, in the sense of ceasing to identify with it; then, once craving and the other mental defilements are dissolved, we can give it safely to others. The verse therefore presents two distinctive elements of Śāntideva's characterization of generosity. Giving is (or is closely related to) abandoning; and giving/abandoning, in leading to or even constituting nirvāṇa, is in one's own highest self-interest. This suggests one of the most intriguing aspects of Śāntideva's account of generosity; initially, it benefits oneself, and only secondary if at all, does it benefit others.

A second set of verses on giving appears in the fifth chapter of the *Guide*, which is devoted to the mental skills of introspection (*saṃprajanya*) and mindfulness (*smṛti*). The quote on giving comes as a response to an objection raised by an opponent, following a long passage characterizing the importance of the mind:

> If the perfection of generosity (*dāna-pāramitā*) consists in freeing the world of poverty, then since there is still poverty in the world

> today, how can it have been developed by the protectors who came before? (BCA 5:9)

> The perfection of generosity is said to result from intending to give away (*tyāga*) everything to all people, along with all resulting fruit of this gift. Therefore, the perfection of generosity is only a mental attitude (*citta*). (BCA 5:10)

The verses raise a hypothetical objection by the opponent of the Mahāyānist who points out that since poverty still exists, previous buddhas must not have perfected generosity. Śāntideva's response is that the perfection of generosity is a mental attitude (*citta*), the intention to give (*tyāga*) everything to all sentient beings. This perfect willingness to give/abandon can occur even in the absence of any noticeable effect on the world. Altruistic impact, in the sense of the actual benefit of another person, is not one of generosity's success conditions. We also find again in these verses the identification of generosity (*dāna*) and abandonment (*tyāga*); the essence of perfect generosity is not transferring possessions to a specific person but is rather mental relinquishment of these items to sentient beings in general.

Several significant features of Śāntideva's conception of giving appear in this passage. Most centrally, the verse tells us that generosity is a mental willingness to give rather than an actual exchange of goods to someone in need. There is a sense, then, in which perfect generosity is private and does not necessarily benefit any specific person. Nevertheless, it remains giving in an intuitively plausible sense, since possessions are given/abandoned to sentient beings as a whole. Finally, generosity is radical in that it is total; giving is abandoning *everything* to sentient beings. We will find each of these themes presented in more detail in the *Training Anthology*.

The last set of verses on giving in the *Guide* that I will consider appears in the seventh chapter which focuses on the development of effort (*vīrya*). This chapter offers meditations to inspire the bodhisattva to enthusiastically engage in bodhisattva practices. One of the obstacles to developing this enthusiasm is the seeming demandingness of the bodhisattva's path, which requires giving one's life and limbs multiple times in the service of sentient beings. Responding to this concern, Śāntideva emphasizes that trainings on the path will be attuned to the level of development of the practitioner. Unlike the previous passages, this verse focuses more directly on ordinary giving, in the sense of offering gifts to others:

> In the beginning, the Guide (the Buddha) enjoins giving vegetables and other small things. Later, little by little, one gives more, until eventually one can give/abandon (*tyajet*) even one's own flesh.[12]
>
> When one achieves insight (*prajñā*) into the similarity between one's own flesh, and vegetation, then how would giving/abandoning even one's flesh and bones be difficult? (BCA 7:25–6)

This verse suggests that ordinary giving is not only difficult, but can even be dangerous; over time, however, with the proper training, even the supreme gift of one's body can be done without mental distress. Giving one's flesh and bones without suffering a loss to well-being does, of course, depend upon Mahāyāna Buddhist presuppositions, in particular that the only lasting causes of suffering are the pathological emotions which create negative karma; and moreover, that if a sufficiently developed bodhisattva dies as a result of sacrificing their body, this itself strengthens propensities for virtuous mental states to arise, that are passed onto the next life, thereby constituting progress on the bodhisattva path. The basic insight, however, is generalizable outside of a Buddhist framework; ordinary giving can be harmful, but when supported by other virtues it may be done safely. Here Śāntideva characterizes wisdom (*prajñā*), the insight into the non-existence of any enduring unified self, as a protective virtue, enabling even radical giving without distress. Śāntideva's choice of *tyāga* to indicate the giving of one's flesh is significant; this gift is perfect because one has abandoned self-identification with one's body, seeing it instead as similar to a plant, in that it is uncontaminated by any sense of "I."

The characterization of perfect generosity which emerges from these sets of verses is remarkable and somewhat startling. Generosity (*dāna*) is equated with both abandoning (*tyāga*) and nirvāṇa; the second of these equivalences indicates that perfect giving is a self-nurturing activity, conducive to or even constitutive of our highest well-being. It is essentially mental, and private in the sense that it does not depend on direct interaction with any person. For this reason, immediate altruistic impact is not one of its success conditions. Nevertheless, it remains giving in an intuitively plausible sense, in that one abandons/gives everything to sentient beings in general. It is radical, in that one gives away everything. Ordinarily giving can be difficult and dangerous, but once any sense of self has been abandoned, one can give anything safely and with ease.

There is one more verse on giving/abandoning in the *Guide* that is highly relevant to understanding Śāntideva's conception of generosity. It precedes 3:11, considered above, which equates giving with nirvāṇa:

> I, without regret, abandon/give (*tyajami*) my being/bodies (*ātmabhāvān*), enjoyments (*bhogān*) and merit (*śubham*) of the three times, for the sake of accomplishing the well-being of all sentient beings. (BCA 3:10)

Most of this verse reoccurs in the *Training Anthology*, where it is commented on in detail, and I wait to examine it until the next section. We will also find there additional support for and explication of each of the characteristics of generosity introduced above. Most importantly, we will gain a clearer understanding of what Śāntideva achieves through the identification of generosity and abandoning.

2.3. *Generosity in Śāntideva's* Training Anthology

2.3.1. *The totality of giving: Person (*ātmabhāva*), enjoyments (*bhoga*), and merit (*śubha*)*

The *Guide* and the *Training Anthology* are in many ways closely related presentations of the bodhisattva path. They share an opening passage stating their purpose as presenting an introduction to developing the virtues of bodhisattvahood (BCA 1:1; Goodman 2016a, 1–2). Their presentation differs, in that the *Guide* is in Śāntideva's own voice. The *Training Anthology*, in contrast, is composed of twenty-seven root verses, each of which receives commentary which is primarily in the form of sutra quotations, supplemented occasionally with prose or additional verses by Śāntideva. Nevertheless, they touch on many of the same themes and concepts, such as the dissatisfactory nature of saṃsāric success, the beneficial nature of the perfections, the importance of faith in the Buddha and so on. In fact, the *Guide* invites us to read the *Training Anthology* as a supplement to working with the *Guide* itself (BCA 5:105). I am following this suggestion by supporting my analysis of generosity within the *Guide* by reference to the verses and sutra quotations of the *Training Anthology*.

Nonetheless, the two texts have very different structures. The *Guide* presents the six perfections (*pāramitās*) as the essential elements of the bodhisattva path. Generosity is the only perfection which is not given its own chapter.[13] Intriguingly, this omitted virtue not only receives a chapter in the *Training Anthology*, but giving (*dāna*) in the form of abandoning (*tyāga*/*utsarga*) is used as its central structuring concept. Each of the other perfections appears as well, and several have their own chapter, but their role is to support the perfection of giving. The fourth verse of the *Training Anthology* is central, both for its emphasis on giving, and its articulation of the overall structure of the text (Goodman 2016a, 20; see also Mahoney 2002 and Clayton 2006):

> Giving away/abandoning (*utsarga*) one's person (*ātmabhāva*), enjoyments (*bhoga*), and merit (*śubha*) in the three times to all sentient beings; and moreover protecting, purifying, and increasing them. (SS 17; verse 4)[14]

This verse closely parallels BCA 3:10 quoted at the end of the last section, with two noteworthy differences. First, the term translated as "abandoning" in the *Training Anthology* verse is *utsarga*, a frequent synonym of *tyāga*, the term used in the *Guide*. The meaning of these terms is virtually identical, and they are used interchangeably in the *Training Anthology*. We have already seen that the *Guide* identifies giving (*dāna*) and abandoning (*tyāga*), and we find this same interplay of meanings in the *Training Anthology*'s fourth verse: abandoning (*utsarga* = *tyāga*) is giving oneself and one's possessions to sentient beings.[15] Second, a list of three additional activities of protecting (*rakṣā*), purifying (*śuddhi*), and increasing (*vardhana*) are introduced.

As both Mahoney and Clayton have shown, this verse presents the basic structure of the *Training Anthology* (Mahoney 2002, 72–91; Clayton 2006, chapter 3). The three preceding verses of the root text discuss preliminary topics for the bodhisattva's training, such as developing faith, relationships with a spiritual mentor, and study of the scriptures. In verse 4, giving/abandoning is introduced as the central practice of the bodhisattva. Three types of objects are given: one's person (*ātmabhāva*), enjoyments (*bhoga*), and merit (*śubha*). Giving these objects is further supported through the activities of protecting (*rakṣā*), purifying (*śuddhi*), and increasing (*vardhana*). The remaining twenty-three verses of the root text explicate or further develop one or another of the elements indicated in this verse: verses 5–13 explain the topic of protecting the person, while verse 14 explains protection of objects and karmic merit, and further verses go on to explain purifying and increasing the three objects. These verses are then further developed in the main body of the text through sutra quotations, interspersed with brief commentary and occasionally additional verses by Śāntideva. Shortly, we will turn to a selection of those passages that will help us understand the importance of Śāntideva's identification of giving and abandoning.

Both SS verse 4 and BCA 3:10 list the same three items that are given by the bodhisattva to all sentient beings: one's person (*ātmabhāva*), possessions (*bhoga*), and karmic merit (*śubha*).[16] The term used for the first of these, *ātmabhāva*, often means physical body, but I follow Mahoney 2002, Clayton 2006, Lele 2007, and Mrozik 2007 in taking its meaning here to be broader, indicating all five of the aggregates (*skandhas*) which constitute the conventional person.[17] Giving up his *ātmabhāva*, therefore, means the bodhisattva abandons/gives his entire person—all physical and mental elements with which he identifies—to sentient beings. In Abhidharma terms, giving one's person means offering one's entire conventionally existing (*saṃvṛtisat*) self.

The second term, *bhoga*, literally means enjoyment, but here it refers to the causes of enjoyment, that is the external objects that we can possess (Clayton 2006, 47). In giving up enjoyments, the bodhisattva abandons everything in his legal and physical possession. The final term, *śubha*, is used by Śāntideva interchangeably with *puṇya*, and refers to good karmic merit (Clayton 2006, 49). What the bodhisattva abandons/gives, therefore, is quite literally everything; anything that could even be conceived of as belonging to him or as constituting an aspect of his being is mentally abandoned and offered to sentient beings. The bodhisattva gives it all. Verse 4 of the *Training Anthology* reinforces in the strongest possible way Śāntideva's characterization in the *Guide* of giving as total (BCA 5:10).

To give most effectively, the bodhisattva supports giving with three further activities: protection (*rakṣā*), purification (*śuddhi*), and increase (*vardhana*) of the objects that are given. In the body of the text, Śāntideva equates these activities with the four right strivings (*samyak-prahāṇas*) of early Buddhism, which are identical to right effort (*samyak-vyāyāma*), the sixth factor of the noble eight-fold path (Mahoney 2002, 38–9). I will return to these three additional activities in my fourth section, in which I examine the relation between giving and the right strivings.

2.3.2. *Giving as abandoning in the* Training Anthology

Although I have noted the frequent identification of giving (*dāna*) and abandoning (*tyāga* or *utsarga*) in the *Guide* and the *Training Anthology*, I have not yet offered a clear explanation of the importance of their overlap in meaning. The terms are often used interchangeably in the first chapter of the *Training Anthology*, which provides commentary on giving as presented in its fourth verse quoted above. I begin with two short quotations from SS chapter one, the first from the *Dhāraṇī that Opens Doors without Limit* (*Anantamukhanirhāradhāraṇī*) sutra, and the second from the *Vows of Individual Liberation* for *Bodhisattvas* (*bodhisattvaprātimokṣa*):[18]

> The primary cause of discord among sentient beings is grasping at possessions (*parigraha*). Therefore, one should abandon (*tyajed*) that with respect to which craving (*tṛṣṇā*) might arise. (SS 19)
>
> Moreover, Śāriputra, a bodhisattva conceives of all things as belonging to others and does not acquire anything whatsoever. Why? Because appropriation (*upādānaṃ*) is dangerous. (SS 19)

The first verse signals that the cause of social disputes among human beings is an acquisitive attitude toward possessions and instructs us to abandon any objects that stimulate craving (*parigraha*). However, presumably possessions need not be physically abandoned if they can be held without craving, and this is exactly the advice we find in the second quoted verse. What the bodhisattva needs to give up is *upādāna*, a term meaning to appropriate or take for oneself. In Buddhist psychology, appropriation, which is caused by craving, occurs when we erroneously identify with an element of our experience. We appropriate the aggregates by falsely taking them to belong to or constitute an enduring unified self. Based upon this fundamental error, we then appropriate external objects, seeing them as belonging to this constructed self, and deepening emotional attachment to them. As a result, we become angry and act aggressively when these possessions are threatened, suffer when they are lost and so on. This is why the *Vows of Individual Liberation* says that appropriation is dangerous.

The solution to addressing this danger, according to the *Vows of Individual Liberation*, is not to throw possessions aside, but rather to think of them as belonging to others. This is the attitude we take toward an item a friend has loaned us that must soon be returned. The bodhisattva is advised to adopt such a mental standpoint toward all his possessions, which as we have seen, in the context of SS 4, also includes his body and mental states (*ātmabhāva*) and good karma (*śubha*). The bodhisattva, therefore, attenuates identification with every moment of his experience, resulting in mental flexibility and freedom from craving.

This helps us understand why Śāntideva identifies giving/abandoning with nirvāṇa, as claimed in BCA 3:11. The nirvāṇa intended here is an early Buddhist conception of liberation called "nirvāṇa with remainder" (*sopadhiśeṣa-nirvāṇa*), in which a practitioner ceases pernicious identification with the aggregates, and therefore eliminates appropriation and the generation of the pathological emotions. The aggregates, however, continue to function until the person dies, after which they are not reborn. As we will see in my sixth chapter, Śāntideva rejects the early Buddhist conception of final liberation as the escape from rebirth. However, he incorporates the psychological transformation of nirvāṇa with remainder, in which craving and appropriation are perfectly abandoned, into the bodhisattva path, identifying it with the perfection of generosity. In so doing he incorporates nirvāṇa with remainder as a constituent element of progress on the way to full buddhahood.

This pair of verses, therefore, help us see that what abandoning (*tyāga/utsarga*) means for Śāntideva is primarily the giving up of any sense of craving (*parigraha*) and appropriation (*upādāna*) toward objects, and only secondarily if at all surrendering physical control over these items. Both quotations also emphasize the danger of our ordinary attitudes toward material possessions, in that possessiveness generates social strife as well as mental anxiety. This is why giving is self-beneficial. Giving, in its sense of abandoning possessiveness, protects the bodhisattva from the arising of the pathological emotions, and in particular craving, the root cause of suffering.

Śāntideva continues to develop the relation between giving and possessions by citing and discussing one of his favorite Mahāyāna sutras to quote, the *Questions of Ugra* sutra (*Ugra-paripṛcchā*). This text is natural to consult for guidance on how to alter one's attitude toward possessions, since many of its instructions are directed toward household bodhisattvas who remain legal owners of property and live with their families, even while dedicating themselves to awakening.[19] Such a situation provides an ideal opportunity to consider what attitude a bodhisattva should take toward possessions:

> Therefore, oh householder, a household bodhisattva should not develop a sense of ownership (*mamatvaṃ*) or grasping (*parigraha*) toward anything, nor exertion, nor restriction, nor the propensity to crave. (SS 20)[20]

Notice that the household bodhisattva is *not* instructed to physically abandon/give away his possessions, but instead eliminates grasping (*parigraha*) and the sense of ownership (*mamatvaṃ*: literally "mineness"), meaning a strongly possessive attitude which conceives of property as belonging to oneself. A quotation from the *Questions of Nārāyaṇa* (*Nārāyaṇa-paripṛcchā*) sutra repeats this claim, but also brings into view the connection between giving/abandoning as elimination of grasping and appropriation, with giving in its ordinary sense of transferring items to those in need:

> One should not appropriate (*upādāta*) anything which one has not mentally renounced ... One should not appropriate any property which has not been mentally renounced ... Indeed, oh noble son, the bodhisattva, the great being, should think in this way: "My entire person (*ātmabhāva*) is abandoned (*parityakta*) and given (*utsṛṣṭa*) to all sentient beings, how much more so external objects. I will give whatever existing thing can be found to whoever among sentient beings has a need for it, and to whoever needs to accomplish something with it. I will give a hand to those who need a hand; a foot to those needing a foot; an eye to those needing an eye; flesh to those needing flesh; blood to those in need of blood ... what need to say anything further about external objects, such as money, grain, gold, silver, gems, ornaments, horses, elephants, chariots, vehicles, towns, cities, nations, kingdoms ... In the same way, any of these things should be given to that sentient being who has a need for it, or who needs to accomplish something with it. I will give whatever is at hand. I will give without grief, without regret, without expecting karmic fruit. I will give impartially. I will give for the purpose of serving sentient beings, with compassion and sympathy for sentient beings, for the purpose of gathering sentient beings together, thinking 'let these gathered sentient beings come to know the dharma, when I have attained awakening.'" (SS 21)[21]

The bodhisattva is instructed to refrain from acquiring material goods until they can relate to possessions as if they are not the owner, and therefore can give them up without hesitation or regret. As we saw in previous passages, this is accomplished through the abandonment (*tyāga*) of any sense of grasping (*parigraha*) and ownership (*mamatvam*), that constitutes the appropriation (*upādāna*) of possessions. In the current quotation, these insights are applied to giving in its ordinary sense of the transfer of property to another person without return payment. Based on her prior abandonment of any sense of ownership, the bodhisattva effortlessly gives items away when an occasion arises.

Giving emerges as a two-step process: first, mental appropriation is eradicated, and second, physical property is transferred. The first, rather than the second of these steps, however, is what Śāntideva means by the perfection of generosity (BCA 5:10). Certainly, the bodhisattva wants to benefit others through giving items, but for this to be deeply effective, perfect giving must have already taken place, privately, by mentally turning over everything to sentient beings in general. Perfect gifts are made to nobody in particular, and this is why it is most natural to think of them initially and primarily as acts of abandonment.

The quotation from the *Questions of Nārāyaṇa* also refers to the common Mahāyāna trope of the bodhisattva sacrificing his body for sentient beings, and this should make us think of BCA 7:26 discussed above, in which the bodhisattva gives his flesh and blood with ease after recognizing that, like a vegetable, it is empty of self. The passage we have been examining from the *Questions of Nārāyaṇa* continues, and makes this same suggestion:

> Moreover, oh noble son, just as when people are harvesting material from the root of a medicine tree, or from its joints or branches or bark or leaves or when they are harvesting its flowers or fruit, or are harvesting its sap, the tree does not think: "Something is being removed from my root" and so on. Moreover, the tree does not think that the diseases that are being cured belong to inferior, average or superior sentient beings. In the same way, oh noble son, the bodhisattva, the great being, should conceive of this body, which is made up of the four great elements, as medicine, thinking: "Let those sentient beings who require a hand take a hand, let those who need a foot take a foot . . ." and so on. (SS 21)[22]

The analogy with medicinal vegetation illustrates that the generous bodhisattva has absolutely no feelings of possessiveness toward his person and the items in his control: once the sense of ownership has been completely abandoned, giving even one's flesh is no more difficult than breaking off leaves from a medicinal herb. The passage also links the perfection of generosity to wisdom, since it is insight into the selfless nature of experience which enables recognizing the unowned nature of the body. It is significant as well that the bodhisattva conceives of himself as a source of healing; no matter how severe the gift, the bodhisattva is merely fulfilling his purpose for existing in offering it. Finally, notice that the bodhisattva gives impartially, displaying no favoritism toward the beings he aids.

This Mahāyāna imagery, in which bodhisattvas gladly chop up their flesh and slice off their limbs as gifts, sometimes conceals the fact that many of these insights are translatable into intuitively plausible examples which do not depend upon Buddhist presuppositions. We can imagine a wealthy person who transfers a large portion of their accumulated wealth into a legally irrevocable trust to be dispersed to various good causes which will be chosen in the future. Until this time, the benefactor remains the administrator of the fund, managing its investments and helping coordinate disbursements to worthwhile charities. In a legal, social, and presumably psychologically robust sense, the benefactor has given up her ownership of the wealth, even while temporarily maintaining control over it. The example helps us get some sense of why Mahāyāna Buddhists claim this attitude of dispossession causes profound psychological transformation. When an opportunity to transfer money from the trust to a good cause arises, there will likely be no hesitation or distress on the part of the trustee, since the wealth is quite literally no longer hers. This is the strategy used by the bodhisattva, except that it is not only part of her wealth, but rather every possession and every element of her experience which is offered fully and irrevocably to sentient beings.

2.4. *The four right strivings and generosity*

In verse 4 of the *Training Anthology*, we have seen that giving provides the overall framework for the text's representation of the bodhisattva path but is also supported by three further activities of protecting (*rakṣā*), purifying (*śuddhi*), and increasing (*vardhana*). Śāntideva equates these activities with the four right strivings of early Buddhism, which are identical to right effort, the sixth factor of the noble eight-fold path (Mahoney 2002, 38–9). These are: i) preventing negative mental states (*akuśala-dharma*) like anger and greed from arising; ii) eliminating existing negative mental states; iii) causing the arising of virtuous mental states (*kuśala-dharma*), such as non-greed and non-malice; and iv) increasing these virtuous mental states. Śāntideva equates protecting with the first right striving, purifying with the second, and increasing with the third and fourth (Mahoney 2002). Basically, what this means is that the giving of one's person, possessions, and karmic merit, when performed perfectly, is done with a mind uncontaminated by pathological emotions, and filled with the mental qualities conducive to awakening.[23] Śāntideva's acceptance of the four right strivings is of itself not unusual; virtually all Mahāyāna authors endorse the major categorical schemas of mainstream Buddhist traditions. What is remarkable is the intimate connection he fashions between the right strivings and the Mahāyāna perfection of generosity; the right strivings enable and bring to completion the bodhisattva's perfect giving.

Having analyzed the central features of generosity in Śāntideva's two texts, I can now give a better account of what he achieves through so closely entwining elements of the early Buddhist and Mahāyāna paths in relation to possessions. We can get a sense of what is at stake by referencing another of the central early Buddhist categorical schemas, universally accepted by Mahāyāna authors: the twelve links of dependent origination (*pratītyasamutpāda-nidhana*). Here, pleasure and pain (*vedanā* = link 7) are said to be the cause of craving (*tṛṣṇā* = link 8) which causes appropriation (*upādāna* = link 9). As we have seen, craving and appropriation are used frequently by Śāntideva to indicate the harmful attitudes that the bodhisattva must remove toward possessions. In the twelve links, these two negative mental factors stand in for all other pathological emotions; just as craving arises when we experience pleasure, anger arises when we experience pain and so on.

We have also seen that both of Śāntideva's texts comment on how difficult and even dangerous ordinary giving can be. This is implied by BCA 7:25–6, in which training in giving is adjusted to the bodhisattva's level of development. It is also referenced in the SS quotations emphasizing the necessity of abandoning possessiveness prior to giving possessions away. Link 7 of the twelve links spells out where the danger lies. In ordinary saṃsāric consciousness, pleasure and pain trigger craving and anger. When we obtain objects that reliably produce pleasure, they arouse craving, causing appropriation of the items. When we lose the objects, because of this craving, we become angry and suffer. In a Buddhist karmic universe, such mental reactions are fraught with terror since one can acquire horrible rebirths as a result of a moment of craving or anger. Moreover, these cosmological descriptions of rebirth realms also have a psychological dimension, in illustrating the helpless and terrified nature of a mind under the influence of the psychopathologies.[24] Likewise, each occurrence of pathological emotions stimulates the habitual tendency (*anuśaya*) for them to arise in the future. Possessions, as the *Vows of Individual Liberation* puts it, are dangerous.

Theoretically, one way of addressing our harmful and dysfunctional relationship with external objects is to successfully protect the ones we have. Given the dependent nature of human lives, and the radical impermanence of the universe, however, preventing the loss of possessions is impossible. Śāntideva frequently stresses the futility of attempting to do so, reminding us that the body is like a borrowed object (BCA 4:16), and that fragile material possessions will soon be lost (BCA 6:93). An equally futile strategy would be to give up possessions entirely, not only because we need basic material resources to survive, but also because Śāntideva is using an expansive sense of possession and possessiveness which includes mind and body (*ātmabhāva*), as well as karmic potencies. Suicide is not a viable option either, since killing oneself worsens rather than escapes karmic effects.

The only way to rectify our dysfunctional relationship with possessions, therefore, is to transform our attitude toward them. This means gradually eliminating propensities for pathological emotions like craving and anger to arise whenever we encounter pleasure and pain, and the objects which cause them. It is natural, then, for Śāntideva to employ the four right strivings to express how we should relate to the three sets of objects (person, possessions, and karmic merit) that are given, for it is by perfectly applying the strivings that we free our interactions with these objects from craving and the other pathological emotions. When we encounter a new object, we reflect on its impermanent nature as a way of preventing craving from arising; when craving does arise, we meditate on death or another antidote to dissolve it; we generate and nurture virtuous mental states to prevent all future pathological emotions from arising and so on.

Conversely, why is giving such a potent counterpart for developing the four right strivings? One of the reasons is that it takes a long time to develop virtue and eradicate delusion and the other pathological emotions, and we must practice constantly to progress toward this goal. This requires tackling the psychopathologies over and over, recognizing and eliminating them whenever they arise. The world gives us plenty of opportunities for this kind of practice, by constantly taking away the things we love, but these interactions are dangerous for beings of limited capacity; we risk not being able to respond virtuously in circumstances where what we love is ripped from us unexpectedly.

This is why ordinary giving, in which possessions are transferred to others, is such a useful training tool. Giving is voluntary losing. We can do it on our own schedule, and we can choose which items are given. Beginning with vegetables and small items (BCA 7:25) is a way of training our minds to respond well in situations of loss, where craving and anger are likely to arise. Likewise, making mental offerings such as those in chapter two of the *Guide* helps accustom the mind to the joy and reverence which can accompany skillful acts of giving. Slowly we work our way up, to fruit, coins, gems, houses, and finally, in the imagery of the Mahāyāna, our flesh and blood and bones. The various levels of giving, and the right strivings, reinforce each other on a developing trajectory toward perfect abandoning which is itself the perfection of generosity. We practice the right strivings and train at controlling the pathological emotions through eons of gradated practice of offering gifts. Thus, we strengthen our ability to give more virtuously, free of negative emotional reactions. We can then offer more valuable possessions, resulting in deeper mastery of the right strivings and so on.

We can now characterize a second way giving and the four strivings interact. Perfect giving, as the mental attitude of abandoning possessiveness, and eliminating the appropriation of the aggregates which creates our false sense of self, is itself what the strivings aim to achieve. Ordinary giving is an instrument by which to practice and improve the strivings, and perfect giving is the goal toward which we employ them. This could have been stated using only the language of early Buddhism, were Śāntideva to limit himself to talking about the relationship between the right strivings and abandonment (*tyāga*). The Mahāyāna twist Śāntideva introduces is that total abandonment of self-grasping and appropriation can also be described as giving up everything to all sentient beings. If we do this, then the elimination of craving and the realization of selflessness, as the culmination of the early Buddhist path, becomes a progress point on the bodhisattva's road to full awakening. The *arhat*'s nirvāṇa with remainder, represented as the perfection of generosity, is incorporated into the bodhisattva's project of remaining in saṃsāra forever.

Matching giving with the four right strivings also helps us to think more clearly about the relationship between ordinary giving and the perfection of generosity. All activities, ultimately, are beneficial only insofar as they lessen the arising of the pathological emotions and help one to generate virtue. Ordinary giving is sometimes virtuous, when motivated by compassion (*karuṇā*) and love (*maitrī*), but it can be selfish as well, when we give out of pride (*māna*), or spite (*upanāha*). It participates in the perfection of generosity only to the extent that it is free of selfishness; otherwise, giving merely manifests craving and aggression.

This takes us to one of the deepest and most challenging insights of Śāntideva's treatment of generosity. Real giving can never be merely self-interested, but it is not simply altruistic either. Successfully done, it diminishes the pull of the pathological emotions, and ultimately this is the only way to deeply contribute to anyone's happiness. We give for our own sakes, as a way of abandoning our saṃsāric selves, and we do it by offering ourselves to sentient beings forever.

2.5. Conclusion

It is only recently that contemporary academic scholars are in a position to draw deeply on both the *Guide* and the *Training Anthology* in our analysis of Śāntideva's moral thought. I have argued that doing so helps us reconstruct a powerful and challenging conception of generosity at the heart of his thinking. Perfect giving, for Śāntideva, is private, but other-focused; self-benefiting, yet radically benevolent; total, and yet not self-injurious. These positions are developed by wielding together insights from both early Buddhist and Mahāyāna traditions, and in so doing Śāntideva encourages his listener to think beyond the dichotomy of the *arhat* and bodhisattva ideal. In a more explicitly philosophical vein, giving for Śāntideva undercuts tensions between altruism and self-interest, fusing pursuit of one's own happiness with complete dedication to the well-being of the world.

Suggestions for further study

Good treatments of Buddhist accounts of generosity include Banks 2003, Heim 2004, and Wright 2009, chapter one. An English translation of the *Training Anthology* with extended scholarly introduction is Goodman 2016a. Philosophically sensitive treatments of the *Training Anthology* include Clayton 2006 and Mrozik 2007. Lele 2013 offers an interesting analysis of the puzzle of why bodhisattvas give apparently harmful gifts to those who ask for them. Ohnuma 2006 provides an excellent treatment of the theme in Mahāyāna literature of bodhisattvas offering their bodies and lives as gifts to those who request them.

Questions for reflection

1. When, according to Śāntideva, can giving be harmful? When is it beneficial?

2. What are Śāntideva's reasons for claiming that giving is often more beneficial to the giver than the one receiving the gift? Do you find them convincing?
3. When (if ever) is a gift excessive? Do you think Śāntideva would agree or disagree with your answer?
4. Contrast the account of generosity described in this chapter with that of an author from another philosophical tradition. How do the two accounts differ? How does each relate to what you think generosity is?

Chapter 3

PATIENCE AND THE IRRATIONALITY OF ANGER

3.1. Introduction

Śāntideva's goal in the *Guide*'s sixth chapter is to develop the mental state of patience (*kṣānti*) which acts as the antidote to anger (*krodha/dveṣa*), an aggressive state of mind which lashes out at whatever frustrates desire. To do so, he argues that anger is irrational through a series of connected arguments, most of which appeal to the core Buddhist tenet of dependent origination (*pratītyasamutpāda*). Throughout the chapter, Śāntideva argues that anger arises from false beliefs, or from a narrow perspective which does not consider all relevant factors. Acceptance and repeated contemplation of these arguments will weaken, and eventually eliminate anger.

Nevertheless, the chapter is not simply a toolkit containing a series of arguments against anger to be applied depending on the situation and one's current temperament, although it admirably serves this function. The chapter is divided into three parts: an outer frame, and two inner sections. The outer frame, given in the opening and the concluding verses (BCA 6:1–6; 6:133–4), focuses on the bodhisattva's own well-being, characterizing patience as beneficial in offering protection from the destructiveness of anger. Becoming angry, therefore, is irrational in conflicting with self-interest, with the implied premise being the universal desire for one's own happiness.[1] This opening section also articulates the importance of patience for the bodhisattva path.

The remaining two sections of the chapter each offer a strategy for eliminating anger. The first, which I will call the "subject-oriented strategy," is introduced in verses 6:7–21, and picks up again at verse 6:52, continuing for much of the rest of the chapter. The strategy applies the Buddhist tenet of dependent origination to the bodhisattva's own mind, by offering treatments to remove the psychological causes of anger. According to Śāntideva, anger's immediate cause is mental pain which is itself caused by the frustration of self-centered desires (BCA 6:7). Eliminating self-centered desires requires radically reshaping the bodhisattva's character, which Śāntideva achieves by arguing that ordinary self-centered conceptions of well-being are deluded, and therefore the desires which they cause are irrational.[2]

This subject-oriented strategy is paired with a distinguishable approach, which I will call the "object-oriented strategy" in which Śāntideva argues for the irrationality of anger by focusing on its object, the enemy who harms us (BCA 6:22–51). Anger toward enemies, Śāntideva argues, is irrational in that it arises dependent on false beliefs or an overly limited perspective: we incorrectly think that we were harmed by an autonomous agent (BCA 6:22–33) or fail to acknowledge our own contribution to the harmful situation (BCA 6:41–9) and so on. As with the subject-oriented strategy, virtually all the arguments in this section appeal to the tenet of dependent origination, but this time applied to the external world, rather than the bodhisattva's own experience.

We will turn to a more extended consideration of both strategies below. Before doing so, however, we can note another important aspect of the chapter's structure. The *Guide* frequently offers gradated trainings, in which relatively easy and appealing exercises are given to novice initiates to prepared them to engage in more severe trainings.[3] We find Śāntideva allude to the need for gradated trainings explicitly elsewhere in the text (BCA 7:23–7), but it is particularly important in the sixth chapter since developing the ability to endure severe abuse from enemies will be beyond the power of early or even mid-level trainees. This may explain Śāntideva's choice to begin the chapter by emphasizing the harmfulness of anger, and the benefits of patience. Moreover, these opening verses stress patience's intuitive benefits; most of us agree that too much anger can be harmful, and therefore developing at least some degree of patience will benefit oneself. They provide, therefore, the ideal starting point for those outside of, or just entering, the bodhisattva path.

Applying this strategy to the development of patience, however, results in a tension. Ordinary persons and early-stage bodhisattvas focused primarily on their own well-being would be motivated to develop moderate patience, but not to perfect it. This is because, although almost everyone accepts excessive anger can be harmful, many persons would agree with the Aristotelean position that moderate anger is sometimes appropriate and perhaps even a constituent of a flourishing life.[4] Moreover, the role patience plays in the bodhisattva path appears severe; the bodhisattva will sacrifice her body and eventually her life without complaint, and visits the hell realms to benefit beings there.

Self-centered practitioners, therefore, would be motivated to develop only moderate patience, disengaging from trainings at the point where they become too extreme.

The genius of chapter six is that it is arranged so that this motivational problem will be solved without ever needing to be explicitly addressed. This is because Śāntideva's subject-oriented strategy for developing patience, to be explained in detail shortly, requires eliminating self-centered desires which stimulate anger. A self-centered person developing moderate patience for his own benefit will gradually lessen his selfish desires and reshape his conception of well-being, resulting in a willingness to take on more severe trainings in patience, further weakening self-interested desires and so on. The result of *practicing* patience will be a commitment to perfecting it for the sake of all beings. This explains as well why arguments against anger which incorporate *bodhicitta* and compassion as premises are not extensively developed until the latter parts of the chapter. In the end, patience will be perfected for the sake of all beings, even if this is not the initial motivation.

My exploration of the chapter will progress as follows. In the immediately following section, I explain what anger and patience are, according to Śāntideva, and introduce the chapter's opening characterization of how it benefits its possessor. The next section explicates the subjective-oriented strategy, in which Śāntideva offers arguments to eliminate deluded conceptions of well-being and self-centered desires which are the psychological causes of anger. The longest part of this section examines his arguments that physical pain cannot harm a virtuous person's well-being, and that developing patience results in an ability to bear unavoidable pain with mental equilibrium. The final section turns to the object-oriented strategy for eliminating anger and analyzes a selection of Śāntideva's arguments that anger toward the person who harms us is irrational. The last part of this section focuses on Śāntideva's appeal to *bodhicitta* and the commitment to the bodhisattva path as providing reasons and motivation to abandon anger. I argue that in addition to being part of the object-oriented strategy, this emphasis on *bodhicitta* also represents a furthering of the subject-oriented strategy of purifying the bodhisattva's character of self-centered desires.

3.2. Patience and its benefits

Śāntideva uses several synonyms to refer to anger in the *Guide*'s chapter six (*krodha*, *dveṣa*), but he introduces it with the term *pratigha*, which means to strike out, or to destroy (BCA 6:1). He describes anger as a mental attitude which internally lashes out at whatever is frustrating one's desires (BCA 6:7). In an earlier chapter, Śāntideva defines patience as the mental attitude which resists or eliminates anger, which is there defined as the wish to harm sentient beings (BCA 5:12). However, chapter six also explores how patience eliminates harmful aversion caused by physical pain (BCA 6:12–21), suggesting that the scope of both anger and patience is not limited to conflicts with living beings. Likewise, the *Guide* describes the patient mind as possessing resoluteness (*dṛḍhatva*) and being invincible (*duryodhana*) in difficult circumstances (BCA 6:18). Patience, therefore, can be understood as the mental state which keeps the mind tranquil in the face of adversity.[5] In the *Guide*'s sixth chapter, Śāntideva presents two forms that it can take. The first, referred to as "patient endurance of physical pain" (*duḥkhādhivāsanākṣānti*) by many Mahāyāna texts, is the mental state which enables the bodhisattva to withstand any amount of physical pain with mental tranquility. The second, called "patient endurance of others' wrongdoings" (*parāpakāramarṣaṇakṣānti*), allows the bodhisattva to remain tranquil in the face of physical or verbal abuse by sentient beings.[6]

Śāntideva begins the chapter by emphasizing the benefits of patience for both the bodhisattva and ordinary people:

> Anger destroys all virtuous actions accomplished over thousands of eons, such as generosity and venerating the buddhas.
>
> There is no vice that is anger's equal, and no spiritual training is the equal of patience. Therefore, one should diligently cultivate patience with various techniques. (BCA 6:1–2)

In traditional presentations of the bodhisattva path, the bodhisattva must accumulate vast amounts of positive karmic merit (*puṇya*) from good actions. Patience protects the bodhisattva's progress by preventing anger, which destroys these potencies (BCA 6:1–2).[7] Śāntideva's basic point in these verses, however, is not limited to those who have taken the bodhisattva vow. His claim is that a moment of anger can destroy achievements into which people have invested great time and energy. Think of the damage angry words or actions inflict on long-standing friendships and family relationships, and their potential to jeopardize business opportunities. Śāntideva is arguing that anger threatens to destroy whatever of value that we have achieved.

Śāntideva continues arguing for the benefits of patience by providing a list of anger's dangers:

> When the dart of anger is stuck in one's heart, the mind cannot become tranquil, nor enjoy pleasure and joy, nor can it rest or become stable.
>
> Even dependents who are given wealth and treated with respect want to harm a master who is disfigured by anger.
>
> Even his friends fear him. He receives no recognition for his gifts. In short, there is nothing that can benefit an angry person.
>
> Therefore, one who recognizes anger as the enemy that causes these kinds of sufferings, and destroys it with dedication, he is happy in this world and the next. (BCA 6:3–6)

The verses offer a series of intuitive benefits gained by increasing patience and thereby reducing anger: this results in psychological peace, better health, and improved social and work relations. The reference in the last line to happiness "in this world and the next" means that eliminating anger benefits one in both this and future lifetimes, given its protection of good karmic potencies. Perry Schmidt-Leukel points out that these verses invert the typical conception of anger, which is usually thought to harm others, but here is described as harming its possessor (Schmidt-Leukel 2019, 257). The rest of the chapter continues to defend and amplify these claims about the badness of anger.

It is important that Śāntideva begins the chapter by emphasizing commonsense benefits of patience which would appeal to ordinary people. Since the pathological emotion of anger causes suffering, weakening it to any degree benefits all persons, regardless of whether they have committed to the bodhisattva path. Moreover, ordinary people will have *some* degree of recognition of these benefits. They are therefore likely to be convinced by these opening arguments to take up the task of lessening anger's influence.

These opening appeals to well-being are, in a certain sense, a Trojan Horse. Developing patience and eliminating anger *will* benefit all persons, but as we will see, the processes by which patience is developed will radically deconstruct a practitioner's sense of value, reshaping ordinary conceptions of well-being to deemphasize concern for external goods like possessions, and bodily health. Śāntideva, in this opening section, targets the common ground between the psychology of ordinary persons and highly realized bodhisattvas. Both wish for their own happiness, but to achieve this aim, the ordinary person's motivations must be carefully refined, broadened to become like the advanced bodhisattva to include concern for all beings. This process will continue for the remainder of the *Guide* but is systematically undertaken for the first time in chapter six.

3.3. The subject-oriented strategy

3.3.1. The psychological causes of anger

After emphasizing the harmfulness of anger in the opening verses, Śāntideva turns to the task of eliminating it. His initial strategy for doing so, in what I am calling the "subject-oriented strategy," is to identify its psychological causes and target them for removal. As Barbara Nelson has shown, Śāntideva's method in this section is clearly laid out in verses seven and eight:[8]

> Consuming the fuel of mental pain (*daurmanasya*), which originates from the frustration of desire (*iṣṭa*), or through encountering the undesirable (*aniṣṭa*), scornful anger destroys me. (BCA 6:7)
>
> Therefore, I will destroy the fuel of this adversary, since this enemy's only purpose is my destruction. (BCA 6:8)

The term that Śāntideva uses for "desire" in 6:7 is *iṣṭa*, which of itself is relatively neutral in connotation. We will see later in the chapter, however, that altruistic motivations like compassion and *bodhicitta* do not cause anger—in fact, developing *bodhicitta* is a key method for eliminating it. The desires in question, therefore, are those which arise out of an inflated conception of one's own importance, which itself arises from delusion about the self. When these self-centered desires are frustrated, whether by encountering what one does not want or failing to get what one does want, one experiences mental pain (*daurmanasya*), which is the immediate causal condition for anger (6:7).

As we will see below, an essential component of Śāntideva's strategy in this section is to distinguish physical pain (*kāyika-duḥkha-vedanā*) from mental pain (*mānasika-duḥkha-vedanā* = *daurmanasya*), which is referred to in 6:7. Both are kinds of hedonic sensation (*vedanā*), but physical pain arises based upon contact between one of the five senses and the external world. We turn to Śāntideva's strategy for dealing with it in the next section. Mental pain, by contrast, depends only on the mind, and can arise as a response to either physical pain or disagreeable ideas. It is also distinct from anger, which is an aggressive response to mental pain. For example, I feel physical pain from the contact between my foot and a sharp rock. For ordinary persons, this is followed by a mentally painful sensation, which is itself followed by anger, an internal lashing out at the situation which caused the mental pain.

These psychological distinctions, which are articulated in early Buddhist texts, are applied by Śāntideva here to fashion a strategy to prevent anger.[9] Since mental pain causes anger, keeping the mind happy is an effective way to prevent it (6:8–9). Mental pain in turn is generated when self-centered desires are frustrated (6:11). Eliminating these desires, therefore, prevents mental pain, keeps the mind happy, and thereby eliminates anger.[10] Identifying anger's psychological casual factors, therefore, creates two strategies to eliminate it. The first is to develop practices which target mental pain directly; if it is eliminated, anger cannot arise. Śāntideva uses this strategy in the two verses which immediately follow:

> Even in undesirable circumstances, my joyful mood must not be disrupted. When mental pain (*daurmanasya*) is felt, my desires are not fulfilled, and virtuous activity ceases. (BCA 6:9)
>
> If there is a remedy, then what's the use in feeling mental pain (*daurmanasya*)? Moreover, if there is no remedy, then what's the use in feeling mental pain (*daurmanasya*)? (BCA 6:10)[11]

The undesirable circumstances, mentioned in verse 9, can refer to any unpleasant situation, including verbal abuse, loss of property, and experiencing physical pain. Verse 10 offers a single argument to prevent or eliminate mental pain in such situations. The passage resembles the prayer for serenity from the Christian tradition. In unpleasant situations in which one can remove the cause of distress, the sensible thing to do is act effectively. If one is powerless to alter the situation, however, then experiencing mental pain simply heaps unnecessary hardships upon oneself.

This verse targets mental pain for removal, not the unrealistic desires which cause it, nor the anger which results from it. Mental pain accompanies anger but is not itself a pathological emotion (*kleśa*) but rather painful hedonic sensation (*vedanā*).[12] Since mental pain also precedes anger and acts as its immediate cause, there will be at least a split instant in which we are mentally distressed but not yet angry, where we suffer, but do not yet mentally lash out in retaliation. This provides a slight psychological gap in which the bodhisattva can intervene. If mental pain can be prevented, or dissolved immediately, then anger will not arise. These are the only verses in chapter six which employ this technique, however. The strategy Śāntideva uses more frequently to prevent or dissolve anger is to delve deeper into its causal structure, targeting the selfish desires whose frustration results in mental pain. This strategy is introduced in verse 11:

> We do not want (physical) pain, contempt, verbal abuse, or disgrace for ourselves or our loved ones. But we want the reverse for our enemies. (BCA 6:11)[13]

When we experience physical pain, or are treated with contempt, verbally abused or humiliated, we experience mental pain, which causes anger (Nelson 2021, 202, 210–11). This happens because we desire the opposite of these unpleasant situations, and Śāntideva's solution is to eliminate these desires and instead accept with composure physical pain (*duḥkha*), contempt (*nyakkāra*), verbal abuse (*pāruṣya*), and disgrace (*ayaśas)* when they are encountered (Nelson 2021, 217–20). Much of the remainder of the chapter focuses on one or another of these four purportedly unfortunate circumstances, offering arguments that suggest the bodhisattva should be willing to accept them with equanimity or even joy, when they cannot be avoided. Śāntideva's strategy, consistently, is to argue that the apparently unpleasant situation does not really have disvalue, or perhaps even helps the bodhisattva progress along the bodhisattva path. The arguments against the badness of physical pain are presented from verses 6:12–21. Arguments to eliminate the other three forms of self-centered desire begin on verse 6:52 and continue for most of the rest of the chapter. I treat a selection of these arguments in the following subsections.

Śāntideva's subject-oriented strategy for eliminating anger, therefore, is to deploy arguments to refine the bodhisattva's motivations and radically transform his conception of well-being, until he no longer experiences mental pain in situations which ordinarily cause anger. This is consonant with basic Buddhist soteriological strategies, laid out in the four noble truths and the twelve links of dependent origination, which conceive of desire as a primary cause of pathological emotions, and stress the contamination of ordinary goods with subtle forms of suffering.[14] We should recognize, however, the radical nature of Śāntideva's application of these techniques. Anger is not eliminated merely through intermittent contemplation of premises and conclusions of argumentation but requires a commitment to compete transformation of character. If a person is to fully eliminate anger, then their entire personality will need to change as well.

3.3.2. Patience as enduring physical pain (duḥkhādhivāsanākṣānti) (BCA 6:12–21)

As we have seen in BCA 6:7–9, Śāntideva's subject-oriented strategy to eliminate anger is to provide meditations and arguments that target its causal factors, mental pain and the frustration of self-centered desire. The first of these desires attacked by Śāntideva is the wish to be free of physical pain, meaning pain that is caused by sense organ contact with the external world. I step on a sharp thorn, or smell manure, or hear a harsh sound and I experience visual, olfactory, or auditory bodily painful sensation *(kāyika-duḥkha-vedanā)*. Since I wish to be free of these painful physical sensations, mental pain (*daurmanasya* = *mānasika-duḥkha-vedanā*) arises and in turn causes anger, the wish to strike back at whatever frustrates me. It is mental pain, anger, and the other pathological emotions, however, which are the real sources of suffering (BCA 4:28–36); physical pain is bad only to the extent that it gives rise to mental pain and contributes to the causal chain which results in anger. Fortunately, physically painful sensations do not inevitably cause mental pain; even early Buddhist texts refer to *arhats* and the Buddha himself experiencing them with tranquility.[15]

Śāntideva's strategy in these passages, therefore, is to argue that physical pain does not harm the well-being of a virtuous person developed in patience. Moreover, the beginning bodhisattva can gradually increase patience, learning to remain mentally tranquil when experiencing gently increasing amounts of physical pain. This is done by altering his attitude toward physically painful sensations, seeing them as neutral, or as having positive value, and thereby eliminating his desire to be free of them and thus severing their link to mental pain and anger.[16] He will still avoid pain for pragmatic reasons, as a way of preserving his body which is a valuable tool for Buddhist practice (BCA 5:66). Early-stage bodhisattvas must also try to avoid pain until they develop the ability to response to it with virtue (BCA 7:25–6).[17] Physical pain of itself, however, does not damage one's happiness if it is not responded to with mental pain and anger; moreover, developing the ability to experience it with equilibrium is essential for progressing on the bodhisattva path.

Śāntideva begins slowly by arguing that some ordinary people, even without Buddhist training, can withstand physical pain without mental distress. One of his clearest presentations of this argument comes earlier in the text, in the fourth chapter, as part of an extended encouragement to eliminate the pathological emotions:

> If people like fishermen, outcasts, and farmers, for the sake of making a living, endure discomforts like cold and heat, then why would I not endure them for the sake of benefiting the world? (BCA 4:40)
>
> Despite having promised to liberate the world from the pathological emotions up to the limit of space in all ten directions, I have not even liberated myself of the pathological emotions! (BCA 4:41)

There is a rhetorical strategy at play in contrasting ordinary workers with the bodhisattva who vows to liberate the world but cannot stand pain even a fisherman endures without complaint. But there is also a philosophical point being made in these verses. Śāntideva is arguing that we can change our attitude toward physically painful sensations by considering their relation to our goals. Fishermen and farmers brave the elements in order to produce food; the bodhisattva likewise should accept pain as a necessary part of developing virtue and liberating sentient beings. Awareness of context alters our attitude to physically painful sensations, and this lessens the severity of any mental pain and anger which arises.

Śāntideva also gives examples of non-Buddhists enduring pain in the early verses of chapter six:

> The people of Karṇāṭa, who are devotees of Durgā, needlessly endure the pain of practices like cutting and burning (their bodies). Why then am I, who am aiming at liberation, a coward? (BCA 6:13)

The verse refers to the practices of the followers of the goddess Durgā, who believe that ritually inflicting pain on oneself brings liberation. Like the example of the fishermen, this verse illustrates that human response to pain is malleable; despite having no bodhisattva training, the followers of Durgā can bear it with ease. More importantly, they illustrate the strategy Śāntideva has laid out in verses 6:7–8. The followers of Durgā view physical pain as essential to their goal of liberation, and this lets them endure it without experiencing mental pain, thereby preventing anger. According to Śāntideva, their beliefs about liberation are false, and their practices will achieve nothing. Nevertheless, the bodhisattva can adopt this same psychological strategy, by understanding her experience of physical pain as contributing to her goal of achieving buddhahood for the sake of all sentient beings.

The verses quoted so far illustrate the possibility of eliminating harmful adverse mental response to physical pain, and instead enduring it with an undisturbed mind, by viewing it as valuable in terms of one's goals. The way to perfect patience is by repeatedly practicing this technique:

> There is nothing which remains difficult after repeated practice. Therefore, by practicing (*abhyāsa*) with mild pains, great torments can be endured. (BCA 6:14)
>
> Do you not see as insignificant pain from things like the bites of gnats and mosquitoes; the sensations of hunger and thirst; and the discomfort of a great itch? (BCA 6:15)
>
> One must not be delicate in the face of cold and heat, rain and wind, travel and illness, imprisonment and beatings. Otherwise, one's distress will increase. (BCA 6:16)

Inspired by examples like the fishermen and the followers of Durgā, the bodhisattva sets herself to the long task of perfecting patience. To do this requires repeated practice (*abhyāsa*), in which the meditations and arguments provided in chapter six are continually reapplied (BCA 6:14). Quotidian events like enduring a mosquito bite without complaint are transformed into sacred spiritual practice through taking up this attitude.[18] Just as she begins to develop generosity by offering vegetables (BCA 7:25), she sets out to practice patience by enduring the relatively small sufferings listed in verse 15. These increase slowly in intensity, as suggested by the somewhat stronger list of painful occurrences given in verse 16. The next set of verses emphasize the mental attitude the bodhisattva must develop to successfully endure pain:

> When seeing their own blood, some people display extraordinary valor; others proceed to faint from the mere sight of the blood of other people. (BCA 6:17)

That comes from resoluteness or timidity of the mind.
Therefore, one should become invincible to suffering, and overcome pain. (BCA 6:18)

Even in pain, a wise person will not let the serenity (*prasāda*) of their mind be disturbed, since the battle is against the pathological emotions, and in battle pain is easy to come by. (BCA 6:19)

The first verse reintroduces the battle imagery frequently favored by Śāntideva to describe the bodhisattva's struggle against the pathological emotions.[19] It also reemphasizes the great variation in people's ability to endure pain, thereby arguing that the ability to tolerate it can be increased. Verses eighteen and nineteen make explicit Śāntideva's claim that any level of physical pain can be endured with a tranquil mind. By first training to remain tranquil while experiencing bug bites, hunger, and bad weather, eventually the bodhisattva achieves an invincible (*duryodhana*) mind which can endure any amount of physical suffering without mental distress. In verse 19, Śāntideva uses the term *prasāda* to characterize a patient anger-resistant mind. This multivalent term has connotations of tranquility and purity, suggesting the bodhisattva's lack of mental distress and the absence of anger. Yet *prasāda* also has rich undertones of joy, and its use suggests the possibility that the bodhisattva can take delight in physically painful experiences which help him develop virtue.[20] This is necessary, since as Śāntideva has already said, keeping the mind joyful prevents the arising of mental pain and anger (BCA 6:9).

It is easy enough to provide intuitive examples that capture at least something of the sense in which the bodhisattva's painful experience can be joyful. There is the runner's delight at finishing the marathon, accompanied by painful gasping for breath; the pleasure of the weightlifter testing her endurance; and the gratification of the mother choosing to experience natural childbirth. The relevant insight captured in Śāntideva's reasoning is that the valence of painful physical sensation is affected, if not wholly determined, by our awareness of its context, and our perspective on how it fits into the overall structure of our goals. Although grounded in these commonsense intuitions, Śāntideva's position becomes radical when combined with his claim that the mind is infinitely malleable and can be trained to eventually withstand any level of physical pain without mental distress.

Śāntideva continues to develop this strategy by arguing that physical pain can even have positive value for the bodhisattva:[21]

> The virtue of suffering is unsurpassed, since because of its violent agitation (*saṁvega*), there is a lessening of lust, compassion for those in saṃsāra, fear of bad actions, and longing for the Buddha. (BCA 6:21)

In this verse Śāntideva intensifies his strategy by arguing that physical pain can actually benefit the bodhisattva dedicated to attaining buddhahood. Deep reflection on one's own pain increases compassion for those who suffer in similar ways, and it enhances *saṃvega*, a term translated here as "violent agitation."[22] *Saṃvega* is the affective awareness that there is no lasting happiness to be found in saṃsāric pursuits. It is gained by reflecting on suffering and the inevitability of death and inspires escape from saṃsāra.[23] The verse also suggests that experiencing pain motivates us to stop creating the karmic causes for future suffering (*pāpa*), and therefore will inspire following the Buddha's teachings. This range of motivations aroused by pain illustrates a reoccurring theme of the *Guide*. In emphasizing *saṃvega*, the verse draws upon early Buddhist motivations to escape from saṃsāra for the practitioner's own benefit. The verse, however, integrates this with the Mahāyāna emphasis on compassion which inspires infinite commitment to remaining within saṃsāra to benefit sentient beings. Śāntideva's solution to this tension, which he develops throughout the *Guide*, is to conceive of the fully virtuous bodhisattva as able to flourish within the realm of rebirth itself, completely free of the pathological emotions which are the sources of all suffering. Patience, in particular, acts as a bridge between early Buddhist and Mahāyāna motivations, since it immunizes the bodhisattva to the badness of physical pain, and thereby removes the last vestige of suffering experienced by enlightened persons.

Chapter six does not discuss in detail the torments of the later stages of the bodhisattva path, such as the gift of the body and voluntary visits to the hell realms, even though patience as endurance of physical pain would be vital in these circumstances. Nevertheless, we find encouragement to maintain mental tranquility or even joy in extremely painful circumstances elsewhere in Śāntideva's writing.[24] The most detailed treatment of this kind is given in the patience chapter of the *Training Anthology*, in which Śāntideva quotes a long passage from the *Meeting of Father and Son* sutra (*Pitāputrasamāgama*). The passage describes a meditational concentration called "All Things are Overcome by Happiness" (*sarva-dharma-sukha-ākrānta*), in which extreme pain is experienced with great joy. Śāntideva introduces the passage as follows:

> Just as, through the power of habituation, one conceives of the suffering of other sentient beings as pleasurable, in the same way, through habitually remaining connected to happy thoughts in relation to anything that causes one suffering, one can abide exclusively in thoughts of happiness. (SS 181)[25]

The *Meeting of Father and Son* sutra goes on to suggest that joy can be experienced even while being tortured in a hell realm. Śāntideva's commenter Prajñākaramati quotes part of this passage in his commentary to BCA 6:14, considered above, which emphasizes becoming accustomed to physical pain through repeated practice (Nelson 2021, 286–7). Prajñākaramati understands Śāntideva to be claiming that the strategy of becoming habituated to painful physical sensations can be developed to an infinite degree, to enable mental equilibrium or joy when experiencing any level of physical pain. Here is how this ability is described by the sutra, as quoted in the *Training Anthology*:

> Oh Blessed One, there is a meditative concentration called "All Things are Overcome by Happiness." Bodhisattvas who attain this absorption feel only happy sensations (*vedanā*) toward all things encountered and never sensations of suffering (*duḥkha*) or unhappiness (*asukha*). Even for a person who is tortured with the agony of hellish experience, only happy thoughts (*saṃjñā*) occur. While being tortured by human forms of suffering also, even when their hands are being cut off and their feet and ears and nose as well, only happy thoughts arise. (SS 182)

The passage goes on to list numerous additional graphic forms of torture experienced by the bodhisattva, including being fried in hot oil, beaten with whips, eaten by lions, and crushed by elephants.[26] According to the passage, those who develop this meditative state "feel only happy sensations" (*sukhām-eva-vedanām*) toward all these experiences, and no feelings of suffering (*duḥkhām*). This might be understood as the bodhisattva no longer experiencing physical pain; if he has a hand cut off in hell, this would presumably feel like a massage rather than losing a limb. However, the passage goes on to describe the bodhisattva as thinking only happy thoughts (*sukha-saṃjñā*) even while experiencing any of these torments. This suggests that the bodhisattva does experience physical pain, but due to his advanced meditative training, it no longer causes him mental pain. Instead, in line with Śāntideva's recommendation in BCA 6:9, he maintains a joyful mind in response to physical pain of even the severest magnitude.

In this interpretation, the sutra's claim that the bodhisattva does not experience painful sensations refers only to painful mental sensation (*mānasika-duḥkha-vedanā/daurmanasya*), not physical pain (*kāyika-duḥkha-vedanā*) which continues to be experienced. In other words, he has perfected the strategy Śāntideva lays out in BCA 6:7–11, by ensuring that physical pain never causes mental pain.[27] The meditative state of All Things are Overcome by Happiness is the limit case of the commonsense examples of the marathon runner, the weightlifter and so on, who are joyful while experiencing what some of us would consider agony. In essence, the passage distinguishes between pain, as a variety of hedonic affect accompanying extreme physical experience, and suffering, as an adverse mental reaction to those affective responses. For the high-level bodhisattva, physical pain is quite literally no longer bad, not because she no longer feels it, but because she responds to it with virtue.[28] Reading the *Training Anthology*'s descriptions of this meditative state alongside BCA 6:14, as Prajñākaramati encourages us to do, suggests there is no limit to the extent to which the bodhisattva can develop his ability to transform his attitude toward physical pain.

3.3.3. The other self-centered desires: Esteem, praise, fame, and material goods[29]

At the conclusion of the selection of trainings to endure physical pain, Śāntideva presents a series of arguments for the irrationality of anger which reference mistaken conceptions about the enemy who harms us, or lack of attention to the broader causal factors contributing to the event of harm (BCA 6:22–51). I return to these object-oriented arguments in the following section. Beginning in verse 6:53, Śāntideva resumes the subject-oriented strategy of focusing on the underlying desires whose frustration causes mental pain and therefore anger. Śāntideva begins the section by referring to three additional unpleasant situations, already introduced in verse 6:11, of which the bodhisattva desires to be free:

> Contempt, verbal abuse, and disgrace—this gang cannot harm the body. Why then, oh mind, do you become angry! (BCA 6:53)

> Will the disfavor that others bear toward me consume me now, or in another life, that it is so undesirable to me? (BCA 6:54)

As Roger Jackson points out, Śāntideva groups contempt, verbal abuse, and disgrace together in verse 6:53 because they are all examples of apparent harm done by the speech of sentient beings (2019, 170–1). Just as we experience mental pain and become angry when we are physically harmed, sentient beings also enrage us by insults, engaging in calumny and so on. In this section Śāntideva also provides arguments about why we should not be distressed when we lose material goods or when our reputation suffers when other sentient beings are praised. Śāntideva uses the same strategy to eliminate these self-centered desires as the one examined above in relation to physical pain. He argues that these items are not really bad, and are even beneficial in certain respects, such as their conduciveness to bodhisattva practice. In 6:54 he gives the first of these arguments, that abusive speech and so on cannot physically hurt us, and so we do not need to fear them. As a result of altering our perception on these situations, mental pain is not experienced, and anger is prevented. In all these cases, Śāntideva is not denying that real harm can be done when abuse occurs but is insisting that the actual suffering is the experience of mental pain and the pathological emotions, not the verbal abuse or loss of possession themselves which merely trigger negative mental response.

Śāntideva's arguments in this long section are often standard applications of early Buddhist insights about suffering and the contamination of saṃsāric success. I provide only a brief analysis of a few selections below. More important for our purposes is to understand how these arguments fit into Śāntideva's goals for the chapter. They reveal his recognition that anger's psychological causes are deeply rooted in habitual valuations and overarching saṃsāric goals. This entails that isolated arguments against the rationality of any particular instance of anger, no matter how effective, will be insufficient to achieve his objective. Eliminating anger completely is possible, but it requires radical transformation of an individual's character, refinement of her conception of value, and alteration of the structure of her desires.

One of Śāntideva's early targets in this section is the desire for material possessions, which he attacks with Buddhist insights about the impoverishment of pleasure and ordinary success. The verses here are reminiscent of early Buddhist accounts of the suffering of change (*vipariṇāma-duhkha*):[30]

> If I am adverse to this (disfavor of others) because it is an obstacle to the pursuit of wealth, my wealth will be lost in this life, but my harmful actions will certainly endure. (BCA 6:55)
>
> It is better to die right now, then to have a long badly lived life, since, even if I live for a long time, the exact same suffering of death will be mine. (BCA 6:56)

Contemplations on impermanence, the fragility of ordinary success, and the inevitable approach of death are perhaps the most frequent motif in the *Guide*. Moreover, as pointed out in BCA 6:55, the karmic effects of harmful actions performed in the pursuit of wealth cause suffering in future lives. Here, Śāntideva deploys these insights to eliminate attachment to saṃsāric goods as a way of eroding the causes of anger. Elsewhere, as we have seen, reflections on impermanence and death are given to inspire commitment to the bodhisattva path (BCA 2:28–65), to keep this commitment (BCA 4:4–26), to maintain mindful awareness as a way of guarding against the pathological emotions (BCA 5:20), and as we will see in the next chapter, they also inspire abandonment of saṃsāric relationships to prepare for strengthening compassion (BCA 8:30–84). These arguments reinforce each other, with each illustrating some aspect of the way suffering arises through misperception of the world and showing how virtue can be developed by eliminating these mistaken perceptions.

Another of Śāntideva's targets in this section is the desire for reputation and prestige which, when frustrated, causes mental pain and then anger:

> For the sake of fame, they squander their wealth and even bring about their own deaths. Can words be eaten? And who can enjoy fame, once dead? (BCA 6:92)
>
> Like a child howling in pain when his sandcastle is knocked down, just so my mind appears to me, when losing praise and fame. (BCA 6:93)

In order to eliminate this pernicious desire, Śāntideva argues for the worthlessness of building an admired reputation in the shadow of the certainty of death. Moreover, one sacrifices valuable resources in pursuit of reputation which might have been put to better use. Verse 93 deepens the critique by emphasizing the danger of attaining reputation for a person subject to craving. Eventually, such a person will lose their esteemed position, resulting in emotional suffering. These verses critiquing reputation and possessions need to be read alongside Śāntideva's characterization of generosity, analyzed in the last chapter. His position is not that these items are intrinsically bad; rather, for the ordinary person, they are dangerous in that they stimulate pathological emotions, and therefore should not be pursued. Nevertheless, a virtuous person who has abandoned craving for these ordinary goods can interact with them freely, possessing them strategically in order to benefit others.

I close this section by considering two of Śāntideva's arguments against envy, the wish to harm another because of their success at acquiring possessions or gaining reputation.[31] These arguments continue the subject-oriented strategy, in arguing that one should abandon the desire for an admired reputation, given that it causes emotional suffering and social strife. They are also relevant to the object-oriented strategy, which I analyze in the following section, given that they focus directly on the irrationality of aggressive attitudes (here, envy) toward sentient beings:

> If others take joy and pleasure in praising a person who acquires good qualities, why, oh mind, do you not praise them and rejoice? (BCA 6:76)
>
> This pleasure from rejoicing is a blameless source of happiness. It is not forbidden by the virtuous ones and is supremely attractive to others. (BCA 6:77)

In these verses, Śāntideva argues for the importance of rejoicing, the joy resulting from perceiving another person's success.[32] This shows that desiring a reputation superior to others is irrational, given that doing so prevents accessing this stable and dependable source of joy. Here, Śāntideva continues his emphasis on the importance of maintaining a joyful mind to prevent anger. Throughout the text, we find him distinguish impoverished experiences of pleasure, particularly those gained from sensual enjoyment and social status, from joy which is conducive to liberation. There is a partial parallel here with authors like Aristotle, who claims that pleasure accompanies virtuous activity (2009, 1174b32–1175a; 188–9). For Śāntideva, virtuous joy is not just an outcome of developing virtue, but a necessary component of it. The bodhisattva cannot stably guard against anger without expanding his capacity to feel joy in challenging situations which ordinarily generate pathological emotions. As a way of preventing envy, rejoicing in others' success itself becomes a matter of moral importance. I return this topic in my fifth chapter.

As the chapter progresses, Śāntideva's appeals to *bodhicitta* and gratitude for or trust in buddhas and high-level bodhisattvas become more extensive. His critique of envy continues below through stressing its incompatibility with the bodhisattva's commitments:

> Having generated *bodhicitta* out of a wish for the happiness of all sentient beings, why are you angry at those sentient beings who attain happiness themselves? (BCA 6:80)
>
> Indeed, you desire buddhahood, which is worthy of reverence in the three worlds, for sentient beings. Why then do you burn within when seeing them honored a little? (BCA 6:81)
>
> What would one who wants awakening for sentient beings not wish for them? How could one who is angry at the success of others possibly possess *bodhicitta*? (BCA 6:83)

Śāntideva points out the obvious incoherence of dedicating one's life to promoting sentient beings' happiness, while simultaneously becoming envious when they achieve success. Part of Śāntideva's purpose in juxtaposing argumentative strategies like these with arguments emphasizing the bodhisattva's own well-being is to appeal to persons of different dispositions or different levels of training, or even himself in various moods. However, alternating between self-interested and other-regarding premises also reinforces one of Śāntideva's main goals in the *Guide*: the elimination of any tension between altruism and pursuit of one's own well-being. Developing patience represents progress on the bodhisattva path, but it also offers continual benefits to the bodhisattva by protecting him from the torments of anger and unquenchable desire.

3.4. *The object-oriented strategy: Patience as endurance of others' wrongdoings* (parāpakāramarṣaṇakṣānti)

3.4.1. *Introduction*

In the last section, we examined Śāntideva's strategy of preventing anger through eliminating its psychological causal conditions, mental pain which itself is caused by frustrated desires. The arguments in the current section focus instead on anger's object, the sentient beings who cause harm. We can illustrate the difference between these two approaches through the following example. Imagine that I am dejected from not getting a promotion at work. Upon returning home, I become angry at my roommate, who has left unwashed dishes in the sink. In this case, the object of my anger, the roommate, is distinct from its psychological causes, which according to Śāntideva would be my mental pain resulting from not getting the wanted promotion. This suggests two strategies to eliminate my anger.[33] First, I can recognize that I am disappointed that I did not get the promotion, making me more susceptible to becoming angry. This parallels the strategy we have seen Śāntideva employ in the last section, in which mental pain caused by frustrated desire is identified as the cause of anger. But I can also turn my analysis to the object of anger, here the roommate, and consider whether he is really deserving of blame. I might remind myself that he has recently lost a loved one and has been struggling with depression, or that I myself frequently leave dirty dishes in the sink and am being inconsistent when I blame him for not immediately cleaning his own. In these cases, I recognize that my anger toward the roommate is undeserved. This corresponds to the strategy we find in the arguments surveyed below, in which Śāntideva stresses that anger toward enemies who harm us is irrational.

A reoccurring feature of the arguments in this section is that they attempt to undercut anger by broadening the perspective of the one who is harmed, through drawing attention to the myriad causal factors which contribute to the harm experienced. Underlying this strategy is Śāntideva's belief that anger arises because of delusion, here taking the form of an overemphasis on the importance of a single causal factor, the harm-doer, and an exaggeration of their autonomy in choosing to perform harmful actions. We will find Śāntideva broadening attention to the overall causal nexus through asking the bodhisattva to contemplate the psychological condition of his adversary (BCA 6:34–8) and how his actions are influenced by external conditions (BCA 6:22–33), but also the relevance of the past behavior of the one harmed (BCA 6:41–9), as well as the incompatibility between anger and the bodhisattva's goal of buddhahood (BCA 6:80–5; 100–27).

3.4.2. The universal causation argument (BCA 6:22–33)

Śāntideva begins the first argument of the section by drawing an analogy between enemies who hurt us, and harm caused by inanimate processes, here using stomach acid as an example.

> I am not angry at things like bile, even though they cause me great suffering. Why be angry at sentient beings, who are likewise enraged by causal conditions? (BCA 6:22)

> A stabbing pain arises, even though it is not wanted. Likewise, anger, which is not wanted, arises forcefully. (BCA 6:23)

The comparison between bile and sentient beings who harm us emphasizes the mechanical nature of anger's arising. Given a disorder of the body, caused by bad food or sickness, bile arises as a natural process. In the case of bile, there is clearly no intention to harm; the pain which results is merely the result of causal factors. Drawing upon the phenomenological work he has conducted at the beginning of the chapter, Śāntideva claims that the case is similar regarding anger. When its causal factors, mental pain resulting from the frustration of desire, are present, then anger mechanically arises, and as a result, the enemy hurts us.[34] In both cases, the process is not initiated deliberately by an agent.[35]

There are, however, two ways to understand how this reasoning supports the conclusion that anger is irrational. Śāntideva may be understood as appealing to anger's specific causal properties; the confusion and psychological distortion it causes are so strong that the harm-doer under its influence is not culpable for their acts (6:23). The argument here would be similar to an insanity defense in a court of law. Śāntideva presents an argument with this form in 6:35–8, which I examine in the next section. As we will see, however, this is not the way he develops the present argument. Instead, Śāntideva is here appealing to the broader metaphysical principle of universal causation, the claim that every event has a cause. His argument is that given the truth of dependent origination, all events occur because of causal factors which are, ultimately, outside the harm-doer's control. Therefore, anger toward them is irrational. Universal causation, rather than the mind-distorting properties of anger, entails that they do not deserve blame. Anger is only alluded to as a salient causal factor of the enemy's harmful action.

It is a bit strong to suggest that we are never angry toward inanimate processes and objects, as anyone who has banged their laptop in frustration understands. The real point is that if anger arises toward an inanimate object, we quickly realize that this reaction is irrational, since it does not intend to harm us. Śāntideva wants to extend this strategy toward human enemies. An obvious objection, however, is that unlike inanimate objects, humans have awareness, beliefs, and intentions, and appear to harm us deliberately. In the next set of verses, Śāntideva responds to this concern:

> A person does not become angry by choice, thinking "I will get angry," and anger does not arise, having intended, "I will arise." (BCA 6:24)
>
> All these various transgressions and harmful actions exist because of the force of their causal conditions; they do not exist independently. (BCA 6:25)
>
> A collection of causal conditions does not possess the intention, "I will cause these things to arise," nor does what is produced have the intention, "I will be produced." (BCA 6:26)

Since both bile and human enemies harm us, and it is not rational to be angry at bile, the fact of harm itself cannot justify anger toward enemies. The relevant difference seems to be that unlike bile, sentient beings harm us deliberately. Moreover, anger is the desire to harm another sentient being. This explains why Śāntideva begins by focusing on anger in verse 6:24; if someone harms me accidentally, then given that no intention to harm exists, the case parallels that of harm done by inanimate entities. In determining whether blame toward the enemy is rationally acceptable, there are therefore two relevant questions. First, is the enemy blamable for the anger itself? Second, is he blamable for acting on that anger and harming us, once it has arisen?

Śāntideva argues for a negative response to the first of these questions in verse 24. The unstated assumption is that an enemy must have freely chosen to become angry to deserve blame for doing so. Śāntideva's argument that this is not the case is again phenomenological, drawing upon the work he has completed in the previous section. When its causal conditions are present, anger arises spontaneously, without choice on our part. In verse 6:25, Śāntideva moves down the causal chain to tackle the second of the questions, arguing that enemies are not responsible for acting on their anger, when committing transgressions and performing harmful actions (*aparādhāś* and *pāpāni*), since these actions have their own set of causal conditions. The chief among these causes are, of course, anger and the other pathological emotions. Once these are present, unless contravening causal factors intervene, the harmful action will proceed. Given the universality of causal conditioning (6:25–6), we must conclude that there exists no freely chosen intentions (*cetanā*) or other motivational states among the causal factors relevant to human action. Instead, at each link of the causal chain, one meets more conditions which, when analyzed, are themselves dependent on causal conditions and so on. Given that harmful actions are caused by factors outside the enemy's control, anger toward him is irrational.

In the next four verses, Śāntideva offers a series of brief arguments against the possibility that the eternal self (*ātman*) of either the Brahmanical Sāṃkhya or Nyāya schools could act as an agent independent of causal influence (6:27–30). Anger might be a rational response toward such an independent agent; however, this would require accepting a metaphysical core of personhood to ground agent-causation, and an account of how such a metaphysically independent agent could intervene in the causal order. Śāntideva argues extensively against the first of these conditions elsewhere in the text (9:57–74). In the present verses, however, he focuses on the second condition. Although I cannot examine his arguments in detail, an important premise is that an eternal unchanging self could not engage in action, given that acting itself entails alteration of the agent (6:30ab).[36]

Having disposed of the possibility of causally unconstrained agent-causation, Śāntideva summarizes his reasoning in this argument in the next verse:

> In this way, everything is under the control of something else, and that on which it depends is also dependent. Since beings are inactive, like illusions, who is there to be angry with? (BCA 6:31)

We should notice that Śāntideva's conclusion emphasizes the second of the strands of argumentation, distinguished above; the fact of universal causation entails that no action is done with sufficient autonomy to entail blame. Śāntideva also introduces a new element in this presentation of his conclusion, by describing enemies who harm us as "apparition-like." References to illusion in Madhyamaka texts indicate that an object appears in a way it does not exist. In this case, the ordinary person inaccurately perceives the harm-doer as an autonomous agent who freely chooses to harm. As Śāntideva has argued, however, the act of harm is merely one link in a beginningless series of causal factors, none of which arise freely. Recognizing the dependent nature of harmful action entails seeing that one's anger is irrational.

Having concluded the main argument with verse 31, Śāntideva has an opponent raise an objection regarding the consistency of his argument with his broader soteriological commitments:

> If it is argued that preventing anger is not possible, for who would be able to prevent what? Our position is that it is possible; since there is dependent origination, there can be the cessation of suffering. (BCA 6:32)

The opponent here suggests that Śāntideva's appeal to the negation of agency in the universal causation argument undercuts his project of eliminating anger, since it also negates the bodhisattva's ability to apply the trainings of chapter six. If we accept that the enemy does not choose to become angry, the opponent charges, then it follows that the bodhisattva cannot choose to eliminate his own. Śāntideva's response is to emphasize that he has not negated dependent origination, nor the conventionally existing person who intervenes to eliminate anger. Here, we can remember that it was dependent origination which was employed in laying out the psychological causes for removing anger earlier in the chapter. There is nothing mysterious about how anger is removed, any more than it is mysterious how bile is eliminated from the body. The conventional agent simply intervenes in these mechanical processes by eliminating a causal condition: fatty food (in the case of bile) and mental pain and self-centered desires (in the case of anger).

One can still be concerned, however, that without autonomous agency, it remains mysterious how the bodhisattva could actively intervene in these processes to prevent anger and remove suffering. This is another reason Śāntideva uses illusion-like language to describe conventionally existing agents in verse 6:31. His position, shared with Candrakīrti, is that conventionally existing phenomena function when not analyzed (Candrakīrti 2004: 6:35; 6:109–14; 6:158–60). Just as chariots provide speedy travel, humans engage in decision making at the conventional level, although such agency has no ontological ground. Conventionally existing persons, therefore, can intervene in psychological processes and eliminate anger, just as they can take the bodhisattva vow and progress along the path. They are not, however, metaphysically robust enough to warrant blame and anger, given that they do not meet Śāntideva's condition of acting freely, independent of causal influence.

One can accuse Śāntideva of being inconsistent at this point. If conventional persons are metaphysically robust enough to eliminate anger and progress on the bodhisattva path, then they would seem to have sufficient metaphysical depth to rationally ground attitudes of anger. Tensions like this are frequent in Mahāyāna texts, and often apparent contradictions like empty bodhisattvas eliminating the illusion-like suffering of empty sentient beings are embraced, without clear resolution.[37] In the current case, however, the tension is not as strong as it appears. Śāntideva's purpose in this chapter is to use argumentation as a therapeutic treatment which removes anger, not theorize exhaustively about anger's impermissibility in all conceivable situations. In Buddhist psychology, anger arises from the misperception of the enemy as being an enduring unified independent self. Upon realizing that its referent does not exist in this way, our ordinary practices of anger will lose their ground. Anger toward beings perceived of correctly as empty of intrinsic existence may be conceivable, but it does not in fact happen.[38] Śāntideva, therefore, need not consider its theoretical justifiability. Rather, in these verses, he has identified a necessary condition of the anger that actually occurs toward our enemies, the misperception of beings as possessing causally independent autonomy. Arguing that these current manifestations of anger are irrational is all he needs to do to achieve his goal.

Śāntideva once again summarizes his argument to conclude the section, in a verse which also instructs the bodhisattva to apply this reasoning as a training tool to eliminate anger:

> Therefore, when one sees a friend or an enemy performing a harmful action, one should think to oneself, "Such are his causal conditions," and remain joyful (*sukhi*) (BCA 6:33).

The reasoning given in this verse is a straightforward restatement of that already provided in 6:31: realizing that harmful actions occur in dependence on causal factors which are ultimately outside the harm-doer's control entails anger toward her is irrational. There are, however, several additional points to be recognized in the way Śāntideva presents his conclusion. First, the verse shows that Śāntideva is not *simply* doing theoretical moral philosophy, but rather is using reasoning as a therapeutic tool. In ordinary life, when harmed by another person, the bodhisattva is to recall the steps or at least the conclusion of the argument, thereby preventing or eliminating anger. Second, the conclusion in this verse is applied to harmful actions done not just by enemies, but also by friends. Friends and loved ones can, of course, hurt us deeply, in which case applying the present argument toward them is fitting. But this addition also suggests the all-encompassing nature of Śāntideva's conception of patience. Even slight harms done by persons affectionate toward us can stimulate subtle feelings of hostility in return, and these too are targeted by Śāntideva for removal.

Finally, notice that the conclusion of the verse urges the bodhisattva to "remain joyful" (*sukhi*) upon recognizing the irrationality of anger toward the harm-doer. This shows the complementary nature of Śāntideva's subject-oriented and object-oriented approaches to eliminating anger. Recognizing that anger toward its object is irrational itself improves the bodhisattva's own subjective condition, here by recovering or allowing him to maintain his joyful mood. In other words, contemplating the universal causation argument considered in this section is itself a way of fulfilling Śāntideva's instructions to the bodhisattva to remain joyful at all times (BCA 6:9). In so doing, the bodhisattva prevents mental pain from arising, thereby eliminating the subjective causal condition of his anger.

3.4.3. The diminished capacity argument (BCA 6:34–8)

Śāntideva next introduces a distinct argument that focuses on the specific causal properties of anger and the other pathological emotions. He argues that those inflicting harm are dominated by these pathological emotions and are therefore unable to resist their distorting influence. In previous chapters he has conducted much relevant psychological work, through contemplating the low-level bodhisattva's lack of control over his emotions and actions. In the opening chapter, he claims that those outside or at the beginning of the bodhisattva path have almost no ability to engage in virtuous activity and to resist performing bad actions (BCA 1:5–6). Likewise, in the fourth chapter, he compares the power of the pathological emotions to black magic, dark forces which impel behavior (BCA 4:26–8):

> Somehow or other, I have obtained a favorable situation that is difficult to gain. Even knowing this, I am lead to those same hells once more.
>
> Here, as if bewitched by spells, I have no will (*cetanā*) of my own. I do not know by whom I am deluded, or who dwells in me.
>
> Enemies such as craving and anger are deprived of hands, legs, and so on. They are neither courageous nor wise. How have they made me their slave? (BCA 4:26–8)

Under the influence of the pathological emotions, the bodhisattva finds himself repeatedly engaging in unvirtuous activity which results in unfortunate rebirths. Notice the reference to the lack of will (*cetanā*), as the bodhisattva is driven about by the force of the pathological emotions. By the time we reach chapter six, the bodhisattva has become intimately familiar with his own susceptibility to their power, giving him a deep appreciation for his enemies' inability to resist their force. In addition, he is now aware through firsthand contemplation that the enemy's anger arises because of mental pain stemming from the frustration of his goals (BCA 6:7). He has also contemplated the involuntary nature of anger's arising at the beginning of the universal causation argument which we have just considered (BCA 6:22–4).

Beginning in verse 6:35, Śāntideva offers additional evidence that the wrongdoer, overwhelmed by pathological emotions, has little control over his actions.[39] The bodhisattva cannot directly examine the mind of his enemies to confirm this.[40] He can, however, infer their lack of control by observing their external behavior:

> Out of carelessness, they afflict themselves with thorns and other torments, or hunger and other punishments, driven by anger, or the lust for unattainable women and other desired things. (BCA 6:35)
>
> Some people kill themselves by hanging or jumping from a cliff, by consuming poison, bad food, and other harmful substances, or by unwholesome conduct. (BCA 6:36)
>
> If under the control of the pathological emotions they kill even their own beloved selves, then how could they avoid treating the bodies of others in the same way? (BCA 6:37)
>
> How can you feel anger, rather than only compassion, for these people, driven mad by the pathological emotions, who have set about killing themselves? (BCA 6:38)

Contemplating the harm that they do to themselves reveals that enemies, dominated by anger, cannot control their behavior. Notice that the strategy here differs from the previous argument, since it implies that the trained bodhisattva, who has developed mental factors of attention such as mindfulness and introspection, and has familiarity with meditations on patience, will be able to intervene in the causal trajectory leading to anger. By applying the meditations of chapter six, he will eliminate mental pain, or uproot harmful self-centered desires, and therefore gain control over his behavior. Enemies, who have not developed these abilities, cannot control themselves.[41] Therefore, as Śāntideva claims in verse 38, the rational attitude toward them is not anger, but compassion.

3.4.4. The shared responsibility argument (BCA 6:42–6)

As chapter six progresses, Śāntideva widens his analysis of the causal grid further and draws attention to the bodhisattva's own contributions to the harm he experiences. The bodhisattva has created negative karma in the past which ripens into present suffering (BCA 6:42) and causes rebirth in a body which is susceptible to pain (BCA 6:43–4):

> Previously, I caused sentient beings these kinds of pain. Therefore, they are completely suitable for me, who afflicted these beings. (BCA 6:42)
>
> Both his weapon and my body are the cause of suffering. He has grasped a weapon and I have grasped a body. Toward whom should I feel anger? (BCA 6:43)
>
> Blinded by craving, I have taken up this open sore in the form of a body which cannot bear to be touched. When it feels pain, where should my anger be directed? (BCA 6:44)
>
> I do not seek suffering, but being a fool, I seek the causes of suffering. When suffering occurs because of my own transgressions, why would I be angry at anyone else? (BCA 6:45)
>
> Just as the forest of razor-leaves and the birds of hell are born from my actions, so is this present suffering. With whom would I be angry? (BCA 6:46)

The argument appeals to karmic regularities as a way of emphasizing shared responsibility between harm-doer and victim. Verses 42 and 45 point out that the bodhisattva's previous karmically negative actions are a condition for his present suffering. Verses 43 and 44, similarly, appeal to the Buddhist belief that rebirth in a vulnerable human body results from past karmic actions. This shows that the bodhisattva's own actions are also a causal condition for the harm he experiences. Verse 46 further develops the argument by referencing the tortures of a hell realm, such as being sliced by trees with razor-sharp leaves, or picked apart by vultures, which result from karmic misdeeds. Śāntideva's point is that rebirth in hell is caused by one's own anger. Moreover, as he has shown in 6:31–2, it is our mistaken interpretation of the harm-doer as possessing autonomous agency which resulted in anger, not the actions of the harm-doer.

For Śāntideva's audience, belief in karma was almost ubiquitous, so this argument would be cogent. However, there is also a broader philosophical point being expressed in these verses. One of the ways anger deludes us is by artificially narrowing our focus to a single individual who appears as the most salient cause of our suffering. Śāntideva's emphasis on dependent origination encourages stepping back from this narrowed perspective to examine how a particular harmful event is brought about by a vast array of causes and conditions. When we do so, inevitably, we will find that actions we have taken contribute in significant ways to the suffering we experience.

We should also remember that cosmology and psychology are intricately linked in Indian Buddhist texts. For Śāntideva, the hell realms are places of physical torture, but graphic descriptions of unfortunate rebirths also illustrate the pain and chaos of an anger-filled mind, even in a human rebirth.[42] When read psychologically, Śāntideva's claim in verses 6:45–6 is that we are responsible for the mood in which we find ourselves. If we respond to difficult circumstances with anger, it is because we have not put into practice techniques to stabilize the mind and eliminate the pathological emotions. Combined with the claim that the pathological emotions are the deepest source of suffering, this entails that all individuals bear the primary responsibility for any suffering they endure. 6:43–4 can be read similarly, as criticizing the bodhisattva for not developing the ability to bear physical pain with equilibrium.

Later in the chapter, Śāntideva even more strongly emphasizes the individual's responsibility for his own suffering:

> Some commit offences out of delusion, and others, being deluded, become angry. Which of them should we call innocent and which the offender? (BCA 6:67)

Previously, Śāntideva has identified the pathological emotions as the sources of all suffering in saṃsāra (BCA 4:28–36). Many verses in chapter six continue to develop this theme, by arguing that the loss of saṃsāric goods, like reputation, material possessions, and even bodily health, are harmful only to the extent that this loss generates anger and other pathological emotions.[43] In verse 6:67 Śāntideva draws the conclusion that the overall contribution to harm by victim and harm-doer is equal, in that both have generated pathological emotions during the dispute. The enemy harms the bodhisattva motivated by his anger, and the bodhisattva becomes angry in response. Therefore, blame and anger are no more appropriate toward the adversary than for the bodhisattva. The relevant conception of rationality in this argument is consistency. If one is not angry at oneself when one has generated the pathological emotions, anger toward others is inappropriate as well.

It is natural to wonder whether Śāntideva's emphasis on responsibility for the harm one experiences entails the problematic position of blaming the victim for their own suffering, and a corresponding passivity toward preventing physical and mental abuse. This does not follow, however. The bodhisattva's compassion entails a commitment to removing suffering wherever it occurs. Moreover, abusive situations can act as very real causes of suffering, given their role in causing the emotional suffering of the psychopathologies. It is only the highly developed bodhisattva, protected by patience and the other virtues, who can experience situations of deprivation without mentally afflictive response. Until their training is sufficiently advanced, bodhisattvas also must avoid these circumstances (BCA 5:87; 7:23–6). What Śāntideva is arguing for in chapter six is that the harm-doer, just as much as the victim, suffers from the anguish of the pathological emotions. This entails that compassion is the rationally appropriate response toward both parties. It suggests as well that the bodhisattva will commit to preventing abusive situations whenever doing so is feasible.

3.4.5. The benefits of enemies argument (BCA 6:104–8)

We have seen how Śāntideva's causal analysis of anger enables him to lay out various strategies to eliminate it. Anger can be destroyed by removing either of its subjective causal factors, mental pain and self-centered desires. Likewise, it can be eliminated by removing false beliefs about its object, the enemy who harms us. If this exhausted Śāntideva's strategies to prevent anger, the ensuing eradication of desire would result in the renunciation of ordinary existence and entry into final nirvāṇa after death. Instead, in line with his Mahāyāna commitments, Śāntideva emphasizes developing altruistic motivations to replace self-centered desire, and therefore references *bodhicitta* frequently as the chapter progresses.

There are two ways *bodhicitta* is relevant to eliminating anger. First, Śāntideva appeals to it, and the resulting commitment to the bodhisattva path, as premises in arguments for the incompatibility of anger with the bodhisattva's goals. These include his argument that jealousy is incompatible with caring for sentient beings' happiness (BCA 6:80–3), as well as an argument that we should benefit beings to repay the debt that is owed to buddhas and high-level bodhisattvas (BCA 6:119–26). But we should also recognize the repeated references to compassion and *bodhicitta* as completing the psychological treatment that Śāntideva prescribes for the bodhisattva at the beginning of the chapter. Developing altruistic motivation eliminates the self-centered motives whose frustration causes mental pain and thereby anger. Desire is not merely tamed in the sixth chapter, but it is also purified and intensified as the wish for saṃsāric well-being is transformed into the aspiration to benefit all beings.

An influential argument toward the end of the chapter appeals to *bodhicitta* as motivating the bodhisattva's aspiration to develop the virtues of patience and generosity. In this argument, the usual attitude toward enemies is inverted; they are now seen as beneficial, in acting as a condition for progressing toward buddhahood:

> We describe a cause as a thing without which something else does not exist, but which is present when the other thing exists. How can that thing be called an obstacle? (BCA 6:104)
>
> A mendicant approaching at the right time does not impede generous action. The arrival of an ordained person is not called an impediment to becoming a monastic. (BCA 6:105)
>
> Those requesting gifts are easy to find in the world, but wrongdoers are hard to find since no one will harm me if I have not harmed anyone. (BCA 6:106)
>
> Therefore, like a precious treasure found at home, that is gained without effort, I should long for my enemy since he assists me in my bodhisattva trainings. (BCA 6:107)

Like many theorists of virtue, Śāntideva conceives of virtuous mental states as the qualities which enable responding well to situations of adversity. This entails that fully developing virtuous character requires encountering crises. In 6:105, Śāntideva references the example of generosity, which is developed by offering gifts to those in need.[44] Likewise, one devoted to bodhisattva training should rejoice when encountering enemies, since they facilitate the development of patience (6:106–7). We should also connect this argument to Śāntideva's claim that keeping the mind joyful in situations of adversity prevents anger. Recognizing abuse by enemies as an opportunity to develop patience is a reliable way to do this. As Nicolas Bommarito points out, Śāntideva develops patience by widening our perspective to consider the significance of seemingly unpleasant events for our broader goals and commitments (Bommarito 2014, 273–4).

This does not exhaust the strategies for eliminating anger that are found in chapter six; however, it gives us a good understanding of Śāntideva's overall approach for developing patience toward those who harm us.

3.5. Conclusion

Anger, for Śāntideva, is a mental attitude which internally lashes out at whatever is frustrating one's desires. Patience, as its antidote, is the mental state which lets the virtuous person remain calm in difficult circumstances. In addition to eliminating anger, it also enables experiencing any level of physical pain without mental distress. In so doing, patience protects the bodhisattva from the harms of anger, including the psychological, social, and karmic disruption which it causes. Likewise, it is central to progress on the bodhisattva path, both as being one of the perfections constituting virtuous character, and in protecting positive karmic merit from destruction.

Contemporary academic treatments of the *Guide*'s chapter six have tended to focus on Śāntideva's arguments for the irrationality of anger toward enemies, sometimes placing him in conversation with hard determinist theories of free will (Goodman 2002) or ancient Greek thought (Vernezze 2008). I have also emphasized the importance of these passages in what I have called the "object-oriented strategy," in which Śāntideva argues for anger's irrationality by drawing attention to the myriad causal factors which contribute to the moment of harm. It is important, however, to recognize that chapter six uses argumentation as a tool to craft character. Anger can only be completely eradicated by eliminating its psychological causes, self-centered desires whose frustration causes mental pain. The key to doing so is to keep the mind joyful, which is achieved through refining one's conception of well-being, thereby transforming self-centered motivations into *bodhicitta*. These objective and subjective strategies complement each other throughout the chapter; we miss an essential feature of Śāntideva's method if we remain focused on particular arguments in isolation.

Attention to Śāntideva's analysis of the psychology of anger also helps us appreciate the cyclic organization of the chapter, itself a manifestation of Śāntideva's commitment to presenting a gradated path accessible to untrained persons. Patience is introduced as providing commonsense benefits such as mental peace and improved social relationships that would be attractive to non-Buddhists and low-level bodhisattvas. Once undertaken, however, the practices which develop patience will lessen selfish desire and reshape the practitioner's conception of well-being, resulting in a reduction in anger and increased altruistic motivation, leading to an even stronger commitment to further training in patience and so on.

Śāntideva's method in chapter six is also phenomenological in important respects. Throughout the chapter, Śāntideva portrays patience as the rational response to a fragmented but interconnected world. We falsely perceive transient phenomena as able to provide lasting satisfaction and suffer terribly when our desires are frustrated. The solution is not to alter the fundamental nature of the world, which is impossible, but to transform self-centered grasping into deep concern for the well-being of all. Likewise, we are patient when we perceive other sentient beings accurately, as radically dependent and fragile, prey to the controlling influence of the pathological emotions from which they suffer. Compassion, rather than anger, is the only rational response to sentient beings perceived accurately, alongside the bodhisattva's own recognition of the role that she plays in generating their and her own distress.

Cross-culturally, Śāntideva's account of anger is in sharp contrast with more moderate positions, which hold that anger is an appropriate response to situations of injustice, or abuse. These include classical authors like Aristotle, but also many contemporary philosophers, who stress the motivational and epistemic benefits of anger (Nussbaum 1994, Lorde 1997, Bell 2009).[45] Further work is needed to consider what challenges such positions raise for Śāntideva, as well as the resources his psychological and argumentative strategies contribute to contemporary discussions. Likewise, Śāntideva's emphasis on the relationship between anger and desire invites comparative study with Hellenistic traditions such as Epicureanism and Stoicism, as well as Confucian authors like Mencius and Xunzi, who stress the need to refine desire and eliminate harmful emotions.

As we have seen previously in Śāntideva's account of generosity, and as we will find again in his development of compassion, Śāntideva's conception of patience is totalizing, in that when perfected it encompasses virtually every moment of experience. Maintaining patience requires keeping the mind forever joyful, through a complete transformation of character which overhauls motivation and radically alters one's conception of value. Doing so fully will require the development of all the other virtues, including the repeated application of wisdom. It will also require the perfection of ethical discipline which we have seen for Śāntideva means the proper and continual application of mindfulness and introspection.[46] As a result, every unpleasant situation encountered, every tinge of physical pain or potentially annoying behavior by others, will not disturb the mind. I return to the question of the relation between Śāntideva's virtues, and their mutual penetration of all experience, in the conclusion to this book.

Suggestions for further study

An excellent analysis of Śāntideva's understanding of patience in the *Guide*, compete with translation of Prajñākaramati's commentary to BCA chapter six, is given in Nelson 2021. Cozort 2013 provides a sensitive treatment of the *Guide*'s attitude toward pain. Influential treatments of Śāntideva's universal causation argument (BCA 6:22–33) include Goodman 2002 and Breyer 2013. Vernezze 2008 provides a comparative study of Buddhist and Stoic arguments that anger is irrational. Bommarito 2014 gives an elegant argument emphasizing the role of proper perspective in Śāntideva's arguments for anger's irrationality. Barnes 2020 offers a broader argument that anger is never a valid response to situations of distress and injustice. A commentary on the *Guide*'s patience chapter can be found in Dalai Lama 1997.

Questions for reflection

1. What is patience, according to Śāntideva? What is its relation to anger?
2. What does Śāntideva identify as the psychological causes of anger? Do you think this is accurate?
3. What, according to Śāntideva, is the relation between anger and physical pain? Do you agree?

4. Śāntideva claims that anger arises in part because of a distorted perception of the world. Do you think this is right? Is anger sometimes an appropriate response to certain situations, such as those of gross injustice?
5. Contrast two or three of the strategies Śāntideva uses to eliminate anger. Which do you think would be most effective? Are any of the techniques incompatible with any of the others?

Chapter 4

Compassion and Desire

4.1. Introduction

The eighth chapter of the *Guide* interweaves a complex web of themes central to Śāntideva's conception of the bodhisattva path. Its descriptions of saṃsāric societal dysfunction, and the repulsiveness of the body, interspaced with graphic charnel-ground contemplations, are among the most visceral depictions of suffering and the faults of saṃsāra in the text. The second half of the chapter is composed of meditations to develop compassion, including Śāntideva's influential equalizing self and other argument, which reasons that selfishness is irrational, given the commonality of suffering, and the non-existence of an enduring unified self. It also contains the exchanging self and other meditation sequence, in which the bodhisattva imaginatively takes up the standpoint of others as a way of strengthening compassion.

What is less clear is how the various parts of the chapter cohere, and in particular how the first half of the chapter, largely dedicated to meditating on the faults of saṃsāra, connects with the second half, devoted to developing compassion. The situation is made more difficult by Śāntideva's relative disinterest in explicating the perfection from which the chapter takes its name, concentration (*dhyāna*).[1] More than half of the chapter's 186 verses were added at a later date (Saito 1993 and 2000), and so it may be tempting to treat it as an anthology of important but not clearly connected meditations relevant to the bodhisattva path.[2] Nevertheless, I will argue that we need to understand how the parts of the chapter function together if we are to fully appreciate Śāntideva's presentation of the benefits of compassion.

We can understand the chapter better if we view it as a study of the relationship between three items: craving, and particularly the way it manifests as inflated self-interest (*svārtha*); and two strategies to lessen its negative effects, seclusion (*viveka*) and compassion (*karuṇā*). Early verses of the chapter (8:5–25) analyze how craving contaminates social relationships, generating pathological emotions like envy and arrogant pride, and inspiring harmful actions. Śāntideva then introduces two solutions to address these problems. The first, seclusion, is modeled on the early Buddhist path aiming at liberation for oneself; the practitioner abandons society to escape relationships which trigger craving and other negative emotions. The wish to flee society is introduced in verse 8:14, and is carried out in verse 8:26, where we find the bodhisattva retreat into the wilderness to practice contemplations designed to lessen lust until 8:89. The most graphic of these meditations are a series of charnel-ground contemplations which develop awareness of the impermanent and impersonal nature of the body.

These practices provide the foundation for the chapter's second, and deeper antidote to craving: the development of universal compassion for all beings. Meditations and arguments to develop compassion make up the entire second half of the chapter (8:90–186). Here, Śāntideva will argue that the initial strategy of seclusion was insufficient in two ways. First, given that everyone wants happiness and freedom from suffering, it is irrational to prioritize one's own well-being (8:90–106). Second, inflated self-interest and the grasping at self (*ātma-parigraha*) from which it emerges are the root of all suffering. Therefore, one cannot escape suffering through social isolation, but only by transforming self-centered attitudes into compassion (8:116–86). These arguments are most centrally presented in the influential sequences referred to as "equalizing self and other" and "exchanging self and other," respectively.

Although each part of the chapter does important work in its own right, it is essential to understand their relationship in order to fully appreciate Śāntideva's conception of the self-benefiting properties of compassion. This is because the second half of the chapter, and in particular the exchanging self and other meditations, illustrates how compassion acts as an antidote to inflated self-interest, and the afflictive social emotions of arrogant pride, competitiveness, and envy, which are a primary focus of the chapter's first twenty verses. This shows how compassion, according to Śāntideva, eliminates a pernicious kind of emotional suffering arising from craving-infected relationships, and as a result deeply benefits the bodhisattva. Just as importantly, it enables him to engage skillfully with sentient beings, in his work of benefiting the world.

I divide my explication of the chapter into three parts. The section following this introduction explains Śāntideva's analysis of how craving infects social relationships and causes emotional pain. It then presents the first of Śāntideva's strategies to lessen craving: seclusion, in which the bodhisattva flees saṃsāric society into the wilderness to meditate. This section includes a brief treatment of some of Śāntideva's charnel-ground contemplations which are designed to eliminate lust. The next section analyzes the first of Śāntideva's compassion practices, called "equalizing self and other," and the last section focuses on the second set of compassion meditations, the "exchanging self and other" exercises. In this last section, I will also show how Śāntideva deploys compassion as an antidote to self-interest and the fundamental grasping at self from which it arises, thereby destroying the pathological social emotions which destabilized the bodhisattva's societal relationships.

4.2. *The strategy of seclusion*

4.2.1. Craving, self-interest and saṃsāric society

A surprising feature of the eighth chapter of the *Guide* is that, although its title and stated purpose is to develop the perfection of meditative concentration (*samādhi/dhyāna*), the chapter provides relatively little guidance about how this is done. Nevertheless, Śāntideva opens the chapter by commenting on the importance of concentration:

> After invigorating effort in this way, one should station the mind in meditative concentration. A person whose mind is scattered stands between the fangs of the pathological emotions. (BCA 8:1)

Meditative concentration is a mental state of intense focus on a single object. It is often presented by Buddhist texts as progressing through four states of absorption, the *dhyāna* stages, resulting in a phenomenological merging with the object of concentration and a temporary cessation of the pathological emotions.[3] Given that the title of chapter eight is *dhyāna*, and that Śāntideva introduces concentration as its topic in this verse, one would expect that he would proceed to explain what concentration is, how to progress through its stages and so on.[4] Although there are occasional references to concentration throughout the chapter (8:1–2, 4, 6, 89), however, it never becomes an extended subject of discussion.

Instead, we find Śāntideva transition to one of his deeper interests in the chapter: describing the drawbacks of saṃsāric society and the pain caused by craving. Craving is introduced, however, in a way that connects it to the topic of concentration, by emphasizing its capacity to impede meditative focus. This allows Śāntideva to build a double meaning into many of the verses that follow:

> Because of bodily and mental seclusion, distraction does not happen. Therefore, having abandoned the world, one should abandon distracting thoughts. (BCA 8:2)
>
> Because of social attachment (*sneha*) and craving (*tṛṣṇā*) for possessions and other desires, one does not abandon the world. Therefore, to renounce these things, the wise person should reflect as follows: (BCA 8:3)[5]

On one level of meaning, verses 2 and 3 can be read as giving instructions for preliminary practices conducive to developing meditative concentration. One such practice referred to frequently in Buddhist texts is going to a secluded place to minimize distraction, as indicated by Śāntideva in 8:2.[6] Moreover, concentration instructions also list five mental states called hindrances (*nīvaraṇāni*) which impede concentration and therefore must be weakened before concentration practice proper begins (Gunaratana 1980, 56–105). Śāntideva's reference to social attachment (*sneha*) and craving (*tṛṣṇā*) in verse 3 can be understood as an allusion to one of these hindrances: craving, in the form of sensual desire (*kamācchanda*). Many of the verses which follow, that give meditations and arguments to lessen craving, can be partially understood as treatments to weaken this hindrance.

Actual instructions on how to engage in concentration meditation, however, do not appear in the chapter, or anywhere in the text, and this suggests that Śāntideva's deepest concern is not developing concentration, but rather compassion and the elimination of selfish desire. He transitions to these topics through exploiting the multiple roles played by the pathological emotion of craving, which is not only a hindrance to concentration, but also acts as one of the root causes of the suffering of saṃsāra. These verses can be read in this dual manner, as offering treatments to weaken the hindrances, while also exploring the broader pernicious effects of craving:

> How could attachment toward an impermanent person be worthwhile for an impermanent person who will not see his loved ones again for thousands of births? (BCA 8:5)
>
> He becomes displeased when not seeing them and cannot remain in meditative concentration. Even when he sees them, he is not satisfied, but is tormented by craving just as before. (BCA 8:6)

Verse 8:6 briefly signals continued interest in concentration meditation, by indicating the role romantic love and sexual lust play in impeding mental focus. The real topic of these verses, however, is the analysis of how craving infects relationships and thereby generates suffering. Throughout this part of the chapter, Śāntideva draws upon early Buddhist critiques of the impoverished nature of sense pleasure, which are elsewhere referred to as the suffering of change (*vipariṇāma-duḥkha*).[7] Verse 8:5 emphasizes the anxiety caused by the realization that one's relationships with loved ones will end in death. 8:6 describes the impoverished nature of craving, which by its nature can never be satisfied. Śāntideva emphasizes the inevitability of suffering by a craving-infected mind through presenting a dilemma. When we are separated from a loved one, we suffer from longing. Sensual desire, however, is addictive, and the presence of the loved one increases its force, causing jealousy and the emotional pain of clinging. Inevitably, affectionate relationships, contaminated by selfish desire, are filled with anguish.

Śāntideva deepens his critique of saṃsāric social interactions by examining a series of negative emotions arising from hierarchically structured relationships between persons pursing their own self-interest:

> They are envious of superior persons, competitive with equals, and full of arrogant pride toward inferiors. They become conceited when praised and angry when criticized. What good can come from interacting with a foolish person? (BCA 8:12)
>
> From one foolish person to another, unwholesome behavior is inevitable, such as boasting about oneself, criticism of another, or conversing about the delights of saṁsāra. (BCA 8:13)

The verses continue to illustrate how craving contaminates relationships by examining its emotional manifestations in social interaction. Verse 12 takes the form of a trilemma, a strengthening of the dilemma about desire used in 8:6. We stand in three possible social relationships to persons, all of which are dominated by a social pathological emotion. Those who are inferior to us are filled with envy (*īrṣya*) for our superior position. Our relationships between our equals in social status are dominated with competitiveness (*dvandva*), a socialized manifestation of anger, while those in a superior position look down on us with arrogant pride (*māna*). Each of these pathological emotions are a manifestation of selfishness, the propensity to value one's own well-being over others. As a result, every relationship becomes a hierarchical struggle for better status.

Verse 12 then describes how the bodhisattva is unable to have a positive influence on people in saṃsāra. If he subordinates himself to them and tries flattery as a way of encouragement, this inflates their self-worth, causing them to become conceited. If he presents himself as their superior, however, and takes up the position of educator, then they become angry. Verse 13 turns to the verbal behavior of beings in saṃsāra, who conceitedly praise themselves, or spitefully criticize others, or encourage pursuit of unstable saṃsāric goods that cannot bring lasting satisfaction. Śāntideva uses dilemmas and trilemmas in these verses as a way of illustrating the inevitability of emotional disfunction, aggression, and anguish in relationships between persons infected with craving. As he contemplates the seeming inevitability of social strife, the bodhisattva's sense of despair grows.

Śāntideva presents these verses from the standpoint of a bodhisattva observing the unbalanced behavior of others without recognizing her susceptibility to these same faults. In the second half of the chapter, the bodhisattva will be shown the error of this assumption. During the exchanging self and other meditations, imaginatively taking up the standpoint of others reveals that she is perceived by them in the same way: as filed with envy, competitiveness, and arrogant pride. This insight, as we will see, enables the bodhisattva to purify herself of dysfunctional social emotions and replace them with compassion.

These verses show that the suffering caused by saṃsāric relationships results from their hierarchical nature; the social superior is envied by her social inferior and so on. Purifying afflictive social emotions, therefore, requires equalizing these relationships. Śāntideva will accomplish this in the second half of the chapter, through an extended meditative argument called "equalizing self and other" which develops compassion by stressing the equal wish for happiness and freedom from suffering possessed by all beings (8:90–106). At this point in the chapter, however, the bodhisattva does not understand that compassion can assuage his mental anguish in this way.

Instead, Śāntideva has the bodhisattva reject a possible solution to the social trilemma described in 8:12. Why can't the bodhisattva strive to always maintain the higher social position, thereby achieving his aims?

> A mortal person thinking "I am wealthy and well-respected and sought after by many people" experiences fear as death approaches. (BCA 8:17)

That very thing in which a mind, infatuated with pleasure, takes delight will become suffering, multiplied a thousand times. (BCA 8:18)

Therefore, the wise do not desire it. Fear is generated from desire, but passes away on its own. Be composed and behold it with indifference. (BCA 8:19)

Many people have been wealthy, and many people have been famous. Where they went with their possessions and fame is unknown. (BCA 8:20)

The most desirable of the three social positions introduced in verse 8:12 would seem to be that of the social superior who is proud of his status and is envied by others. Śāntideva rejects this view by appealing once again to the pernicious nature of craving which stimulates negative emotions like fear. Upon achieving a good reputation and obtaining material success (8:17–18), craving manifests as a neurotic desire to guard one's accomplishments, resulting in continual anxiety (8:19). Moreover, all saṃsāric success is impermanent, and so the anguish of losing one's possessions is unavoidable (8:20). Finally, the inevitability of death is a constant terror for successful people (8:17). We should also recall the various arguments Śāntideva has been making throughout the *Guide* about the pernicious nature of saṃsāric success, such as its proclivity to cause anger (chapter 6) and impede spiritual commitment (chapter 7).

Śāntideva now identifies the cause of the dysfunctional nature of saṃsāric relationships:

The buddhas said, "A fool is a friend to none, since their affection is never without self-interest." (BCA 8:24)

Affection entered into with self-interest is affection for oneself only. It is similar to feeling anxiety about losing a treasured possession, not for the sake of the object, but for being deprived of enjoying it. (BCA 8:25)

The cause of the social suffering described in these opening verses is that participation in these relationships is motivated by self-interest (*svārtha*: 8:24–5), the inflated valuation of one's own well-being as more important than that of others. Eventually, in the second half of the chapter, Śāntideva will further analyze self-interest as being caused by the fundamental grasping at self (*ātma-parigraha*: 8:134), a deeply engrained selfishness which arises out of the erroneous belief in an enduring unified self. Śāntideva is not, however, rejecting the importance of caring for oneself; rather he is illustrating the harmful results of an inflated concern for one's own happiness. This inflated self-interest causes human relationships to be conceived of as analogous to material possessions, in being valuable only to the extent that they benefit the individual. The affection one feels for such friends is like the distress one feels at losing a treasured possession; in both cases, one's only concern is in the pleasure the person or object brings to oneself (8:25).

These verses, then, distinguish self-interested affection from compassion, the pure concern for the well-being of others, which is the topic of the second half of the chapter. Affection contaminated by self-interest is the root of social suffering, since it ensures that all relationships are structured hierarchically, resulting in envy at those who are more successful, contempt toward those less successful, and competitiveness toward social equals. For ordinary persons, all saṃsāric relationships are infected with self-interest, and therefore even friendships and romantic partnerships will be interpreted through the lens of how these relationships benefit oneself. Such selfishness eliminates any possibility for genuine connection with others, preventing meaningful affection based upon concern for the other person's welfare.

Śāntideva presents two solutions to the problem of inflated self-interest in chapter eight. The first is seclusion (*viveka*). Since relationships contaminated by craving for one's own well-being are reliable generators of suffering, the bodhisattva can temporarily escape social suffering by fleeing society altogether. He thereby avoids triggering his own pathological emotions while escaping the aggressive behavior of others. Śāntideva presents this solution at the conclusion of this opening section, by portraying the bodhisattva as fleeing society into the wilderness.

There is a certain limitation to this strategy, however, which Śāntideva already hints at by identifying inflated self-interest as the root cause of social suffering. Social isolation, of itself, will not eliminate the bodhisattva's deeply rooted selfishness. Therefore, this array of disadvantages will be experienced again, anytime the bodhisattva encounters beings in the future. If he is to keep his bodhisattva commitment, moreover, he will need to reengage with society. The better solution is to eliminate inflated self-interest by developing its opposite, compassion which cares equally for all beings. The entire second half of the chapter will be dedicated to meditations and arguments to achieve this goal.

At this early point in the chapter, however, the bodhisattva does not recognize the social benefits of compassion; therefore, flight into the wilderness appears to be his only option:

> One fool, through association with another, encounters misfortune in many ways. I will happily live alone, with an unafflicted mind. (BCA 8:14)
>
> One should go far away from a fool. One should conciliate people encountered with pleasantries, not with intimate relationships but with a benevolent indifference. (BCA 8:15)
>
> Taking only what is of use for the Dharma, like a bee takes nectar from a flower, I will wander everywhere as a stranger, like someone who did not previously exist. (BCA 8:16)

These verses introduce the first of Śāntideva's solutions to the problem of craving, in its manifestation as inflated self-interest, and the societal pain it causes. This solution is seclusion (*viveka*), removing oneself from society.[8] Śāntideva introduces this strategy by describing the bodhisattva's wish to live alone with an "unafflicted mind" (*akliṣṭa-mānasa*: 8:14). The phrase can be taken literally, since in the wilderness the bodhisattva will enjoy a temporary respite from the pathological social emotions of envy, pride, and competitiveness.

The next two verses acknowledge that basic material needs entail that complete avoidance of people and possessions is not realistic. When interaction is necessary, it should be done without emotional involvement, with kindness but also with indifference (8:15). The idea is to avoid engaging in intimate relationships which generate pathological emotions. Verse 8:16 explains how the renunciate should relate to pleasure gained from satisfying necessary desires, like the enjoyment of eating. It should be enjoyed just as a bee drinks nectar, that is without lingering over the pleasure and without thoughts of ownership. The reference to living "like someone who did not previously exist" references the bodhisattva's abandonment of reputation, thereby protecting himself from the envy of others, and his own propensity for arrogant pride.

Verse 8:16 also describes the solitary bodhisattva's period of seclusion and restraint as being in accord with Dharma, meaning that it is a part of spiritual practice. The bodhisattva in the wilderness temporarily takes on the role of the solitary realizer, a Buddhist practitioner who attains awakening for his own sake without guidance from a buddha or monastic community. The meditations in the wilderness can also be seen as standing in for the entire set of practices and aims of the vehicle of the disciple, the early Buddhist path which seeks to eliminate craving in order to attain nirvāṇa for oneself, leaving saṃsāra behind. In the compassion meditations to follow, Śāntideva will critique and reject this conception of liberation. However, he acknowledges that early Buddhists correctly identify the impoverished nature of craving, and its ability to infect societal relationships. Śāntideva's strategy in chapter eight is to incorporate these early Buddhist insights into his conception of the bodhisattva path, as preparatory practices which weaken the force of the pathological emotions and prepare the bodhisattva's mind to develop impartial compassion.

Śāntideva then begins to describe the mental peace experienced when society is abandoned:

> Trees do not harass anyone, and do not need to be appeased by a special effort. When might I live among those whose company is pleasurable? (BCA 8:26)
>
> Residing in an empty temple, or at the foot of a tree, or in caves, when will I travel, untroubled, without looking back? (BCA 8:27)
>
> When will I wander as I wish through unowned wild expansive regions, with no fixed resting place? (BCA 8:28)
>
> When will I wander without fear, with an unprotected body, wearing a robe that would not attract a thief, having as property merely a clay bowl? (BCA 8:29)

The overall effect of these verses is to illustrate the mental peace that the bodhisattva experiences in the wilderness, while temporarily freed from the pathological emotions.[9] The verses target the specific kinds of societal suffering which Śāntideva has described in the preceding verses as being caused by inflated self-interest. The suggestion to take trees as one's companions (8:26) is a poetic presentation of the use of social isolation to avoid the pain of sensual craving (see 8:5–6) and the negative emotions of envy, pride, and competitiveness (see 8:12). The lack of concern for the past referenced in verse 8:27 indicates the bodhisattva's abandonment of reputation, freeing him from the emotional pain of occupying esteemed social positions (see 8:17 and 8:20). Finally, the reference in 8:29 to the worthlessness of the wandering bodhisattva's possessions indicates that he has escaped the fear of loss and intensification of craving which accompanies material prosperity (see 8:17–20). Having given up saṃsāric success and reputation, the bodhisattva no longer needs to fear impermanence and death (see 8:17).

The bodhisattva's sojourn in the wilderness, and the meditations he enacts there which we examine in the next subsection, are effective in weakening craving, and the pathological emotions which arise from it, a point suggested by Śāntideva's beautiful descriptions of the peace the bodhisattva experiences in solitude.[10] Nevertheless, the praise of seclusion given here contrasts sharply with the bodhisattva's way of life, which requires passionate dedication to sentient beings, coupled with a deep concern for their welfare. Part of what Śāntideva is doing in chapter eight is contrasting early Buddhist attitudes to practice and liberation, represented in the first half of the chapter, with Mahāyāna soteriological conceptions of liberation within saṃsāra. In the second half of the chapter, Śāntideva will sharply critique the early Buddhist perspective, as being virtually incoherent in its simultaneous emphasis on eliminating inflated self-interest, while taking as primary the aim of one's own liberation from suffering. Early Buddhist insights about the impoverished nature of craving, however, are not rejected, but are incorporated into Śāntideva's conception of the bodhisattva path by providing the psychological foundation for developing compassion.

4.2.2. The charnel ground (BCA 8:30–88)

The sections of chapter eight that we have examined thus far, on the dissatisfactory nature of saṃsāric society, and the bodhisattva's flight into the wilderness, are followed by a long section in which the bodhisattva engages in a series of contemplations on rotting corpses, interspersed with meditations on the repulsive aspects of the human body. The primary purpose of these exercises is to reduce craving, in the form of sensual lust. In so doing, they continue the work of the previous section, in which Śāntideva contemplated the dysfunctional nature of saṃsāric relationships. These meditations lay the ground for the compassion meditations to follow, by weakening craving to the point where deep concern for others can begin to emerge. Some of the meditations also emphasize the impersonal nature of the body, thereby preparing the bodhisattva for the exchanging self and other meditations to come, which require imaginative disengagement from one's own body.

As is usual in the complex interweaving of themes in chapter eight, these verses fulfill other functions as well. In terms of the formal purpose of the chapter, Buddhist texts often describe charnel grounds as suitable places for engaging in concentration meditation (Gunaratana 1980, 55). Likewise, bodies in various stages of decay are one of the objects focused on during these meditations (Gunaratana 1980, 49). Therefore, the bodhisattva can be thought of as having entered the charnel ground to engage in these practices. Nevertheless, the charnel-ground meditations Śāntideva actually presents do not seem to be intended to develop meditative concentration. They emphasize various aspects of decomposing bodies in quick succession and are highly discursive, drawing conceptual conclusions regarding the incoherence of valuing the body and the worthlessness of romantic love. This would limit the development of concentrative focus. The real purpose of the section is not nurturing concentration, but rather deepening insight into impermanence and selflessness and weakening sensual desire.

These verses are also where the existential themes of the chapter emerge most forcefully. Chapter eight as a whole can be read as an existential journey of separation from, and then reconnection to the ordinary world. In the opening section just considered, the suffering the bodhisattva experiences in society causes the breakdown of his ordinary set of values. This is analogous to the existential collapse of meaning referenced by European authors like Kierkegaard and Heidegger. The bodhisattva's flight into the wilderness and the charnel ground plays the role of the breakdown state of existential death in Heidegger's *Being and Time*, or despair in the thought of Kierkegaard, in which all ordinary motivations and value systems collapse.[11] The bodhisattva will not remain in this nihilistic state, however, but will reconnect with the world through engaging in compassion meditations which make up the second half of the chapter. These awaken the new master value of *bodhicitta*, the commitment to eliminate the suffering of all beings, which inspires the bodhisattva's reconnection with society. I will not be able to develop this aspect of the chapter in detail here, but the existential themes of chapter eight emerge so strongly in the charnel-ground contemplations that it deserves mention.

My treatment of the rich and complex set of meditations and arguments in this section is necessarily brief; I restrict myself to drawing attention to Śāntideva's presentation of the insights just summarized:

> When will I go to a nearby charnel ground to compare my own body, whose nature is to decay, with the skeletons of others? (BCA 8:30)

> Indeed, this very body of mine will become so fetid that even a jackal would not creep close because of its stench. (BCA 8:31)
>
> If the co-arisen bones of this single body are breaking to pieces, how much more will other beloved persons depart, one by one. (BCA 8:32)

These verses initiate the bodhisattva's contemplation of corpses in a charnel ground, a practice which occurs intermittently for much of the next sixty verses. The primary purpose of these passages is to decrease sensual desire, accomplished here through contemplating decaying bodies (8:30) while observing their rotting stench (8:31) and exposed bones (8:32). Verse 8:32 also stresses the fragile nature of the body, and its disunity, the fact that it is a contingent collection of bones which are now disintegrating. Metaphorically, this sets up a parallel with the fragmentation and disunity of the social relationships the bodhisattva experienced in saṃsāric society. Just as affectionate relationships dissolve in the acidic emotional adversity of the pathological emotions, likewise the physical body is only a temporary configuration always on the verge of collapse. We will find additional attention to the contingent nature of the body in the compassion meditations to follow, particularly in the exchanging self and other meditations where the bodhisattva, having recognized the body's impersonal nature, will imaginatively disengage from it and take up the perspective of others.

> A person is born alone and dies completely alone. No one else can share in this suffering. Of what use are loved ones who act as hindrances? (BCA 8:33)
>
> Having neither affections nor hostility, the renunciate owns only his body. He has died to the world a long time ago, so has no regrets when dying. (BCA 8:36)

The verses continue the theme of the unreliability of social relationships, given their radical impermanence due to the inevitability of death. They are also where the existential themes of the chapter emerge forcefully. The bodhisattva, in his role as renunciate in the wilderness, has "died to the world," which is to say he has wholly abandoned all social goals and obligations. Being in the charnel ground metaphorically represents the state in which saṃsāric value has collapsed. Dying to the world also indicates the bodhisattva's complete abandonment of fame and reputation, which triggered hostile emotions from others, and reinforced his own arrogance (8:17, 8:20). The verses also provide a striking example of the contrast between the present strategy of seclusion from society and the compassion meditations to follow. In the current verses the bodhisattva's goal is simply to isolate himself from all social contact and thereby avoid the aggression of others and the stimulation of his own pathological emotions. By contrast, the later compassion meditations not only reestablish, but intensify the bodhisattva's motivation to engage with others, through strengthening and universalizing his commitment to end suffering.

In the following set of verses, Śāntideva transitions from the contemplation of corpses, to considering the disgusting processes of the human body such as digestion and excretion:

> If you do not want to touch soil and anything else defiled with excrement, why do you want to touch the body from which it came? (BCA 8:58)
>
> If you do not desire an impure thing, why do you embrace another body which originated in a field of filth, was born there, and was nourished by it? (BCA 8:59)
>
> Because it is small, you do not desire an impure worm which is born in filth, but you do desire a body that is made up of great quantities of filth and is also born in filth! (BCA 8:60)
>
> Oh you who are voracious for feces! Not only do you not despise your own filthiness, but you desire other vessels of filth! (BCA 8:61)
>
> Since the body causes great terror when its skin is ripped off, how, even after realizing this, can you feel passion nevertheless for that very thing? (BCA 8:64)
>
> Even though it is applied to the body, this scent is merely from sandalwood, nothing else. Why are you enamored of one thing because of a scent belonging to something else? (BCA 8:65)

The most obvious purpose of these passages is to function as another antidote to lust, through contemplating repulsive aspects of the body, such as excretion (58–61) as well as the blood and pus inside the body (64) and the body's naturally foul smell (65). Simply drawing attention to what we find repulsive about the body lessens or eliminates sensual desire. Notice Śāntideva's use of imagination in the meditation, in visualizing the inside of the body and its repulsive fluids.[12] Moreover, all such meditations are facilitated by the virtuous mental factors of mindfulness and introspection, which become aware that craving is arising and facilitate the deployment of these images as an antidote to eliminate it.[13]

The verses also do argumentative work, in drawing attention to the conceptual processes of exclusion which condition sensual lust. Desire arises toward a body only when aspects of visual perception are suppressed: we do not notice spittle on the edge of the lips, or the sweat on the cheeks and nose. Likewise, we ignore our awareness of what goes on beneath the skin—the digestion of food and churning of excrement running through the digestive track. In addition, as Śāntideva points out in 8:65, much of what attracts us to a body is external to it. He uses the example of sandalwood perfume, but the same point applies to clothes, jewelry, and all cosmetic treatments, which are extrinsic to the body, yet facilitate our lust for it. Perceiving bodies as pure and attractive, Śāntideva is arguing, is a delusion, facilitated through processes of confusion and conceptual exclusion. It is irrational, and recognizing this will weaken and finally eliminate sensual desire.

The insights presented in the first half of the eighth chapter must be taken with care. On the one hand, these verses accurately diagnose problems with inflated self-interest and sensual desire, which are insatiable, and which give rise to harmful emotions that contaminate relationships. Moreover, the meditations in the wilderness do important work toward lessening craving and developing awareness of the impersonal and contingent nature of the body. All of this is a necessary precondition for developing compassion. As we move into the second half of the chapter, however, Śāntideva will argue that seclusion is not an acceptable final solution to the problem of desire. This is because concern for oneself alone is irrational, given that we have no justification for giving more attention to our own needs than those of other people. We turn to this argument in the following section. Moreover, as the concluding section will show, developing equal concern for all is the only way to fully eliminate inflated self-interest which is the cause of all other pathological emotions.

*4.3. The equalizing self and other (*parātmasamatā*) argument*

4.3.1. Introduction to the second half of the eighth chapter

After emerging from the charnel ground, the bodhisattva practices two series of contemplations designed to lessen selfishness and develop compassion. The first of these is an argument called "equalizing self and other" whose key premise is that all beings equally want happiness and freedom from suffering. The second, which is called "exchanging self and other" has two parts. The first stresses the disadvantages of selfishness and the benefits of compassion. The second is composed of a series of meditations in which the bodhisattva imaginatively identifies with persons who are socially inferior, equal, and finally superior to him. In this meditation, we will find the bodhisattva conjure up and eliminate the pathological emotions of envy, competitiveness, and arrogant pride which caused him to flee into the wilderness.

Generally, I will describe the passages in the equalizing section as an argument, since they explicitly state premises which support Śāntideva's conclusions, and will refer to the exchanging passages as meditations, since they are presented as a series of contemplations. As we will see, however, both sets of passages do argumentative work, and both are meant to develop compassion. The equalizing passages show that a powerful way of achieving this is through inferential reasoning, but here also we will find Śāntideva employing introspective contemplation as a way of strengthening his premises. Likewise, the empathetic observations described in the exchanging passages deepen awareness of the suffering of sentient beings, thereby entailing compassion, rather than anger, is the rational response to their behavior.

4.3.2. The equalizing argument (BCA 8:90–108)

The section known as "equalizing self and other" develops compassion by emphasizing sentient beings' shared experiences of suffering, and their common wish for happiness. The verses take the form of an extended argument demonstrating the irrationality of selfish behavior. The argument has a consequentialist flavor, given that the bodhisattva recognizes an obligation to help others, even if this will not benefit himself.[14] This will contrast with the exchanging self and other meditations which follow, in which the self-beneficial nature of compassion is more strongly emphasized.

Although the section stretches over nineteen verses (8:90–108), the central argument is elegantly presented in only three. To aid in exposition, I present these first (returning to the intervening verses shortly):

> In the beginning, one should cultivate the equality of self and others carefully, in this way: "Everyone equally experiences suffering and happiness and should be protected just as I protect myself." (BCA 8:90)

> Given that happiness is cherished equally by myself and others, then what distinguishes me so that I strive only for my own happiness? (BCA 8:95)

> Given that fear and suffering are equally disliked by myself and others, then what distinguishes me so that I protect myself, and not them? (BCA 8:96)

Śāntideva begins by asking the bodhisattva to introspect on his experiences of happiness and suffering, and then to extend these reflections to others (8:90). In doing so, he draws upon the psychological awareness that has been building throughout the entire text; all the meditations on death, the fear of negative rebirths, the painfulness of anger, and the panic and fear of being controlled by pathological emotions—in verse 8:90 the bodhisattva reflects on the fact that every sentient being experiences similar kinds of suffering. This has two purposes. First, he feels deep compassion for all sentient beings. Second, evidence is provided for the most important premise of the argument. Recognizing the badness of suffering entails a prima facie commitment to remove all of it, no matter to whom it belongs (8:90).

Verses 95–6 next argue that since happiness and freedom from suffering are equally important to all beings, the egoist must justify his current practice of prioritizing his own well-being. If a relevant distinction (*viśeṣa*) cannot be given, then the egoist must accept that selfish behavior is irrational. Although Śāntideva will support and defend these premises for a dozen verses, the basic argument is complete. It begins by establishing a claim about well-being; by appeal to introspection the bodhisattva recognizes the badness of suffering (8:90). This establishes a prima facie commitment to universal benevolence; since everyone suffers, we should remove all of it, no matter where it occurs (8:90). This in turn shifts the burden of proof from the proponent of altruism to the egoist, who must now provide justification for his self-centered behavior (8:95–6). Shortly, the egoist will take up this challenge, and argue that the fact that his pain belongs to him provides the needed justification. Śāntideva will respond to this attempt at 8:97–103.

In the argument above, the term Śāntideva uses that is translated as "suffering" is *duḥkha*, whose wide semantic range can refer to physical pain, or to both physical and mental pain, or to the emotional suffering of the psychopathologies. We have previously seen that Śāntideva holds that the pathological emotions constitute suffering, and it may be that he intends to refer to them here. The argument does not depend on exact precision about well-being, however, and we can also interpret Śāntideva as leaving open in this argument what precisely constitutes suffering in order to engage a wider audience. The verses then would rely upon the broad agreement that we do suffer, without committing to the question of whether physical pain, mental pain, pathological emotions and so on have intrinsic disvalue.

It is also important to consider how this argument functions in relation to the chapter as a whole. In verse 8:12 we saw Śāntideva identify hierarchical relationships based on self-interest as causing the emotional suffering of envy, pride, and competitiveness. Eliminating these pathological emotions requires adopting a perspective from which all persons are seen as equal, despite differences in wealth and social status. Śāntideva's emphasis on the shared experience of happiness and suffering achieves this, and thereby acts as an antidote to the negative social emotions the bodhisattva experienced in society. We will find Śāntideva provide additional treatments to eliminate these harmful emotions in the exchanging self and other meditations, analyzed in the next section.

Śāntideva takes the next several verses following 8:90 to add further support to the basic argument just outlined. Verse 91 provides a method to universalize the wish to remove suffering:

> Just as the body with its natural divisions into hands and the other body parts should be protected as if it were one entity, in the same way all of this divided world, which is undivided in its character of experiencing suffering and happiness, should be protected. (BCA 8:91)

In verse 90, Śāntideva has argued that the bodhisattva should develop compassion toward everyone. Verse 91 responds to an implied objection that this is psychologically impossible, given the limitlessness number of sentient beings.[15] In response, Śāntideva provides a meditative exercise to facilitate expanding compassion to a limitless degree. In the meditation, one widens identification with oneself to encompass the whole world. In this way, ordinary habits of self-interested concern are extended into universal compassion.[16] We can get a sense of what Śāntideva is suggesting when we think of the affection we feel toward our favorite city. Consider our attitude toward that same city when it is struck by a disaster. Even if we currently know no one injured in the emergency, we are still able to feel compassion toward the city as the aggregate of the beings existing there. Similarly, Śāntideva's suggestion is that we can shift the concern that we usually feel for our own self toward the conceptually constructed aggregation of all people. Moreover, as the verse reminds us, the body is itself an aggregation of body parts, and so the fact that we care about protecting our body suggests we are capable of developing concern for the aggregation of all beings.

This is the first of several verses in chapter eight which employs a technique of altering perspective through imaginative expansion or variation of the boundaries of the conventional self. Each use of the technique is a way of reducing selfishness and nurturing compassion. Later in the argument, Śāntideva will alter perspective again by descending to the level of impersonal *dharmas* and directing attention to the badness of ownerless suffering (8:101–3). Likewise, in the exchanging self and other meditations to follow, the bodhisattva temporarily ceases identifying with her own standpoint, and imaginatively adopts the perspective of others. As will become clear below, the bodhisattva's insight into metaphysical selflessness (*anātman*) grants her the psychological flexibility to enact these techniques.

We saw that verse 90 already introduces the central premise of Śāntideva's argument regarding the impersonal badness of suffering. Verses 92–4 offer additional support for this premise by exploring the nature of suffering's negativity:

> Even though my suffering does not hurt other embodied beings, nevertheless, it is still suffering that is hard to bear because of my affection for myself. (BCA 8:92)
>
> Likewise, even though the suffering of another person is not felt by my own self, nevertheless, it is suffering which is hard for him to bear because of his own selfish affection. (BCA 8:93)
>
> I should remove the suffering of others because of its painful nature, just like my own suffering. I should care for others because of their sentient nature, just as I am a sentient being. (BCA 8:94)

Given that we cannot experience the suffering of others directly, Śāntideva's strategy in these verses is to begin with careful contemplation of one's own suffering. In line with the themes of chapter eight, he recognizes that suffering arises because of an inflated sense of self-interest (8:92). Śāntideva has already shown that this is the case in his study of emotional suffering experienced in society (8:5–25). Moreover, Śāntideva has made similar arguments in chapter six, where self-centered desires were identified as the cause of anger and its harmful consequences (6:7). Introspecting on these facts deepens the bodhisattva's awareness of the intrinsic badness of his own suffering. He then infers, in 8:93, that other people experience the same level of suffering, because of their own selfishness. Śāntideva then reaffirms 8:90's conclusion, by insisting that this impersonally bad suffering should be removed no matter where it is located (8:94).

We have already discussed verses 8:95–6, which challenge the opponent to provide a relevant distinction to justify prioritizing her own well-being. The remainder of the main argument, from 8:97–103, consists of Śāntideva's response to the egoist's attempt to provide this justification. The objection, as is usual in Indian texts, is not fully stated, and Śāntideva will simply begin responding to it in verse 8:97. This response suggests that his opponent is an ethical egoist who holds that it is only rational to care for oneself. This opponent accepts Śāntideva's claim about the badness of suffering, but rejects its normative entailment, that this obligates us to eliminate all of it. Since only one's own suffering belongs to oneself, claims the egoist, one should focus on it alone.

Śāntideva's response comes in two parts. First, he claims that the ethical egoist's position conflicts with his own behavior. To make this point, Śāntideva appeals to their shared belief in rebirth:

> If I do not protect the other person from suffering because his suffering does not hurt me, then why protect against the suffering of my future body, since it does not hurt me? (BCA 8:97)
>
> The thought that "I will also be that person" is false, since one person dies and quite another is born. (BCA 8:98)

Śāntideva and his opponent both accept that karmically potent actions done in this life cause the rebirth of a person with that karmic inheritance in the next life. In 8:98, Śāntideva argues that given the lack of physical and psychological continuity between the dying and reborn person, it is not plausible to claim personal identity spans lives.[17] Nevertheless, Śāntideva assumes that the ethical egoist will be concerned about the karmic consequences of his present actions on the reborn person (8:97). This concern provides an example of the egoist's recognition of the need to remove suffering which does not belong to him. Therefore, it shows that his position that one should not care about the suffering of others is inconsistent with his behavior.

There is also a stronger reading of these verses, taken by some of Śāntideva's Tibetan commentators (Williams 1998, 32–4 and 37–41). In this reading, the "future body" indicated in verse 8:97 is a reference to the future configuration of one's body in this lifetime. Given the lack of an enduring self, this future person is not numerically identical to the present person (8:98). In this reading, the reference to death and rebirth in 8:98 refers to the moment-by-moment dissolution and reconstitution of the collection of aggregates which are conceptually labeled the person. When read in this way, it is natural to discuss this argument alongside the subsequent verse:

> If the idea is that suffering should be guarded against by the very same person who experiences it, then why does the hand protect the foot, even though the hand does not experience its pain? (BCA 8:99)

Given their rejection of an enduring unified self, Buddhists claim that persons exist only as conceptual unifications of discrete and radically impermanent physical and mental events. Moreover, this unification has both a spatial and a temporal element: collections of present aggregates are conceptually unified into the present person, and then are mentally combined with past and future collections to result in an enduring person. In the reading now under consideration, 8:97–8 references the temporal element of this unification, while 8:99, by indicating the causal association among discrete body parts, refers to its spatial aspect. When the egoist benefits his future self a few minutes from now, that is an act of altruism, given that the person is not him. Likewise, when he benefits himself *now*, this is also an act of altruism, since there is no metaphysical unity grounding his experience. The prudent egoist refutes his position at every instant.

The next verse responds to an implied reply by the egoist, who now agrees that his selfish behavior is irrational, but argues that it is inevitable because of deeply rooted processes of delusory self-construction:

> If one replies that even though it is senseless, such behavior occurs because of false reification of the self, we reply that senseless behavior should be prevented with all of one's power, whether it is one's own or that of another person. (BCA 8:100)

The opponent in this verse argues that even if egoistic behavior is irrational, it happens automatically, due to clinging to the non-existent self. The term translated as "false reification of the self" is *ahaṁkāra*, which refers to the spontaneous processes of subject creation in which discrete moments of experience are unified and reified into an enduring self. Śāntideva's response is to reject the opponent's claim that *ahaṁkāra* and the selfish behavior that it causes cannot be eliminated. Although this is difficult, as the practices laid out in the *Guide* themselves show, it is possible. This response suggests a connection between the equalizing argument and the exchanging self and other meditations which follow. The roots of egoistic behavior are so deep that they cannot be wholly removed by argumentation alone like that provided in the equalizing verses. Deeper psychological work must be conducted, which is facilitated by the empathetic meditative practices at the end of the chapter.

Thus far, Śāntideva has pointed out contradictions between the egoist's intellectual commitments and his behavior. In the following verses, Śāntideva considers even more directly whether there is any valid justification for selfish behavior:

> A continuum of consciousness, just like any series, and a collection of aggregates, just like an army and other groups, are unreal. The person experiencing suffering does not exist. To whom would it belong? (BCA 8:101)
>
> All sufferings are ownerless, without any exception. They are to be prevented simply because of their painful nature. Why is any limitation applied? (BCA 8:102)
>
> If one asks why suffering should be prevented, it is because there is no disagreement from anyone in this matter. If it is to be prevented, then all of it must be treated in the same way. If not, then this applies to oneself as much as to other sentient beings. (BCA 8:103)

Verse 101 references the central Buddhist metaphysical commitment to the unreality of wholes, entailing that sequences and collections are not real. Given that persons are collections of impermanent mental and physical events, occurring in a causally connected series, it follows that they are unreal, and therefore all suffering is ownerless. Verse 102 then argues that this ownerless suffering must be removed because of its intrinsically negative feel. It is therefore irrational to appeal to the fact that particular pains are "mine," in prioritizing their removal. In verse 103, Śāntideva concludes that to be rationally consistent, we must commit to removing all suffering, or none of it. He briefly considers whether one might take the second of these options. If persons do not exist, then might his opponent claim that we do not need to remove anyone's suffering, whether our own or that of others? In response, Śāntideva points out that no one believes suffering should not be prevented. This is therefore a merely hypothetical objection and need not be taken seriously. Arguments must end somewhere, and the fact that suffering is bad is the only reason that need be given to justify or motivate its removal. Rational consistency, therefore, commits us to removing the suffering of all persons, without giving any special priority to our own. This commitment to impartial benevolence, for Śāntideva, would entail following the bodhisattva path as the most effective way to eliminate suffering.[18]

Verse 103 completes the main argument of the equalizing self and other section. In summary, the argument is as follows. First, Śāntideva establishes the impersonal badness of suffering through introspection (8:90, 92–3) and appeal to universal agreement (8:103). Second, he argues for a prima facie commitment to removing everyone's suffering, given that it is bad (8:94). The opponent is therefore challenged to provide a justification for egoistic practices of self-prioritization (8:95–6). Śāntideva then argues that the most plausible justification for prioritizing one's own well-being is blocked by Buddhist metaphysics. Since we are not enduring unified selves, we cannot appeal to this fact as rationally justifying self-interested action (8:101–2). A commitment to impartial benevolence follows (8:103). We are responsible for removing everyone's suffering, since it is bad, but are unable to provide a justification for prioritizing the removal of our own.

The verses that follow raise and respond to an objection that helps Śāntideva transition to the next section of the chapter:

> If one asks why we should generate compassion, given that it causes great amounts of suffering, upon seeing the suffering of the world, how can suffering from compassion be considered great? (BCA 8:104)
>
> If the suffering of the many ceases because of the suffering of the one, then that suffering must be produced by one who is compassionate toward himself and others. (BCA 8:105)

The objector points out that compassion causes mental distress for the compassionate person empathizing with the suffering of others. This is a point Śāntideva makes as well in 6:123, where he compares the empathetic pain of compassion to having one's body set on fire.[19] In addition, compassion inspires action to benefit others which may at least seem to diminish the compassionate person's well-being. Notice that in this verse, Śāntideva's response is not to deny that compassion causes pain, but rather to argue that it is inconsequential compared to the suffering the bodhisattva can eliminate. This is the most consequentialist verse of the *Guide*, since it emphasizes the promotion of universal well-being even at the cost of the bodhisattva's own happiness. There is at least the appearance of a tension between these verses, and many of the *Guide*'s early passages which stress reasons of self-interest for adopting the bodhisattva path. This tension is immediately resolved, however, in a striking pair of verses that claim that universal benevolence and self-interest are in harmony:

> The bodhisattvas with cultivated (*bhāvita*) minds and equal concern for the suffering of others dive into the Avīci hell like swans into a pool of lotuses. (BCA 8:107)
>
> When sentient beings are liberated, they become oceans of joy (*prāmodya*). They alone find fulfillment. Why would they seek insipid liberation? (BCA 8:108)

As we saw at the beginning of this book, these verses portray bodhisattvas experiencing bliss while liberating sentient beings in a hell realm. What would have seemed to be the deepest moment of self-sacrifice in a bodhisattva's career instead results in unsurpassable benefits for the bodhisattvas themselves. The image suggests that any tension between self-interest and universal benevolence is only apparent, given that fully virtuous persons are immune to suffering within saṃsāra, and benefit from helping others. The verses presuppose the self-benefiting and protective properties of virtue that Śāntideva has been developing throughout the text, including the ability of patience to protect the bodhisattva from any amount of physical pain.[20] I return to these verses in the following chapter.

In the exchanging self and other meditations, to which we now turn, the self-beneficial aspects of compassion will be emphasized more systematically. We should keep in mind, however, that Śāntideva presents both self-interested and other-regarding reasons for adopting the bodhisattva path. As we see most clearly in the verses to come, Śāntideva holds that these are not in tension, since developing compassion and dedicating oneself to others is the most effective way of benefiting oneself.

4.4. *The exchanging self and other* (parātmaparivartana) *meditations*

4.4.1. Introduction

The section in which the exchanging self and other meditations are given is presented in two parts. The first emphasizes the disadvantages of self-grasping and advantages of compassion, and the second presents a series of meditations in which the bodhisattva develops compassion by imaginatively taking up the perspective of others. Like the equalizing argument, the exchanging meditations draw upon the Buddhist tenet of metaphysical selflessness. As we have seen, the equalizing argument does this at the intellectual level, by using the non-existence of the self as a premise in its argument. The exchanging meditations deepen this work, by focusing on the spontaneous processes of subject and object reification, called I-making (*ahaṁkāra*) and mine-making (*mamakāra*), in which impersonal fragmentary experience is conceptually synthesized and misconstrued as an enduring self that stands out against a realm of enduring objects. Śāntideva's target in this section is the deepest level of craving, which he often calls self-grasping (*ātma-parigraha*), in which one clings to this delusion of an enduring self and craves its well-being. All other pathological emotions arise out of these errors; I cling to objects that I think will benefit this non-existent self, become angry when it is threatened, become proud or envious when I compare it to others and so on. These cognitive errors must be eliminated through practices of cultivation working at a deeper psychological level than propositional knowledge. This is one reason that the exchanging self and other meditations are presented as contemplative exercises, rather than arguments.

In this part of the text, Śāntideva does not try to eliminate these processes of self and object reification, but instead alters how they function, thereby interrupting the generation of pathological emotions and aiding in the cultivation of compassion. In brief, he does this by rechanneling identification with one's own body into temporary identification with the body of another. As a result, craving for one's own benefit is transformed into the aspiration to benefit others. The wish for others to be free of suffering is compassion. Therefore, with this psychological sleight of hand, Śāntideva transforms craving into compassion. The actual meditations where this procedure is enacted begin on 8:140. We will examine them shortly.

Although the equalizing argument and the exchanging meditations employ contrasting styles, we need not overemphasize their differences.

The equalizing passages, though presented in argument form, are meant to be contemplated repeatedly to develop compassion and reduce selfishness. Likewise, the exchanging meditations, though presented as a series of contemplations, do important philosophical work which supports the conclusions of the equalizing argument. First, they deepen the bodhisattva's awareness of the suffering of others. In so doing, they support the equalizing argument's premise that all beings wish to be free of it (8:90, 92–3). Second, their success in eliminating selfish behavior refutes the egoist's claim in verse 8:100 that selfish behavior is unavoidable. Finally, the exchanging meditations articulate how compassion benefits its possessor, thereby providing a powerful set of reasons for the bodhisattva to develop it, which complement those already provided by the equalizing argument.

4.4.2. Disadvantages of selfishness and advantages of compassion (BCA 8:121–39)

In the twenty verses prior to the meditative exchanges themselves, Śāntideva explicates the benefits of compassion and the drawbacks of selfishness. It is this section which stresses most deeply the convergence of impartial benevolence and self-interest that is one of the great themes of the text: given that compassion is the antidote to selfish craving and the harm it causes its possessor, developing it and working for others' well-being is the most effective way to benefit oneself. In this section, Śāntideva employs two terms with deliberate ambiguity. His references to self-grasping (*ātma-parigraha*) refer both to the innate grasping at self which constitutes the fundamental layer of delusion, as well as the resulting motivation to prioritize one's own benefit. Likewise, when he refers to exchanging one's self with others (*parātma-parivartanam*), this refers both to the imaginative exercises of taking on the position of others that begin in 8:140, but also to the motivation to care for others which these meditations stimulate. Both pairings are natural given that the first item in each case causes the second.

Śāntideva transitions from the equalizing argument to this section by introducing the emotional benefits of transforming selfishness into compassion:

> Then, though working for the welfare of others, they experience neither arrogance (*mada*) nor dismay (*vismaya*). One thirsting (*tṛṣṇā*) solely for the well-being of others does not desire the results of their good actions. (BCA 8:109)

Therefore, just as I protect myself from blame until the end, I make an intention to be compassionate and an intention to protect others. (BCA 8:110)

In the beginning of the chapter, Śāntideva claimed that inflated self-interest causes emotional dysfunction which contaminates relationships (8:5–25). Now, he begins to show how compassion eliminates this kind of suffering. Compassion destroys arrogance (*mada*) since the bodhisattva no longer aims at his own aggrandizement. Instead, he regards any success achieved through good actions as important only in that it contributes to his ability to help others (8:109). Compassion also protects against *vismaya*. The term can mean either arrogance or perplexity. If Śāntideva intends the first sense, then he is reinforcing the claim that compassion protects an individual from inflated self-worth. If he intends the second, then he is referring to the single-minded focus of the bodhisattva who has eliminated all doubt about the worth of his goal of benefiting others. Alternately, it can be understood to refer to the bodhisattva's lack of disappointment when taking a low social position, given that his only aim is to benefit others.[21]

In verse 109, Śāntideva also makes the provocative suggestion that the bodhisattva craves (*tṛṣṇā*: literally, thirst) benefiting others. This is one of several instances where he uses a term which usually indicates a pathological emotion to describe an at least provisionally positive mental state.[22] Here, I think his intention is to illustrate a central strategy of the second half of chapter eight. The term *tṛṣṇā* usually indicates craving for one's own benefit which arises out of a deluded belief in the self. Śāntideva will use the exchanging self and other meditations to transform self-centered motivation into compassion, the wish to eliminate the suffering of everyone. Referring to compassion as *tṛṣṇā*, then, is a way of alluding to this transformation. It also suggests that the bodhisattva maintains the emotional intensity of seeking her own benefit while expanding her motivation to encompass the well-being of all.

Verse 110 makes explicit the strategy that allows the bodhisattva to protect himself from these pathological emotions. Defending oneself from blame and other forms of verbal abuse will only stimulate pathological emotions like anger and envy, and thereby increase suffering. Instead, the bodhisattva opens himself up to verbal abuse from others, surrendering attachment to his reputation, and replacing it with the aim to benefit others. This procedure intensifies during the exchanging self and other meditations which follow, in which the bodhisattva imaginatively experiences the aggression of other sentient beings.

After these introductory verses, Śāntideva takes five verses to describe the procedure by which the bodhisattva enacts a deep imaginative identification with the perspective of another person. This section of the text is difficult to follow because the meditative exchanges themselves will not begin until verse 8:140, with the intervening verses praising the benefits of compassion and articulating the disadvantages of selfishness. I will introduce the instructions now, but we will need to reference them again when the actual exchange begins:

> Due to habituation, there is an awareness of a sense of self toward the drops of blood and semen, which are other than oneself, even though nothing exists.
>
> Therefore, why do I not take the body of another person as myself? The otherness of my own body is not difficult to establish.
>
> Having realized that one's own self is filled with faults, while others are oceans of good qualities, one should cultivate renouncing one's self and taking up the self of the other.
>
> Just as hands and the other body parts are loved because of being parts of the body, why are embodied beings not loved in the same way because of being parts of the world?
>
> Just as the idea of a self toward one's own body which is without self occurs because of habituation, why not, through habituation, generate a sense of self toward another person? (BCA 8:111–15)

Starting at verse 140, the bodhisattva will employ the procedure introduced here to facilitate a strong imaginative exchange of perspectives with persons of lesser, equal, and superior social positions. A striking feature of these instructions is that the exchange is facilitated through manipulating delusive processes by which the false sense of self is generated and identified with the body. Verses 111–12 begin by referencing the Buddhist belief that the sense of unified enduring identity is a delusion. Therefore, conceiving of the physical body as belonging to such a unified self is an error. The body, itself a conceptually constructed aggregation of parts, is owned by no one, and our identification with it is the result of the habits of I-making (*ahaṃkāra*) and mine-making (*mamakāra*). This creates a strategic possibility which Śāntideva exploits. We can train ourselves to interrupt habitual identification with our own body, and temporarily superimpose our deluded sense of self onto the bodies of others, facilitating a deep imaginative exchange of positions (8:112–13, 8:115). In verse 8:140, Śāntideva will use this method for the first time to exchange his identity with that of a social inferior.

Before enacting this exchange, however, Śāntideva presents a sequence of verses (8:121–39) explicating the disadvantages of selfishness and the benefits of compassion. Although this has been a theme of the entire text, distinctive to this section is Śāntideva's focus on the deepest cause of suffering, the innate grasping at self (*ātma-parigraha*). The other pathological emotions, and the harmful actions which they cause, arise from self-grasping. Therefore, the contemplations in this section operate at a deeper psychological level then those given earlier in the *Guide*.

In the verses below, Śāntideva explores karmic, social, and psychological dimensions of the suffering caused by self-grasping:

> Due to excessive affection for the self, one fears even small dangers. Who would not hate that self which brings fear just like an enemy?
>
> The self, desiring to resist weakness, hunger, and thirst, slays birds, fish, and deer, and establishes himself as the adversary of the world.
>
> The self, who would kill even his parents for the sake of wealth and honor, and would steal the property of the three jewels, becomes fuel for the fires of the Avīci hell.
>
> What wise person would want this self, protect it, venerate it? Who would not see it as an enemy? Who would idolize it? (BCA 8:121–4)

The list of sufferings and adversities presented here adds little that is new to the horrors of saṃsāra detailed throughout the text. Their contribution, rather, is to attribute these kinds of suffering to their deepest underlying cause, self-grasping (8:121). As a result, fear arises when this non-existent self is threatened (8:121), and various unethical actions are performed for its benefit, leading to social disruption, theft, and disunity in families (8:122–3) as well as karmic retribution in future lives (8:123). The reference to the Avīci hell can be taken cosmologically, as rebirth in a hell realm after death, but can also be read psychologically, as being trapped in a mood dominated by anger and emotional pain, resulting from conceiving of oneself as the center of the moral universe. We can supplement the difficulties referenced here with Śāntideva's descriptions of suffering throughout the *Guide*, since all pathological emotions arise from self-grasping.

Śāntideva's solution, introduced here and enacted in the exchanging meditations to follow, is to abandon self-centered motivations and dedicate oneself to others:

> Having oppressed another for one's own sake, one is roasted in hell and the like. Having oppressed oneself for the sake of others, one succeeds in everything. (BCA 8:126)
>
> After commanding another for one's own benefit, one experiences the condition of slavery. After commanding oneself for the benefit of others, one experiences the condition of being a master. (BCA 8:128)

In these passages Śāntideva inverts the usual attitude to well-being, insisting that pursuing one's own happiness harms oneself, while benefiting others benefits oneself. An important reason for this inversion is karmic consequence: selfish actions cause bad rebirths, while altruistic actions result in good rebirths and so on. However, the passages should also be understood as referring to all the deleterious effects of craving and the other pathological emotions illustrated throughout the text. The reference to rebirth in hell realms (8:126) indicates a mind blazing with the pain of anger even in this life (6:3). The reference to slavery (8:128) indicates a mind controlled by pathological emotions (4:26–36). Correspondingly, attaining the position of a master indicates not just rebirth with high social status, but the ability to control one's mind through eliminating the influence of the pathological emotions. The reference to afflicting the self for the sake of others (8:126) indicates replacing self-grasping with compassion. We will find Śāntideva intensify this use of violent imagery against the self as the chapter continues.[23]

Verse 129 presents one of the clearest statements of the convergence of self-interest and altruism in the text:

> All those who suffer in the world do so because they desire their own happiness. All those who are happy in the world are this way because they desire the happiness of others. (BCA 8:129)

The verse reiterates and summarizes earlier claims about the harmfulness of selfishness and the benefits of compassion, but it also illustrates a puzzling aspect of Śāntideva's approach. It may seem inconsistent to claim that the best way to pursue one's own well-being is to stop pursuing one's well-being. We should keep in mind, however, that the mental state of compassion is the wish for all beings to be happy, with oneself given equal consideration as one among all persons. Compassion as fully developed, therefore, will include the wish for one's own happiness, balanced with concern for all.

Moreover, the verses in this section are still aimed at a developing bodhisattva whose self-interest is stronger than her compassion. For this reason, verses like 8:129 stress the deleterious effects of selfish motivations. Śāntideva's insight here is sometimes discussed in contemporary Anglo-American philosophy as the paradox of hedonism, which claims that the best way to increase one's well-being is to stop directly aiming at it.[24] Consider a person who takes great pleasure in helping others but feels guilty anytime he acts motivated by self-interest. According to many theories of well-being, including hedonism, such a person would effectively promote his well-being by focusing on helping others. Likewise, for Śāntideva, strengthening compassion toward others eliminates inflated self-interest and its harmful effects.

We can become more precise about Śāntideva's position through using a distinction developed in contemporary philosophy between first and second order motivations. A first order motivation is an occurrent desire for an object or state of affairs. For example, I have a first order motivation when I am currently wanting to eat a chocolate bar. A second order motivation is a desire about my first order motivations. For instance, I might have a second order motivation to want to stop having first order desires to eat chocolate bars, because they are making me gain weight.[25]

Verses like the one above are meant to develop compassion in bodhisattvas who have not eliminated inflated self-interest, and whose second order motivation, therefore, is to adopt whatever first order motivations will be most beneficial for them. Śāntideva's claim is that occurrent first order motivations to help others are beneficial to oneself, while occurrent first order motivations to benefit oneself at the expense of others decrease one's well-being. The reasons for this are the ones referenced throughout chapter eight, and the *Guide* as a whole. Even a self-interested bodhisattva, therefore, will engage in meditations to develop compassion and lessen self-interest. Moreover, as compassion deepens, and the boundaries between persons are destabilized through the exchanging self and other meditations which follow, these distinctions between benefiting oneself and benefiting others will start to break down. The advanced bodhisattva will be equally motivated to remove the suffering of everyone at every level of motivation.

As this section draws to a close, Śāntideva begins to shift from the motivational meaning of exchanging self and other, in which one dedicates oneself to caring for others, to the meditational meaning, in which the bodhisattva imaginatively takes up the perspective of others:

> Whatever misfortunes, sufferings, and fears exist in the world, they are all due to self-grasping (*ātma-parigraha*). How is this grasping of value to me? (BCA 8:134)
>
> Until one abandons the self, one is not able to abandon suffering, just as one cannot abandon being burned without abandoning fire. (BCA 8:135)
>
> Therefore, in order to calm my own suffering and to calm the suffering of others, I give myself to others and take them as myself. (BCA 8:136)

Verse 134 attributes all the suffering detailed in the chapter, and the entire text, to self-grasping. The reference in verses 135 and 136 to abandoning the self and taking up the self of others is deliberately ambiguous. Abandoning one's self (8:135–6) means eliminating selfishness, but it also introduces the method explored in the following section, in which the bodhisattva temporarily adopts the perspectives of other persons. Likewise, taking others as one's self (8:136) refers to both adopting a motivation to help them, and to exchanging one's perspective with that of another person during the meditations which follow.

4.4.3. The exchange of perspectives (BCA 8:140–54)

During the meditations on exchanging self and other, the bodhisattva imaginatively takes the perspective of one of three possible social positions: a person who is inferior to him, a person at his own level of prestige, and a person in a higher social position. These are the same three social levels introduced in the beginning of the chapter (8:12). In this earlier verse, Śāntideva claimed that one of three pathological social emotions dominated interaction with each kind of person: the inferior person is envious (*īrṣya*) of the superior, who is arrogant (*māna*) toward the inferior, while persons of equal status are competitive (*dvandva*). The social disfunction resulting from these negative emotions caused the bodhisattva's flight into the wilderness. As a result of the charnel-ground contemplations, as well as the equalizing self and other argument which we have just examined, the bodhisattva has eliminated interest in saṃsāric goals, weakened craving for sensual pleasure and attachment to the body, and increased concern for others. He is now psychologically prepared to target self-grasping directly and destroy the three pathological social emotions.

During the exchanging self and other meditations, upon imaginatively taking up the other's perspective, the bodhisattva observes their habitual reactions toward himself. From the perspective of the inferior person, he observes their envy toward his higher status; from the perspective of the equal person, he imagines their competitiveness, and from the perspective of the social superior, he observes their arrogant pride. Śāntideva describes the thoughts and emotions of the person whose perspective the bodhisattva adopts but is not explicit about what this achieves. This is also not wholly obvious; the bodhisattva engaged in these meditations is literally generating and contemplating negative mental states from the standpoint of the other person, a process far removed from Śāntideva's usual procedure of destroying the pathological emotions directly by generating virtuous mental states. Below I make a few general suggestions before turning to the meditative exchanges themselves.

First and most centrally, the bodhisattva develops compassion toward the person whose perspective she has taken. She does this by contemplating the suffering they experience, through examining how they are driven by the pathological emotions of envy, arrogant pride, and competitiveness. In doing so, she also develops compassion toward herself, for observing these negative emotions in the mind of another deepens awareness of how they function in one's own mind. By cycling through lower, equal, and higher social positions, these insights are universalized to all human beings.

Second, taking the position of the other and generating pathological emotions from their perspective allows the bodhisattva to become familiar with these negative emotions, from a safe psychological distance. Since this is not the bodhisattva's usual perspective, mental states of envy and so on will not become entwined with usual reactive habitual patterns of afflictive response. When contemplating the envy of the inferior person, for instance, these feelings will not stimulate narratives about how the bodhisattva's positive features are not properly recognized. He can therefore contemplate what envy is, and how it manifests and distorts thinking, without risking stimulating anger. Epistemically, this lets the bodhisattva experience more clearly how painful the pathological emotions are, and this in turn further develops compassion, both for the other whose perspective has been taken up, as well as for himself and all other sentient beings, who suffer from the same pathological emotions.

Third, the meditative exchange of self and other is a powerful technique to dislodge the bodhisattva from her usual self-centered narratives, without wholly collapsing the conventional self. We have seen that it is the processes of appropriating and reifying the aggregates (with particular attention to the body) which the bodhisattva manipulates to deepen her identification with the other (8:111–15). Doing so also strengthens the bodhisattva's insight into the contingency and fluidity of these processes of identification. She needs to maintain a conventional identity to progress along the bodhisattva path and work effectively for others. Manipulating this sense of identification skillfully without wholly dissolving it can both aid in developing compassion and weaken the innate self-grasping which is the root of her own suffering.

Fourth, the pathological emotions can be used as weapons to weaken grasping at the self. The afflictions of envy, pride, and competitiveness are destructive forces expressing animosity toward the person at whom they are directed. Envy wishes to see the more fortunate one disgraced, competitiveness wants to subordinate the equal, while pride expresses contempt for the lower person. From the taken-on perspective of the other, the bodhisattva mentally observes these destructive emotions fly back toward his sense of self in its usual position. In the supportive confines of the meditation, he imagines them piercing his deluded self-grasping, thereby weakening it.[26]

Finally, through developing compassion toward persons in all three social positions, the bodhisattva eliminates her own pathological social emotions. The bodhisattva as portrayed at the beginning of the chapter did not have deep concern for the well-being of others, and therefore she was envious of a person in a superior position, arrogant toward the inferior person and so on. Once compassion is developed, she cares deeply for all these persons. Envy when the other succeeds becomes rejoicing for their success (6:77); arrogance in relation to a destitute person is replaced with a deep commitment to end their suffering (chapter ten); and competitiveness for one of equal status becomes complete relinquishment of the bodhisattva's own possessions for the benefit of others (5:9–10). As a result, the bodhisattva is no longer afflicted by the dysfunctional social emotions, and she is therefore able to enter social relations with others harmoniously, whenever doing so will benefit them. Compassion is the antidote to social suffering just as patience is the antidote to the badness of physical pain (6:12–21). The exchanging self and other meditations prepare the bodhisattva to return to society after her long sojourn in the wilderness.

The perspective of the inferior person (BCA 8:140–6)

> Creating a sense of one's own identity toward an inferior person and the other social positions, and a sense of otherness toward oneself, cultivate envy (*irṣyā*) and arrogant pride (*māna*) with a mind free of distractions. (BCA 8:140)

Above, we examined verses 8:111–15, in which Śāntideva instructs the bodhisattva to disrupt and redeploy conceptual processes of identity-construction in order to deeply identify with the perspective of others. In verse 140, Śāntideva uses this technique to imaginatively adopt the perspective of the person of inferior social standing. The pronoun "he" in the verses below refers to the bodhisattva in his usual position, and the pronoun "I" refers to the perspective of the other that the bodhisattva has imaginatively taken up. From this new position, the bodhisattva mentally observes the envy which this kind of person habitually feels toward him. Surprisingly, we will also find that this person remains susceptible to pride, despite his low social status:

> He is honored, not I; I do not possess wealth, like he does. He is praised while I receive blame; I suffer while he is happy. (BCA 8:141)
>
> I do work while he rests at ease. He is said to be a great man in the world. I am said to be lowly, without good qualities. (BCA 8:142)
>
> What can be accomplished by a person without good qualities? Every person possesses good qualities. I am inferior to some people, and to some I am superior. (BCA 8:143)

These verses record the thoughts of the bodhisattva, now that he has taken the position of the inferior person and contemplates himself from that perspective. The thoughts of the social inferior illustrate envy, as he complains about a lack of respect and wealth, the hard work he must do and so on (8:141–2). We should read these passages in conjunction with the insights developed in the *Guide* up to this point, however. The material deprivation and lack of respect experienced by the social inferior is a deep source of suffering, but this is because it causes the emotional pain of the pathological emotions. These verses focus on the suffering of experiencing envy, itself a form of aggression toward the social superior, brought on by unsatisfied craving for material possessions and reputation. Śāntideva has already provided a lengthy analysis of the suffering which anger and envy cause their possessor in the *Guide*'s sixth chapter.[27] Now, contemplating how the mind of the social inferior is consumed by them, the bodhisattva is filled with deep compassion.

Verse 143 introduces a new element into Śāntideva's analysis, by referencing the relativity of the social inferior's position, in relation to others. The social inferior himself experiences arrogant pride by recognizing that he is superior to those of even greater social deprivation. All such social designations are relative and transient, and each person will occupy all three levels of social status at various times and in relation to various persons, suggesting universal vulnerability to the pathological social emotions for anyone infected with self-grasping.

> My failures in discipline and understanding and other shortcomings are caused by the power of the pathological emotions; they are outside my control. I am in need of being cured, to the extent possible. I will accept even painful treatments. (BCA 8:144)

> If I am incurable, then why does he despise me? How do his good qualities benefit me? Yet he is endowed with good qualities himself. (BCA 8:145)

> He feels no compassion for people fixed in the mouth of the wild beasts of hell, but he wants to conquer the wise with his unsurpassed virtue. (BCA 8:146)

The bodhisattva here continues exploring the psychology of the inferior person. The reference to being under the power of the pathological emotions (8:144) should remind us of the meditations on patience in chapter six, in which the bodhisattva eliminates anger by recognizing that enemies are controlled by pathological emotions (6:35–8). Now, these insights are deepened, through imaginatively experiencing these pathological emotions from the perspective of the other person. Moreover, the bodhisattva is contemplating the social inferior's erratic and unstable attitudes toward the bodhisattva *himself*. This will influence the bodhisattva's own attitudes in the future. When experiencing the aggression of social inferiors, he will recall this experiential insight into the way such behavior derives from the emotional pain of envy. This meditation, therefore, not only generates deep feelings of compassion, but nurtures the disposition to respond to envious behavior with compassion in the future.

Verse 145 introduces another new element into the meditation. The inferior person accuses the bodhisattva of "despising" him and failing to eliminate his suffering. The social inferior goes so far as to claim that the bodhisattva lacks compassion, accusing him instead of seeking his own aggrandizement through simulating progress on the bodhisattva path (8:146). Contemplating how he is viewed by others acts as an antidote to the bodhisattva's own arrogant pride, through recognizing his failure to keep his commitment not to harm them. Even if aspects of the social inferior's critique are inaccurate, the bodhisattva's inability to eliminate this person's suffering represents a lack of skillful means.

These verses should remind us of the frustration the bodhisattva felt toward saṃsāric persons at the beginning of the chapter. At that time, the bodhisattva described their behavior as foolish (*bāla*) and fled into the wilderness to escape them. Now, contemplating the pain they feel from their perspective, the bodhisattva experiences deep compassion and recognizes his own limitations and susceptibility to arrogance. Anger in response to their erratic behavior is dissolved by recognizing that their hostile actions resulted from being dominated by the pathological emotions, and the bodhisattva's own failings. After cycling through all three perspectives and developing compassion toward beings in all three social positions, the bodhisattva will wholly eliminate his pathological social emotions, and be prepared to return to society whenever necessary to engage sentient beings with an untroubled mind. Further, the bodhisattva is himself often in a low social position. Therefore, in exploring the mind of the other, he also explores his own, and generates compassion for himself.

The contemplation of envy also acts as an antidote to pride in an even more direct way. Envy is a kind of anger which wishes to strike out at the social superior. The bodhisattva, empathetically observing the social inferior's envy, feels this mental violence coming toward himself with a vividness not possible in his ordinary perspective. In the controlled state of meditation, and in conjunction with compassion generated by the equalizing self and other argument, the bodhisattva lets the mental violence of envy pierce his self-grasping and destroy his inflated sense of importance.

The benefits to the bodhisattva who contemplates the perspective of the inferior person will largely repeat for the meditations on exchanging oneself with a rival and with a social superior. I will therefore treat these sequences more briefly.

***The perspective of the equal* (BCA 8:147–50)[28]**

The bodhisattva now conducts the exchange of perspectives again, taking up the position of a person of equal social stature and examining their experience. In these passages, the mental attitude of competitiveness (*dvandva*: see BCA 8:12) is analyzed as afflicting these relationships. The verses show that simply eliminating social hierarchy will not lead to harmonious interaction as long as pathological emotions continue to structure social experience. The solution, as argued for in the equalizing argument and exchanging meditations, is to develop universal compassion which eliminates the pathological social emotions by recognizing the deeper equality of all persons in terms of wanting happiness and shared vulnerability to suffering.

Only four verses are given for this section of the meditations, presumably because many of the insights developed in the contemplation of the inferior person's experience are applicable here as well:

> Seeing himself as equal to others, he acquires wealth and honor to increase his superior status, even by means of strife.
>
> If my good qualities would become visible everywhere in the world, perhaps no one would hear of his virtues.
>
> If my faults would be concealed, then I would be honored, not him. Now, I easily acquire wealth. I am honored but he is not.
>
> Delighted, we will watch him being pounded into dust for a long time, laughed at by all people, blamed from all directions. (BCA 8:147–50)

All four verses illustrate the contentious nature of relationships between those of equal status, describing their struggle for reputation and material success (8:147), the wish to see the other's status lowered (8:148) and to have one's own faults concealed (8:149), and finally the delight taken in seeing one's rival humiliated (8:150). These meditations presuppose Śāntideva's earlier arguments about the worthlessness of social achievements, such as wealth and honor.[29] They enable the bodhisattva to recognize the absurdity of allowing desires for these worthless items to control one's emotional response to others. In verses 148–9, through contemplating the aggressive impulses of the social equal, the bodhisattva realizes that any good reputation he has is a result of hiding his own faults, rather than real self-betterment. The descriptions in verse 150 of mental animosity suggests the incompatibility of this behavior with the bodhisattva vow.

The results of the meditation parallel those of the exchange with an inferior person, in developing compassion for competitive people, and a greater understanding of the bodhisattva's own tendency to be controlled by competitive impulses. As the bodhisattva cycles through all three social positions, the meditations also develop equanimity, in deepening the bodhisattva's recognition that all persons suffer from these pathological social emotions as they inhabit positions of differing status. Generating compassion and equanimity in this way acts as the antidote to competitiveness, as the desire for the other's possessions and status is replaced with concern for their welfare.

The perspective of the superior person (BCA 8:151–4)

The meditator now takes up the final social position, that of superior status, and contemplates the painfulness and distortions caused by arrogant pride. Śāntideva's treatment here too is brief, presumably because the patterns he establishes in the first two sequences remain the same:

> How dare this wretch compare himself to me! Does he have my level of erudition, wisdom, beauty, noble lineage, and wealth?
>
> When I hear my own good qualities being praised all over the place, my hair stands on end while, thrilled, I enjoy a festival of happiness!
>
> Even if he has possessions, we will take them by force. We will give him only subsistence wages for the work he does.
>
> He should be made to fall from happiness, and always be yoked to our pain! We are all afflicted in saṃsāra hundreds of times because of him! (BCA 8:151–4)

To appreciate Śāntideva's strategy, it is essential to realize that the meditations on the position of the superior person are meant to develop compassion toward socially successful and wealthy people. Numerous chapters of the *Guide*, including sections of chapter eight, have emphasized that possessions, wealth, and reputation are misfortunes, in that they stimulate the pathological emotions.[30] Achievement of high social status makes the individual vulnerable to karmic, psychological, and social adversities in ways explored throughout the *Guide*. Compassion therefore is the appropriate emotional response to socially successful persons who are still dominated by the pathological emotions.

In verse 151, the superior person arrogantly lists his supposed good qualities, and mocks the inferior person for desiring to compete with him. Verse 152 emphasizes his high social status and his delight at his good reputation. That this joy provides no real benefit, however, is suggested by verses 153 and 154, which articulate how arrogant pride impoverishes a life that is successful by ordinary social standards. Bereft of any real concern for the well-being of their social inferiors, the person of high social status remains consumed with greed and aggression, seizing the possessions of impoverished persons for his own use. The behavior is incoherent; since he is in the socially dominant position, he does not need additional wealth. It shows how arrogance inhibits the development of compassion toward those in need and prevents meaningful connection with others. Every saṃsāric relationship, Śāntideva is arguing, breaks down to the same elements. Greed and aggression, deriving from self-interest, manifest in one of the three pathological social emotions which contaminate social interaction. The most efficacious way out of this saṃsāric cycle of social suffering is the path of the bodhisattva, who develops universal compassion which acts as the antidote to these negative emotions.

The vividly strong language used in verse 8:154 also suggests that Śāntideva is using this verse to transition away from the formal meditational sequences of empathetic exchange. One role of the verse is to conclude Śāntideva's depiction of the mind of the social superior, who is characterized as cruelly inflicting pain on the social inferior, and unfairly blaming him for the suffering the superior person experiences. But this verse can also be read as the beginning of a full-frontal attack on the false sense of self which is the source of craving and the other pathological emotions. In this reading, it is this false sense of self which is (accurately) described as causing the sufferings of saṃsāra, and which is destroyed by imaginatively heaping upon it the pain the bodhisattva experiences.[31]

Chapter eight concludes with additional meditations in which the bodhisattva continues to contemplate the benefits of helping others (8:155–60) and engages in meditative techniques to subdue the mind (8:161–73) and subjugate the desires of the body (8:174–84).[32] Some of these verses continue the theme, introduced in 8:154, of heaping violence on the false sense of self to destroy it (e.g. 8:162, 165–6). For reasons of space, I will not comment on these verses.

4.5. Conclusion

Chapter eight is the creative heart of the *Guide*, transitioning from its stated purpose of providing concentration instructions into an existential journey during which societal values are abandoned as the bodhisattva progresses through stages of despair before emerging out of solitude through the power of compassion. It also illustrates Śāntideva's penchant for manipulating the power of delusion for liberative gain with the breathtakingly original strategy of redeploying I-making to fashion a deep imaginative identification with others. Just as striking is Śāntideva's commitment to social harmony that is developed systematically in a chapter whose most salient images are of isolation, fragmentation, and decay. Despite the beauty of the language Śāntideva uses to describe the wilderness, the chapter should be read as providing the means to overcome the need for solitude. The bodhisattva's period of seclusion is spent on contemplative exercises which prepare her to reengage with society. At the conclusion of her training, she returns to the world of saṃsāra, to remain there endlessly, joyful and free of negative emotions, benefiting the deluded persons who flail around in mutual destruction under the power of the pathological emotions which the bodhisattva has vowed to destroy.

The chapter is also where two of the great themes of the *Guide* are treated most clearly. The first part of the exchanging self and other section stresses forcefully the self-benefiting properties of compassion, and thereby illustrates how impartial benevolence and self-interest converge on the bodhisattva path. Moreover, in showing that compassion is the antidote to craving and the pathological social emotions, Śāntideva illustrates how the Mahāyāna conception of the bodhisattva way transcends the path of the early Buddhist disciple, while simultaneously incorporating its deepest insights about suffering. The arguments and meditations to develop compassion in the second half of the chapter illustrate the impoverishment and irrationality of the early Buddhist soteriological strategy of saving oneself alone from suffering. Nevertheless, Śāntideva takes great care to emphasize the benefits of the techniques to lessen lust which are practiced in the period of seclusion. This illustrates the value he places on early Buddhist ideas about the impoverished nature of craving and saṃsāric success. These shared psychological insights provide the foundation upon which Śāntideva's bodhisattva universalizes compassion for all beings.

Suggestions for further study

Good treatments of Śāntideva's attitude toward the physical body in the *Guide* or the *Training Anthology* include Mrozik 2007 and Ohnuma 2019. Both of these sources give attention to the importance of Śāntideva's charnel-ground meditations. Good summaries of Śāntideva's argument in the equalizing self and other section are given by Garfield, Jenkins, and Priest 2015 and Finnigan 2018. Williams 1998, chapter five offers an influential critique of Śāntideva's argument from this section. See Pettit 1999 and Siderits 2000 for replies to Williams. Gyatso 2019 offers a sensitive treatment of the importance of the shift of perspectives that takes place in the exchanging self and other meditations.

Questions for reflection

1. How do the graphic charnel-ground meditations contribute to Śāntideva's goals in the *Guide*'s eighth chapter?
2. How do you think the equalizing self and other argument relates to the exchanging self and other meditations? Are their approaches complementary? Are there ways in which they are in tension?
3. According to Śāntideva, what are the ways that compassion benefits the compassionate individual? Which of these benefits do you find most plausible?
4. The exchanging self and other meditations seem to be constructed to blur the subjectivities of the bodhisattva and the person with whom they conduct the exchange of perspectives. In what ways might Śāntideva think this helps develop compassion and *bodhicitta*? Compare your answers to the ones I suggest in section 4.3. How do your answers differ from my own?

Chapter 5

JOY

5.1. Introduction

My study has focused on Śāntideva's development of the virtuous factors of generosity (*dāna*), patience (*kṣānti*), and compassion (*karuṇā*), with briefer treatments of mindfulness (*smṛti*) and introspection (*saṁprajanya*), and a study of wisdom (*prajñā*) to follow. My primary goal has been to illustrate the self-benefiting properties of these virtues. We have seen that generosity, patience, and compassion benefit the bodhisattva by acting as antidotes that eliminate pathological emotions (*kleśas*), in line with the strategy of most Buddhist virtue theory. For Śāntideva, generosity is the antidote to craving, patience eliminates anger, and compassion weakens self-grasping, and eliminates the negative social emotions of envy, competitiveness, and arrogant pride. The beneficial role of these virtues, therefore, is largely defensive, in protecting the bodhisattva from the ill-effects of the pathological emotions.

By contrast, the *Guide* gives less explicit attention to positive characterizations of the developing bodhisattva's mental experience. Nevertheless, as I argued in my opening chapter, the perfections and other virtuous mental states are not reducible to the mere absence of pathological emotions. A mind developed in mindfulness and introspection, for instance, is fluidly aware of its surroundings; intently focused; able to transition effortlessly to new objects of awareness. Likewise, a compassionate mind attends to the needs of others, is passionately committed to lessening suffering, and remains stable while empathizing with those in pain. In this chapter, I want to focus on a feature of the bodhisattva's experience that deeply connects to the felt quality of each of the virtues, one which plays an almost ubiquitous role in Śāntideva's psychology. The virtuous bodhisattva's experience is suffused with joy (*muditā*).[1]

Śāntideva's positive conception of joy is easy to miss on a first reading of the *Guide*. Dozens of verses explicate in detail the disadvantages of pursuing sensual enjoyments, and the role of pleasure in stimulating craving. The worthlessness of saṃsāric delights is one of the most frequently repeating themes of the text. Nevertheless, Śāntideva recognizes the benefits of rejoicing in the good fortune of others (BCA 5:77, 6:76–7) and affirms the value of pleasure (*sukha-vedanā*) when it accompanies virtue, such as the enjoyment the bodhisattva takes in giving (see Goodman 2016a, 28), or that resulting from compassionate activity (BCA 8:107–8). I return to these examples below.

Although Śāntideva's references to beneficial pleasure are not infrequent, they are always brief and are not systematically developed. Moreover, he uses various terms, without defining or systematically explaining the mental states in question. I am not able to attempt a detailed reconstructive study here. Nevertheless, virtuous joy is so closely related to the major themes of this book that I do not want to neglect it entirely. Therefore, in this short chapter, I discuss many of Śāntideva's scattered references to beneficial pleasure, organizing them where possible in relation to the virtue that they accompany or support. My treatment will usually be brief since we may have studied the relevant virtue in detail already. I give a more extended treatment to the perfection of effort (*vīrya*), which has not been a major focus of this book.

5.2. Enthusiasm for the bodhisattva path

A reoccurring source of joy for the bodhisattva is the attitude of reverence he adopts toward the bodhisattva path. Verses praising buddhas, high-level bodhisattvas, *bodhicitta*, and the path itself occur frequently in the early chapters of the *Guide*. Some of the most beautiful verses in this part of the text come in the third chapter, in which the bodhisattva aspires to save all sentient beings with great exuberance:

> I am a protector for the defenseless; a leader for the caravan of travelers; I will act as a boat, a bridge, or a vehicle for those desiring to obtain the further shore.
>
> Let me be a lamp for those seeking light; a refuge for those seeking rest; a servant for all those beings seeking a servant.
>
> For all beings, let me be a wish-fulfilling gem; a vase of wealth; an efficacious spell; a great medicinal herb; a wish-fulfilling tree; a desire-granting cow. (BCA 3:17–19)

The vow to liberate all sentient beings is taken a few verses later (BCA 3:22–3), after which the new bodhisattva expresses great satisfaction at having joined the noble lineage of buddhas and bodhisattvas:

> The wise person who joyfully grasps *bodhicitta* in this way should rejoice in this resolve repeatedly in order to nourish this wish, as follows:
>
> Today, my life is fruitful! A human birth is auspiciously obtained! Today, I have been born into the family of the Buddha! I am a child of the Buddha now! (BCA 3:24–5)

Shortly after these expressions of joy at having joined the bodhisattva path, Śāntideva compares the development of *bodhicitta* in a polluted human body and mind with the astonishing good fortune of finding a jewel in a rubbish heap (BCA 3:27). The simile communicates the value and rarity of *bodhicitta*, but also conjures up feelings of surprise and delight experienced by the new bodhisattva upon entering the path to complete liberation. Several verses in the first few chapters also describe *bodhicitta* as a source of joy for oneself and others (BCA 1:16; 3:32). Likewise, bodhisattvas who develop *bodhicitta* are great sources of joy for the world (BCA 1:29, 1:33, 1:36).

*5.3. Giving (*dāna*) and patience (*kṣānti*)*

Although generosity is not systematically treated in the *Guide*, we can get a sense of the depth of joy that accompanies giving by examining a quotation in the *Training Anthology*, from the *Vajra Flag* sutra *(Vajradhvajasūtra)*. The passage refers to the gift of the body, in which the bodhisattva offers his flesh to those in need. Śāntideva's quotation uses a string of synonyms for joy to express the astonishing possibility of taking pleasure in this act of bodily sacrifice:

> With aspiring minds (*iṣṭamanā*), with pleased minds (*tuṣṭamanāḥ*), with delighted minds (*prītamanā*), with joyful minds (*muditamanā*), with loving minds (*maitryamanāḥ*), with happy minds (*sukhamanāḥ*), with tranquil minds (*prasannamanā*), with gladness (*pramudita*), delight (*prīti*), and pleasure (*saumana*), they give marrow and flesh from their own bodies to petitioners, with virtuous renunciation. (SS 25)

The passage later references the mental renunciation (*tyāgacitta*) with which the joyful bodhisattva makes these gifts.[2] As we saw in my second chapter, generosity for Śāntideva is initially and most basically an elimination of craving toward one's possessions. Because of this psychological readjustment, the bodhisattva gives fully and freely, no matter how total the gift, a point represented here through the Mahāyāna trope of giving one's body. This purification of one's attitude to possessions facilitates experiencing enormous satisfaction when giving.

The passage also suggests an aspect of joy that is developed more fully in the *Guide*'s patience chapter. As we have seen, joy allows the bodhisattva to endure great physical pain without mental unease. Mental pleasure can accompany physical pain, but mental pleasure and mental pain cannot be experienced at the same time. Therefore, since mental pain causes anger, keeping the mind joyful is an effective way to prevent it (BCA 6:9). As part of his training, the bodhisattva must learn how to produce it reliably, in ways not contaminated by pathological emotions. Although they are not systematically organized in any single chapter, the methods for generating and protecting joy are essential to the progress of the bodhisattva.

5.4. *Effort* (vīrya)

The perfection of effort (*vīrya*), which receives its own chapter in the *Guide*, provides the motivational energy for the bodhisattva's progress on the path. Effort is defined as joyful resolve (*utsāha*) for virtue (*kuśala*) (BCA 7:2), suggesting that it is an enlivening attitude that inspires the bodhisattva during her training. Much of the chapter, however, pays little attention to joy; for instance, Śāntideva provides a graphic description of the terrors of death to act as an antidote to laziness (*ālasya*) (7:4–14). Nevertheless, the chapter does contain two important sequences stressing the importance of joy for progress on the path. The first comes at the conclusion of a set of verses encouraging the bodhisattva to persevere through the difficulties of bodhisattva training:

> Because of abandoning harmful actions, one does not undergo physical pain, and from becoming wise, one does not become mentally despondent, since mental pain arises from false imagining and bodily pain comes from harmful actions. (BCA 7:27)

> The body is happy because of meritorious action and the mind is happy because of wisdom. What could harm a compassionate person remaining in saṁsāra for the sake of others? (BCA 7:28)
>
> Destroying past bad deeds and receiving oceans of merit, by the power of *bodhicitta* alone one quickly passes those on the disciple path (*śrāvakas*). (BCA 7:29)
>
> Obtaining the chariot of *bodhicitta* that removes all lassitude and weariness, what intelligent person would despair at going in this way from joy to joy? (BCA 7:30)

These verses summarize the central insights about the beneficial aspects of *bodhicitta* and the perfections which Śāntideva has been developing throughout the *Guide*. As we have seen in our studies of his accounts of generosity and patience, the bodhisattva develops the mental flexibility to interact with possessions and endure difficult circumstances with mental equilibrium, free of afflictive mental response. Her mind, therefore, remains untroubled in all circumstances. Moreover, any motivation to harm others is eliminated, and therefore the bodhisattva is no longer vulnerable to physical pain caused by the karmic results of past misdeeds (7:27–8). Instead, positive karmic propensities accumulated from beneficial actions will ripen into favorable future circumstances (7:28–9). The only kinds of physical discomfort experienced by the highly developed bodhisattva will be voluntary pain taken on to benefit others.[3] Moreover, as we have seen in my third chapter, patience ensures that the bodhisattva feels no mental distress when experiencing this pain. This lets Śāntideva draw one of the most surprising inversions in the *Guide*. It is not the path of the early Buddhist disciples (the *sravakas:* 7:29), whose explicit aim is self-benefit, which is the most salutary for the practitioner. Rather it is the bodhisattva whose happiness is most secure, given her development of virtue, and the deep and stable joy she experiences as she works to eliminate the suffering of all (7:30).[4]

The second set of verses on salutary joy in the effort chapter comes toward the chapter's end. This sequence of four verses illustrates the role of joy in developing enthusiastic effort for developing virtue:[5]

> One should be intensely addicted to the action entered into.
> One should be intoxicated by that action, insatiable, as if striving for the satisfaction of the fruit of lovemaking. (BCA 7:62)[6]

> An action is carried out to gain happiness; even so, happiness may or may not result. But how can a person who takes joy in the action itself be happy without acting? (BCA 7:63)

> Like honey on the edge of a razor, in saṃsāra there is no sating sense desires. How can one become satiated with the imperishable milk of merit which ripens sweetly and is nourishing? (BCA 7:64)

> Therefore, as soon as an action is concluded, one should dive into the next one, just like an elephant scorched at midday immediately dives into a lake. (BCA 7:65)

This quartet of verses develops a contrast between the impoverished pursuit of sensual enjoyments, and the stable joy experienced while performing virtuous actions. The contrast is made most clearly in verse 7:64, in which Śāntideva uses the visceral image of honey on the tip of a razor to illustrate the danger of sense pleasure, which intensifies rather than satisfies craving. Performing meritorious action (*puṇya*), by contrast, does not stimulate craving, but is instead "nourishing" (7:64). In an almost tantric inversion, verse 7:62 uses the language of sexual desire to describe the attitude with which the bodhisattva should perform virtue. He should be intoxicated (*śauṇḍa*) by it, insatiable (*atṛpta*) for its fulfillment. He should throw himself into virtuous action as if it were the act of lovemaking. The energy of desire (*kāma*), which inevitably ends in frustration when turned to sensual pursuits, can be channeled into the passionate performance of virtuous activity.

Verses 7:62 and 7:64, therefore, instruct the bodhisattva to channel passion away from sensual pursuits and into virtuous action. Verse 7:63 makes several additional points. First, it presages the claim developed in detail in the chapter on meditative concentration that pursuit of one's own happiness is likely to end in frustration and disappointment.[7] But the verse also suggests that even the altruistic agent is vulnerable to frustration if he is overly focused on the results of his actions. If the generous person, for example, takes satisfaction only when he successfully lessens poverty, then in an imperfect world he will be discouraged whenever his attempts fail. This should make us recall Śāntideva's claim in the *Guide*'s fifth chapter that generosity is the mental attitude of wishing to give everything away, rather than physical transference of goods, or the successful elimination of poverty (BCA 5:9–10). As I argued in my second chapter, generosity for Śāntideva can be perfect without benefiting anyone other than the bodhisattva. Similar points can be made about the other virtues (see BCA 5:11–14).

The solution, given in 7:63, is to take "joy in the action itself," that is to take satisfaction in generating the mental attitudes of giving, compassion, patience and so on, and in the performance of verbal and bodily actions motivated by these attitudes, regardless of their results. For this reason, the image of lovemaking is particularly appropriate; lovemaking, motivated by passion, is done for its own sake, for the sake of the pleasure of the activity, rather than for the wish to achieve instrumental benefits like greater intimacy in the relationship and so on. Applying this insight to virtuous activity suggests that performing virtue for its own sake is the deepest reward for the bodhisattva, who has no pernicious attachment to its results. Nevertheless, we must read this sequence of verses alongside others like BCA 8:108, in which the bodhisattva is shown as overjoyed when he benefits others. The virtuous agent, when possible, will try to aid sentient beings and will rejoice when he succeeds. The point brought out in 7:62–4, however, is that generating virtuous mental states and performing virtuous actions is itself beneficial to the bodhisattva, regardless of its effects on the world.

Verse 7:65 then states that this passionate commitment to virtuous activity must be continually renewed, until it pervades every moment of life. Since performing virtue is itself pleasurable, this is yet another way in which the entire experience of the bodhisattva will be suffused with joy. The image of the elephant plunging itself into the lake on a hot day provides an important contrast to temper our reading of the metaphor of lovemaking. On one level, the image simply reemphasizes Śāntideva's claims that virtue is pleasurable, and should be continually engaged in. Notice as well, however, the contrast between the image of submersion and that of lovemaking. Plunging into the lake cools the burning of the hot sun, here indicating respite from insatiable craving. Performance of virtue, unlike pursuit of sense pleasure, extinguishes desire and thereby brings satisfaction. Virtue can be pursued with passion, but it also short-circuits the saṃsāric loop of addiction and leaves the mind tranquil, stable, and satisfied.

Śāntideva's claim made in these verses, that virtuous actions should be engaged in continually, repeats his claim in chapter five, that bodhisattva activity should occur in every moment of life:

> In all circumstances encountered, resulting from one's own or another's actions, one should conscientiously apply the training practices relevant to the situation.

> For there is nothing that cannot be treated as training by the children of the conqueror (the Buddha). For the good person living like this, there is nothing which is not meritorious.
>
> One should act only for the direct or indirect benefit of sentient beings, and for the sake of sentient beings alone, one should dedicate everything to awakening. (BCA 5:99–101)

The basic Buddhist precepts, such as not killing, not stealing and so on, can also take a positive form, such as protecting sentient beings from harm and being generous. Taking them in this expansive way helps us understand Śāntideva's claim in 5:99 that Buddhist trainings apply to all situations. Śāntideva can then instruct the bodhisattva to conceive of all his actions as benefiting others, either directly or by contributing to the bodhisattva's own development of virtuous character and store of karmic merit to enable helping others in the future (5:100–1). As we have seen, chapter five is devoted to developing mindfulness (*smṛti*) and introspection (*saṁprajanya*), two virtues of attention which guard the mind against the pathological emotions at every single moment. Since pathological emotions are eliminated by applying the appropriate virtuous mental state as an antidote, this means that the mindful and introspectively aware bodhisattva will generate virtue continually.[8]

For Śāntideva, however, effort, mindfulness, and introspection are not the only virtues which permeate the bodhisattva's life. As we have seen, generosity is not just the occasional transference of wealth, but a complete transformation of all interactions with possessions. The bodhisattva who has perfected generosity is always giving, since she relates to all experience without craving. Likewise, patience is not only relevant in occasional moments of extreme tension, but when perfected, produces a calm and stable mind which is wholly resistant to disturbance from any subtle daily frustration. It reoccurs almost continually. Compassion, likewise, stabilizes all social interactions by removing the pathological social emotions, and unifies a life through its total commitment to progression on the bodhisattva path. Śāntideva presupposes this expansive conception of virtue in BCA 7:62–5, when he urges unending passionate, and joyful performance of virtue for its own sake. If he is successful in doing so, the joy of the bodhisattva will be never-ending.

5.5. Rejoicing

Rejoicing is an important mental factor in both early Buddhist and Mahāyāna traditions. It is defined as taking joy in others' achievements, and is grouped with compassion (*karuṇā*), love (*mettā*), and equanimity (*upekṣā*) as one of the four divine abidings (*brahmavihāras*), an important early classification of virtue.[9] Śāntideva does not explicitly use the divine abidings as a classificatory system in the *Guide*. He does, however, use various synonyms for joy to express an attitude of rejoicing at the success of others, such as *anu-mud* (BCA 3:1, 3:3), *tuṣṭi* (BCA 5:77), and *hṛṣṭi* (BCA 6:77). In chapter three, Śāntideva emphasizes the role of rejoicing in enlivening the mind before taking the bodhisattva's vow:

> I joyfully rejoice (*anumode*) in the virtuous actions performed by all beings which calm the suffering of unfortunate rebirths. Let those who are suffering abide in happiness!
>
> I rejoice in embodied beings' liberation from the suffering of saṃsāra! I rejoice in the bodhisattvahood and buddhahood of the protectors!
>
> I rejoice (*anumode*) in the arising of the ocean-like *bodhicitta* of the teachers which bears with it the happiness of all sentient beings and brings about their welfare! (BCA 3:1–3)

The verses rejoice both in the achievements of sentient beings and the spiritual attainments of Buddhist teachers. Elsewhere, Śāntideva characterizes rejoicing as a way of producing beneficial joy that is free of the craving which infects sensual pleasure:

> All undertakings are aimed at satisfaction which is difficult to achieve, even through wealth. Therefore, I will enjoy the contentment whose source is the good qualities achieved by means of the efforts of others. (BCA 5:77)

A final use of rejoicing occurs in the patience chapter, where, as we have seen, joy is developed as the antidote to anger. The pleasure of rejoicing is used in the second half of the chapter to eliminate the pathological emotion of envy:

> If others take joy and pleasure in praising a person who acquires good qualities, why, oh mind, do you not praise them and rejoice? (BCA 6:76)
>
> This pleasure (*sukha*) from rejoicing (*hṛṣṭi*) is a blameless source of happiness. It is not forbidden by the virtuous ones and is supremely attractive to others. (BCA 6:77)

Notice that the pleasure of rejoicing is referred to as "blameless" (*niravadyam*: 6:77), indicating that it is not contaminated by the pathological emotions. In addition, the joy of rejoicing attracts others (6:77), suggesting it has a social function, in enabling the bodhisattva to form relationships with the beings he wishes to teach.[10] This kind of joy complements compassion in its role of removing the pathological social emotions which prevent the bodhisattva from interacting skillfully with sentient beings.

5.6. Compassion (*karuṇā*)

We have seen that Śāntideva holds that compassion is strongly beneficial for its possessor, in that it eliminates inflated self-interest and the pathological social emotions of envy, competitiveness, and pride.[11] Moreover, the language with which the impassioned bodhisattva commits to eliminate the suffering of all beings suggests a mind enlivened with joy (for example, BCA 10:55–6). Nevertheless, the relationship between compassion and joy is complex. Compassion arises in response to observed suffering of sentient beings and motivates the bodhisattva to care for them. To the extent that she is successful in doing so, it results in great joy. Until this is accomplished, however, Śāntideva seems to hold that compassion causes emotional pain for its possessor (BCA 6:122–3).

Śāntideva's strongest depiction of compassion's role in facilitating joy is presented in a passage we considered at the opening of this book, which alludes to the Mahāyāna trope of bodhisattvas visiting the hell realms to minister to beings there:[12]

> The bodhisattvas with cultivated (*bhāvita*) minds and equal concern for the suffering of others dive into the Avīci hell like swans into a pool of lotuses. (BCA 8:107)
>
> When sentient beings are liberated, they become oceans of joy (*prāmodya*). They alone find fulfillment. Why would they seek insipid liberation? (BCA 8:108)

We can understand these verses as presenting one of Śāntideva's thesis statements in the *Guide*. In portraying the bodhisattva as finding fulfillment in the Avīci hell, the worst place in the universe, Śāntideva is claiming that a highly developed (*bhāvita*) bodhisattva can flourish in any situation whatsoever.[13] At this point in my study, we understand better how Śāntideva's conception of virtue allows him to make this radical claim. The perfection of generosity eliminates all craving toward any element of the bodhisattva's experience. This enables him to give his body for the sake of others with ease (BCA 7:25–6).[14] Moreover, patience, fully developed, lets him experience any level of physical pain without mental suffering. We should recall that both Śāntideva in his *Training Anthology* and Prajñākaramati in his commentary to the *Guide* link the perfection of patience to the ability to withstand the tortures of the hell realms without mental distress.[15] Finally, compassion gives the bodhisattva access to the deep joy he experiences when liberating sentient beings in situations of distress. These verses, therefore, articulate the radical nature of Śāntideva's account of well-being. Similar to the Stoics in the Ancient Greek tradition, Śāntideva believes virtuous character, and the joyful mental experience which accompanies it, are the primary constituents of well-being.[16] Portraying the bodhisattva as flourishing in Avīci is analogous to the Stoics' depiction of the sage maintaining *eudaimonia* even while being tortured on the rack.

The remaining question to consider is whether compassion will also cause mental pain for the bodhisattva, and if so, whether this mental pain decreases his well-being. There are two verses in the patience chapter which strongly suggest that the bodhisattva's compassion is painful:

> The great sages are pleased when others are happy, and become sorrowful when others suffer. All the great sages take satisfaction from satisfying others. A harmful action toward others is a harmful action toward the sages.
>
> Just as sensual pleasures cause absolutely no enjoyment for a person whose body is on fire, likewise, there is no way for a compassionate person to be happy as long as sentient beings are in pain. (BCA 6:122–3)

The reference to the inability for a bodhisattva (here, "compassionate one") to feel happy as long as others are suffering, as well as the comparison to a body that is on fire, suggests that the bodhisattva experiences empathetic pain when she feels compassion for suffering sentient beings. This interpretation of the verse is not necessarily in tension with verses 8:107–8 just quoted, which portray the bodhisattva experiencing great joy upon liberating sentient beings. Compassion causes empathetic pain until sentient beings are liberated from their suffering, after which it results in joy. We have also seen the bodhisattva voluntarily undergo mental pain while generating compassion for others during the exchanging self and other meditations.[17] For these reasons, we can accept that the bodhisattva experiences mental pain when encountering the suffering of sentient beings. The question that remains is whether or to what extent such compassionate pain decreases the bodhisattva's well-being.

A possible answer suggests itself if we consider Śāntideva's attitude toward physical pleasure and physical pain. Many people think that physical pleasure increases well-being, and that physical pain decreases it. Śāntideva does not fully accept either position. Physical pleasure is not bad per se, but it is dangerous because it stimulates the pathological emotions in untrained persons. Likewise, physical pain is only negative if it causes mental pain and anger to arise. The patient bodhisattva, however, can experience any amount of pain without mental distress or anger, so physical pain does not harm his well-being.[18] Śāntideva's views about physical pleasure and pain seems to be that they are not, of themselves, good or bad, but become negative only to the extent that they stimulate or accompany the pathological emotions.

Although he is less explicit about this, it is natural to extend this analysis to mental pleasure and mental pain. Mental pleasure can be bad, when it stimulates or accompanies pathological emotions such as pride and craving. Likewise, we have seen in this chapter that mental pleasure is often good, when it is conducive to or accompanies virtues like concentration and generosity. Mental pain, likewise, is negative when it stimulates or accompanies a pathological emotion like anger. The mental pain that accompanies compassion, however, is virtuous; it arises out of a deep concern for and wish to remove the suffering of sentient beings. It neither stimulates nor accompanies pathological emotions. It would seem likely, therefore, that Śāntideva would hold that it is not disadvantageous to the virtuous bodhisattva's well-being. Just as patience allows the bodhisattva to endure any level of physical pain without harm, compassion, when developed properly, enables the bodhisattva to experience any accompanying level of mental pain, no matter how severe, without harm.

My argument above depends on the assumption that Śāntideva would treat the well-being value of physical and mental pain as analogous. He does not explicitly do so, however, and an alternate possibility is that the pain of compassion is both virtuous, and well-being decreasing (Edelglass 2017). If we accept this interpretation, then it would follow that aspects of compassion are beneficial, such as its elimination of envy and pride, and its conduciveness to bliss when compassionate action is successful. Other aspects of compassion decrease well-being, as when the bodhisattva suffers from the mental pain of compassion.[19]

Nevertheless, I think that the interpretation that I have offered is better, for two reasons. First, Śāntideva repeatedly stresses that the pathological emotions are the deepest sources of suffering (BCA 4:27–45). Since no pathological emotion is present when compassion is experienced, compassionate pain would not decrease well-being. Second, the claim that compassionate pain does not decrease well-being has some intuitive plausibility. In an imperfect world, all of us will frequently encounter suffering sentient beings. We must ask, therefore, what is the most beneficial affective response to these situations? Feeling unmoved by the suffering of others suggests social alienation and a stunted emotional life. A more reasonable answer is that a virtuous person would feel a deep but also realistic empathetic experience of the pain of the other. Such a reaction would not spiral out of control into paralyzing obsession with the other's suffering, but would acknowledge it, and motivate the individual to eliminate it if this is realistic. The bodhisattva feels the pain of compassion deeply, but his mental experience is stable, supported by virtues like mindfulness, introspection, and patience, which ensure that his painful response is not infected by the pathological emotions. Mental pain, in these circumstances, is plausibly the most beneficial reaction possible for the bodhisattva herself to situations of suffering in an imperfect world.

5.7. Conclusion

There is a common conception of fully enlightened buddhas in Mahāyāna literature as freeing themselves from error by eliminating all conceptual activity and thereafter interacting on behalf of sentient beings as beneficial automaton.[20] There are a few verses in the *Guide* that suggest Śāntideva may have held this conception of the endpoint of the bodhisattva path (BCA 9:34–9).[21] Nevertheless, very little of the *Guide* is focused on these late stages of the path. Instead, Śāntideva is more attentive to the development of early to mid-stage bodhisattvas, whose mental lives become more refined and less contaminated by pathological emotions and suffering as they develop compassion and the perfections. In this short chapter, I have illustrated one more feature of bodhisattvas' mental lives, as they cycle with increasing deliberate control through the various arenas of rebirth. They are alive with joy, erupting into pleasure when sentient beings are saved, delighting in giving away all possessions, enthusiastically committing repeatedly to virtuous action, constantly rejoicing in the achievements of others, and continually reverential of the noble path of the bodhisattvas, upon which they are progressing.

Suggestions for further study

Gold 2018 offers an analysis of the perfection of effort (*vīrya*). Buddhaghosa 1991, chapter nine provides a influential characterization of the Buddhist virtue of rejoicing (*mudita*). Lele 2007 and Mrozik 2007 are studies of the *Guide* and the *Training Anthology* that stress the importance of the bodhisattva's success in developing an attitude of joyful confidence (*prasāda*) in his interlocutors. Arbel 2016 offers an analysis of the importance of joy in early Buddhist accounts of liberation.

Questions for reflection

1. What role does joy play in Śāntideva's conception of the bodhisattva path?
2. According to Śāntideva, what is the difference between beneficial and harmful kinds of joy and pleasure?
3. How does joy support the development of the bodhisattva's virtues?
4. Do you agree with Śāntideva that joy is a matter of moral importance? Why or why not?

Chapter 6

WISDOM AND THE TRANSFORMATION OF EXPERIENCE

6.1. Introduction

Wisdom (*prajñā*), for both early and Mahāyāna Buddhists, is the realization of the ultimate nature of realty, including the non-existence of an enduring unified self, the dependently originated and radically impermanent nature of all phenomena, and the unsatisfactoriness of ordinary experience. We have seen Śāntideva appeal to these grades of wisdom frequently in the *Guide*. It is only in the ninth chapter, however, that he provides an extensive presentation of his core Madhyamaka metaphysical commitment, the emptiness (*śūnyatā*) of intrinsic existence (*svabhāva*) of all phenomena.

Śāntideva opens the ninth chapter by giving pride of place to wisdom among the bodhisattva's trainings:

> The Sage taught all of these trainings for the sake of wisdom. Therefore, longing for the cessation of suffering, one should develop wisdom. (BCA 9:1)[1]

The verse suggests two central features of Śāntideva's treatment of wisdom. First, it is presented as the completion of the bodhisattva's trainings, and so we must understand all the other virtues as in some sense supporting it. Second, the role of wisdom is to eliminate suffering, which for Śāntideva means the suffering of all beings. This verse, then, raises two questions: how does wisdom eliminate suffering, and how does it complete the work of the other perfections?

In broad outline, Śāntideva's answer to both questions corresponds to basic Mahāyāna psycho-soteriological theory. Delusion causes the other pathological emotions, and together they constitute suffering. Wisdom eliminates delusion, and thereby all pathological emotions. Therefore, wisdom eliminates suffering. It thereby completes the work of the other perfections, each of which targets a subset of the pathological emotions, and each of which lessens, but cannot wholly eliminate, suffering.

We will see how Śāntideva fills in the details of this sketch in what follows, but examining its basic contours suggests a new problem that is central to his organization of chapter nine. The realization of emptiness eliminates the pathological emotions, but suffering is also empty, as well as those who suffer, the bodhisattva who removes suffering, and all the techniques and practices which constitute Buddhist training. How then is emptiness compatible with the bodhisattva path? Or, from the side of the subject, how is the realization of emptiness compatible with the mental state of compassion, the intention to benefit (empty) sentient beings by eliminating (empty) suffering?

These are versions of the nihilism objection which is addressed by several major Buddhist authors.[2] The objection is of such central importance to Śāntideva that he considers three formulations of it in the *Guide*'s ninth chapter. His first two treatments focus on different forms of what we can call the "metaphysical problem of nihilism," which arises from a perceived tension between the soteriological goal of eliminating suffering by progressing to buddhahood, and the emptiness of the phenomena necessary for achieving this goal, such as the bodhisattva path, buddhas, bodhisattvas, sentient beings, reliable causal connections and so on. At the chapter's end, Śāntideva also hints at a distinct version of the nihilism objection focusing instead on value: since suffering is empty, why is it bad, and why does it need to be removed? Śāntideva's treatment of this version of the objection is less explicit and he offers no clear solution to it, but nevertheless he emphasizes its importance by placing it at the conclusion of the chapter.

We have, therefore, three questions to consider. The question of efficacy asks how realizing emptiness eliminates suffering. The question of completion asks how it completes the work of the other virtues. Finally, the question of compatibility asks how emptiness is compatible with the bodhisattva path. This chapter focuses mainly on Śāntideva's treatment of the first and third questions. Since the second question requires a review of Śāntideva's development of the other virtues, I give it limited treatment now, but return to it in the conclusion to this book.

As I will explore in more detail below, Śāntideva's answer to all three questions is the same. The realization of emptiness facilitates a global shift of perception, in which conventionally existing phenomena are seen accurately, as being without intrinsic existence. Wisdom is effective since seeing all phenomena as empty is itself the antidote to delusion, and thereby eliminates all the pathological emotions and suffering. Moreover, while individual virtues act as antidotes to a specific pathological emotion, this global transformation of experience eliminates all of them. Wisdom, therefore, completes the work of the other perfections. It also solves the metaphysical variant of the nihilism objection, since dependently arisen phenomena are not negated, and therefore conventionally existing persons can act as the agents and objects of compassion. It therefore provides Śāntideva's answer to the question of compatibility.

My goal in this chapter is to illustrate how Śāntideva's understanding of emptiness facilitates this shift of perception which destroys the pathological emotions and eliminates suffering. In so doing, I provide a more detailed response to the three questions just raised. I begin in the section following this introduction by considering Śāntideva's treatment of two versions of the metaphysical nihilism objection. We will see that Śāntideva's response to both versions is the one Nāgārjuna gives in the *Root Verses on the Middle Way (Mūlamadhyamakakārikā*: hereafter, MMK): conventionally existing empty phenomena are not non-existent, but rather dependently arisen, and therefore function reliably. This provides Śāntideva's answer to the question of compatibility. In partial contrast to Nāgārjuna, however, we will also find that Śāntideva's response to the nihilism objection places more emphasis on psychological and soteriological development as well as phenomenological attention to the experiential content of the compassionate bodhisattva. This section also introduces the global shift of perception in which the bodhisattva transitions to viewing all phenomena as empty of intrinsic existence.

The next section explores Śāntideva's defense of the metaphysics of emptiness, which he presents in an adaptation of the early Buddhist meditation sequence, the four foundations of mindfulness. Although the arguments themselves follow standard Madhyamaka patterns, we will find here as well that Śāntideva emphasizes the experiential and soteriological consequences of realizing emptiness. The following section continues to examine the psychological and soteriological benefits of realizing emptiness, in purifying experience of the pathological emotions, thereby enabling the bodhisattva to remain in the realm of rebirth free of suffering. This section also considers Śāntideva's provocative suggestion that early Buddhist practitioners cannot escape from saṃsāra. These two sections articulate Śāntideva's answer to the question of efficacy, and to a more limited extent, his solution to the question of completion. I close the chapter by considering Śāntideva's treatment of the value nihilism objection, the claim that empty suffering need not be removed because it is not bad. I suggest that Śāntideva recognizes this concern, but that he does not attempt to resolve it. I conclude by offering a suggestion as to why he may not see the problem as in need of a response.

The wisdom chapter is complex and there is no consensus among traditional or contemporary commentators on how to understand many of its positions. I will not attempt anything close to a complete analysis here. My focus will be on the contribution Śāntideva's conception of wisdom makes to the central topic of this study: the self and other benefiting nature of virtue. Since virtue, the pathological emotions, and suffering are all conventional entities, this will limit my focus to Śāntideva's conception of conventional reality and the role of wisdom in realizing its empty nature, thereby facilitating the bodhisattva's skillful interaction with it. I will not take a position on many controversial questions about the chapter, including how much of a role Śāntideva gives to accurate conceptual understanding in the realization of ultimate truth.[3] Likewise, I do not provide an analysis of Śāntideva's complex interactions with competing philosophical Buddhist and non-Buddhist schools.[4]

6.2. Nihilism and the global transformation of experience

Given the counterintuitive nature of the Buddhist rejection of self, and Mahāyāna conceptions of emptiness, Mahāyāna Buddhists are frequently accused of nihilism, the charge that they negate the ordinary world and thereby undercut their soteriological goals. An influential version of this critique is considered by Nāgārjuna in the twenty-fourth chapter of the *Root Verses on the Middle Way* (MMK). An opponent claims that accepting the doctrine of emptiness entails the non-existence of the four noble truths, meditational accomplishments, the Buddha, the community of monks and nuns and so on, and that therefore emptiness negates the path to liberation (MMK XXIV 1–6). Nāgārjuna responds by arguing that emptiness does not equal non-existence (MMK XXIV 7–13); rather, to say something is empty is to claim that it exists conventionally, in dependence on causal conditions, including human conceptuality and social practices (MMK XXIV 18–19).[5]

Śāntideva raises the nihilism objection for the first time early in the ninth chapter:

> [Objection:] How can there be karmic merit from a buddha who is like an illusion?
> [Response:] In the same way, how can you explain receiving merit from a buddha who truly exists?[6]

> [Objection]: If a living being is like an illusion, then how does a person who has died take birth again? (BCA 9:9)
> [Response]: Even an illusion exists as long as its collection of causal conditions lasts. Why would you think that a sentient being is truly real merely because (unlike the illusion) its continuum endures a long time? (BCA 9:10)

> [Objection]: Since it has no consciousness, killing an illusionary person is not an unvirtuous act.
> [Response]: When a person possesses illusionary consciousness, then virtuous and non-virtuous karmic potencies do exist. (BCA 9:11)

> As long as the causal conditions are not destroyed, illusions are not destroyed either. When the causal conditions are destroyed, then illusions do not exist, even conventionally. (BCA 9:14)[7]

Śāntideva's presentation of the objection focuses on the supposed incompatibility between emptiness and karmic connections. The opponent objects that since the Buddha does not exist, worship of him cannot be karmically fruitful (9:9); that no negative karma will result from killing non-existent persons and performing other negative acts (9:11); and that once persons are rejected, the idea of rebirth makes no sense (9:9). Śāntideva follows Nāgārjuna in his response: to say something is empty of intrinsic existence does not mean that it does not exist, but rather that it is dependently arisen (9:10, 9:14). Conventional beings are like illusions, in lacking intrinsic existence, but they are not illusions, because they possess sentience, and therefore karmic consequences follow from intentional actions (9:11). Likewise at conventional levels of description, entities endure and function reliably as long as the relevant causal patterns hold (9:10). Similarly, conventionally existing persons die and take rebirth (9:9–10). One can also intervene in conventionally functioning causal chains; one can eliminate rebirth by eliminating its causes and so on (9:14). In giving these responses, Śāntideva is emphasizing that a metaphysics of emptiness is compatible with conventionally existing objects and causal regularities, and therefore is compatible with the bodhisattva path.

Śāntideva considers another version of the nihilism objection in the middle of the chapter, but this time with attention to the compatibility between emptiness and the bodhisattva's mental experience:

> [Objection]: If no sentient being exists, toward whom is compassion felt?

> [Response]: Toward the one fabricated by delusion that is assented to for the sake of the goal. (BCA 9:75)
>
> [Objection]: If no sentient being exists, then whose is the goal? [Response]: It is true that (the bodhisattva's) activity is also because of delusion. For the sake of calming suffering, delusion related to the goal is not turned away. (BCA 9:76)
>
> However, the reification of the self (*ahaṁkāra*), which is the cause of suffering, increases because of delusion about the self. If this (reification) is not prevented by this (use of delusion), then meditation on identitylessness is the best practice. (BCA 9:77)

The objection remains metaphysical in nature, in that the opponent takes as his premises the supposed non-existence of the bodhisattva and the beings who are saved (9:75–6). Nevertheless, Śāntideva now widens the focus to include phenomenological concerns; according to the opponent, it is not merely the non-existence of sentient beings which undermines the bodhisattva's commitment, but also the corresponding lack of experiential object for the bodhisattva's compassion-filled mind (9:75). The mental state of compassion, as many early and Mahāyāna Buddhist texts insist, must be directed toward sentient beings (Jenkins 2015a). Śāntideva cannot, therefore, meet the objection by merely repeating his previous appeal to dependent origination; the response must show how, from the side of the subject, realizing the emptiness of a sentient being is compatible with continuing to experience them as the object of compassion.[8]

Śāntideva's response, that the bodhisattva can employ delusion (*moha*) to interact with empty persons, is provocative and open to multiple interpretations. A way to understand it that is consistent with most of chapter nine is to interpret the term "delusion" in these verses not as indicating the superimposition (*samāropa*) of intrinsic existence (*svabhāva*), which is the root of all suffering, but rather merely as conceptual unification of fragmentary selfless moments of experience, resulting in conventionally existing bodhisattvas and conventionally existing sentient beings. The bodhisattva developed in wisdom would recognize such entities as dependent on causal conditions and conceptual labeling, thereby eliminating any additional superimposition of intrinsic existence.[9] In this reading, verse 9:77 can be understood as giving advice to developing bodhisattvas who are still susceptible to tendencies to reify conventionally existing persons. As a temporary solution, Śāntideva suggests that they should alternate between meditating on emptiness of self and engaging with conventionally existing beings.[10] When wisdom is perfected, however, this will no longer be necessary, since conventional objects may be experienced as they are, empty of intrinsic existence.

Śāntideva, therefore, gives two related but distinguishable responses to the nihilism objection in the first half of the ninth chapter. At the level of metaphysics, sentient beings, bodhisattvas and so on exist conventionally, dependent on causes and conditions, and therefore the causal patterns upon which soteriological progress depends remain viable. At the level of experience, the bodhisattva developed in wisdom engages with conventionally existing persons who remain the objects of his compassion but are no longer reified as intrinsically existent. The object of awareness therefore remains the same, but the mode in which the bodhisattva experiences them changes, so that suffering, sentient beings, and conventional reality as a whole are experienced as empty of intrinsic existence.[11]

This emphasis on the role of wisdom in transforming the bodhisattva's experience is arguably the central theme of chapter nine.[12] Its importance is suggested by Śāntideva's decision to begin the chapter by focusing on epistemic, phenomenological, and soteriological considerations, leaving metaphysical explication and defense of emptiness until the chapter's second half:

> Truth is considered to be of two sorts: conventional and ultimate. Reality is not within the range of the intellect. The intellect is said to be conventional. (BCA 9:2)
>
> Corresponding to these two truths, two kinds of people are recognized: spiritually adept and ordinary. Of these two, the ordinary are superseded by the spiritually adept. (BCA 9:3)

The connection in verse 2 between the intellect and conventional truth is plausibly interpreted as a reference to the Madhyamaka position that conventionally real objects depend on conceptual labeling for their existence. What is meant by claiming that reality—that is, ultimate truth—is beyond the scope of the intellect is controversial, but Śāntideva seems to be referring to non-conceptual direct perception of emptiness which acts as a condition for liberation.[13] Śāntideva's immediate focus in the chapter is on the way reality is experienced, via conceptual or concept-free awareness. He then transitions to wisdom's soteriological function, by grouping beings according to grades of spiritual advancement relative to their level of insight into the nature of reality, presumably with Mādhyamikas who understand emptiness in highest position (BCA 9:3–4).

Śāntideva next shifts to explicit phenomenological analysis, describing the way bodhisattvas advanced in wisdom experience conventional reality:

> Things are seen and imagined as real by the ordinary people, rather than as illusion-like. In this lies their disagreement with the spiritual adepts. (BCA 9:5)

This verse introduces the bodhisattva's global perceptual shift enacted by wisdom which realizes the emptiness of phenomena. Ordinary people superimpose intrinsic existence on phenomena—that is, "see them as real." The bodhisattva by contrast sees them as they are, as illusion-like in being empty of intrinsic existence and therefore depending on conceptual construction for their apparent unity. Notice that these early verses have already laid the groundwork for Śāntideva's responses to the experiential version of the nihilism objection considered above. Wisdom does not undercut the object of compassion because empty sentient beings do not phenomenologically disappear, but rather are experienced as empty of intrinsic existence. We will turn to the psychological and soteriological consequences of this shift in perception in the following two sections.[14]

The reference to conventional reality as being like an illusion, introduced in 9:5, reoccurs throughout the chapter (9:9–17; 9:26–7; 9:30–1; 9:99; 9:142–4). It is natural for Śāntideva to use this language, given that illusions are reliably experienced, when their causal conditions are present, but they appear in a way in which they do not exist (Westerhoff 2010a, 7). A mirage appears as a lake but is merely the appearance of water caused by refracted light and so on. Likewise, conventional reality is illusion-like in appearing as intrinsically existent, when in fact it is empty of intrinsic reality.

A metaphor Śāntideva uses in the chapter to describe the experiential content of wisdom taking conventional reality as its object is that of the magician conducting a magic show. The context in which the magician example is introduced is a debate with a Yogācāra philosopher who argues that emptiness lacks soteriological efficacy:

> [Objection]: Even when the similarity with an illusion is recognized, why would the pathological emotions cease, since even the maker of an illusionary woman feels lust for her? (BCA 9:30)

> [Response]: In this case, the illusion's maker has not removed the habitual dispositions for the pathological emotions to arise toward the objects of knowledge; therefore, when perception takes place, the disposition to see things as empty is too weak. (BCA 9:31)
>
> The habitual dispositions to see things as real is removed by applying the habitual dispositions to see them as empty. Afterwards, through repeatedly applying the idea that "nothing exists," this (idea of emptiness) is also destroyed. (BCA 9:32)

It is obvious why the magic show is an ideal metaphor to portray the bodhisattva's experience of conventional reality. The magician, who stands in for the bodhisattva, is in a privileged epistemic position in realizing the deceptive nature of his illusionary creations. Ordinary people, fooled by his tricks, take the conjured objects for real things, and as a result may become emotionally attached or fearful in relation to them. The magician, realizing their insubstantial nature, can continue to interact with them without being adversely emotionally affected, just as the bodhisattva does not crave or become averse to conventionally existing objects.[15]

Śāntideva's treatment of the magician example quoted above makes an additional subtler point. The magician is portrayed as being deceived by his own trick and lusting after the illusionary woman (9:30). Śāntideva's purpose here is to distinguish between mere intellectual knowledge of emptiness, which can be attained by listening to teachings or superficial engagement with argumentation, and the deeply embodied realization of the bodhisattva, born out of continued reflection on the reasons for accepting the truth of emptiness combined with meditation. As a result, the high-level bodhisattva eliminates his deeply rooted habitual dispositions (*vāsanā*) to perceive phenomena as intrinsically existent (9:31–2). It is only after this occurs that pathological emotions are no longer stimulated by engagement with conventional entities. Once again we find Śāntideva emphasizing the transformation of experience. The conventional object is not merely intellectually understood to be empty, but is experienced that way, resulting in emotional transformation.

The metaphor of the magician and his magic trick provides a powerful way of representing the bodhisattva's perception of reality for several reasons. Most importantly, just as the magician realizes his creations appear in a way they do not exist, the bodhisattva realizes conventional entities appear as intrinsically existent, when in fact they are empty. Second, this metaphor emphasizes the erroneous nature of conventionally appearing phenomena. Third, the example suggests how the Mādhyamika avoids the nihilistic conclusion that entities are wholly non-existent, since, in a magic show, the illusions which are experienced appear reliably, in dependence on causal conditions and the activity of the magician. This appearing object, moreover, is intersubjectively available; the magician and the spectators look at the same illusionary woman, just as the bodhisattva and ordinary people interact with the same conventional object. Nevertheless the perspective with which they experience these objects differs radically, depending on their level of insight into an object's nature. Finally, the metaphor of the magic show is able to represent the possibility of emotional transformation attained by recognizing the illusion-like nature of conventional objects, although in Śāntideva's presentation the magician himself does not gain this benefit due to the superficiality of his insight. Describing conventional reality as a magic show also suggests its fluid nature, composed of objects which change quickly and whose boundaries can be redrawn. A skilled magician conjures a rabbit and transforms it into a dragon and so on. Likewise, our explorations of Śāntideva's development of generosity, patience, and compassion have found the bodhisattva strategically redrawing the boundaries of conventional reality as an aid in developing virtue.[16]

6.3. The metaphysics of illusion: Emptiness and the four foundations of mindfulness

In the last section I introduced the experiential transformation the bodhisattva achieves in perceiving phenomena as empty of intrinsic existence. We will find Śāntideva's phenomenological focus continue in his explication and defense of the metaphysics of emptiness, for which he adapts the early Buddhist meditation schema of the four foundations of mindfulness. In early Buddhist texts, this series of meditations is used to develop insight into the impermanent and selfless nature of all phenomena, by cycling through contemplations on four sets of meditation objects: the body (*rūpa*), feeling (*vedanā*), the mind (*citta*), and mental objects (*dharmas*).[17] In his adaptation, Śāntideva replaces contemplative exercise with argumentation, with the goal of demonstrating the emptiness of each of the four sets of objects. He gives more extended treatments to the emptiness of the body and feeling, with brief analysis of the last two sets of objects, presumably because he believes the earlier arguments will apply there as well.

Śāntideva's choice to use the four foundations of mindfulness as objects of metaphysical analysis hints at his experiential focus in the chapter. These meditations are used in early Buddhist texts to develop awareness of one's own physical and mental experience, and to realize its nature as impermanent and selfless. Moreover, Śāntideva interprets the four foundations to collectively include all conventional reality. He does this by reinterpreting the meaning of the last item in the scheme, *dharmas*. In early Buddhist treatments of the four foundations, the term "dharma" (Pali: *dhamma*) is used narrowly, to refer to a selection of mental states appearing in several lists of soteriologically relevant factors.[18] Śāntideva exploits the broad semantic range of the term and reinterprets it to mean "factor of experience" so that it refers to all phenomena whatsoever (9:105). Doing so suggests that his arguments apply not just to the body, feeling, and certain mental states, but are applicable with slight modification to all conventional entities. Through this global interpretation of the four foundations, Śāntideva is able to further develop the phenomenological transformation of the bodhisattva's experience by showing that *all* phenomena whatsoever are empty, and therefore can be experienced as lacking intrinsic existence by one advanced in wisdom.

The arguments for emptiness presented in this section are themselves standard adaptations of Madhyamaka patterns of reasoning, such as those developed by Nāgārjuna. Śāntideva begins arguing for the emptiness of the body by noting that it cannot be identified with any particular body part (9:78–9). The unstated presupposition is that if the body had intrinsic existence, we should be able to mentally identify it.[19] Whenever we attempt to do so, all that is found is one or another body part, or a collection of them, suggesting that the body is only a conceptual superimposition. Next, Śāntideva deploys a standard Madhyamaka refutation of intrinsic existence which considers the relation between the whole and its parts. If the body exists intrinsically, it must either wholly, or partially, inhere in each of its parts. If it inheres in its entirety in each part, then the body, which was supposed to be single, becomes plural (9:81). If it is divided among its parts, however, then the body itself loses its unity (9:80). Moreover, it makes no sense to think of a body existing somehow separate from the body parts, given that they compose it (9:82). The body, therefore, should be recognized as a conceptual imputation on its parts, without intrinsic existence. Śāntideva then suggests that the same reasoning also applies to each body part. The foot can be divided into its toes, and cannot be identified with any of them, and the toes can be split into joints and so on (9:85). The final units of division are atoms, which are supposed to be unanalyzable. Atoms, however, can be analyzed into the six directions; the left side is distinguished from the right side and so on. Therefore, atoms also vanish under analysis (9:86). These same arguments can be applied to any external element of physical reality, supporting the conclusion that all of it is empty of intrinsic existence.

In the conclusion of the argument, Śāntideva turns from the deconstructive aspects of emptiness to its compatibility with conventional reality:

> Therefore, the body does not exist. However, through delusion (*moha*) there is the impression of a body in regard to the hands and other body parts, on account of their particular arrangement, just like the impression of a person in relation to a post. (BCA 9:83)
>
> As long as the collection of causal conditions exists, the body appears as a person. In the same way, as long as this collection lasts, the hands and other body parts are seen as a body. (BCA 9:84)

The emphasis once again has turned to the experience of the agent. As with verse 9:75 considered above, Śāntideva's reference to delusion can be interpreted to mean conceptual construction of conventionally existing entities. Verse 9:83 provides a useful example of such conceptual activity. In the dim light of the evening, we may mistake a post seen in the distance for a figure walking toward us. This image of the person walking is superimposed upon what is actually there, the post; absent human mental activity, no walking person appears. The example shows in what way conventional reality is delusive. The object in the example appears (as a person) in a way it does not exist (a post). Likewise, the appearance of all conventional existence is delusive, in that entities appear as possessing intrinsic existence, when in fact they are empty of it. But the example also suggests the reliability and coherence of conventional reality, for given the right lighting conditions, visual abilities and so forth, an image of the post reliably appears.

The last verse of the sequence turns to the psychological and soteriological effects of realizing the emptiness of the body:

> Since form is like a dream, what thoughtful person would be aroused by it? Since the body does not exist, who is female and who is male? (BCA 9:87)

The term translated in the first line as "form" is *rūpa*, which here refers to the parts of the human body, but which can refer more broadly to any physical thing. This suggests that the results of this argument can be generalized to all physical objects. The verse compares physical reality to a dream, in the sense that it is the result of mental construction and disappears upon analysis. Śāntideva is suggesting that recognizing the insubstantial nature of the body undercuts the pathological emotions, eliminating craving toward male and female bodies. This is an application of a basic principle of Buddhist psychology which we have seen employed repeatedly in the *Guide*, that pathological emotions arise because of the superimposition of endurance, unity, and intrinsic existence upon impermanent, fragmentary, and empty phenomena. Stripping away the delusion of intrinsic existence destroys pathological emotions while leaving the conventionally existing object intact.

Śāntideva next turns to the second foundation of mindfulness, feeling (*vedanā*), meaning pleasurable and painful sensations. Śāntideva's strategy in this section is to refute the intrinsic existence of feeling by claiming that it is impossible to give a coherent account of the intrinsic existence of its causal factors. Śāntideva's unstated premise is that if an entity's causes and conditions are empty of intrinsic existence, then the entity must be as well.[20] He then appeals to the widely held Buddhist view that the salient causal condition for feeling is contact between sense object and sense organ.[21] For instance, the sense organ of taste connects with gustatory particles, generating sense awareness of a particular taste, leading to pleasant or unpleasant gustatory sensations. Śāntideva argues, however, that there cannot be contact between the sense faculty and sense object. If there is space between them, then they do not touch (9:93). However, if they do touch, this must happen at the atomic level, since both sense organ and object are physical, and therefore are composed of atoms. Further, by definition, atoms are indivisible, and without parts. If two atoms are in contact, therefore, then they must wholly overlap, which is absurd (9:93–4). Moreover, intuitively, the idea of touch occurring between partless atoms makes no sense (9:95). Since contact between sense organ and object is impossible, contact cannot give rise to feeling (9:97). Feeling, therefore, does not exist intrinsically; like the walking man illusion from the last set of arguments, it is a conceptually constructed mental image superimposed upon its parts in dependence on causal conditions. Although the reasoning once again follows common Madhyamaka patterns of argumentation, it is significant that the intrinsic existence of feeling, which is mental, is deconstructed by an argument focusing on the impossibility of interaction between physical particles. This is another example of Śāntideva's frequent use of the body in developing arguments for selflessness and emptiness.[22]

At the conclusion of the argument, Śāntideva turns to the psychological benefits resulting from insight into the emptiness of feeling:

> Thus, since contact does not exist, how can feeling (*vedanā*) originate? What use is this exertion? Who is afflicted and from what would affliction arise? (BCA 9:97)
>
> If there is no experiencer and feeling does not exist, then, once this state of affairs is realized, why, oh craving, are you not torn asunder? (BCA 9:98)
>
> No one experiences feeling; thus, in reality, there is no feeling. In this selfless bundle, who could be afflicted by it? (BCA 9:101).

Verse 9:97 concludes that rejecting the intrinsic existence of contact entails rejecting the intrinsic existence of its effect, feeling. We need not take this to mean that the bodhisattva does not feel pleasure and pain; rather her experience of it is altered now that it is recognized as illusion-like in being empty of intrinsic existence. Śāntideva then emphasizes the psychological effects which occur from perceiving the emptiness of feeling. In the twelve links of dependent origination, feeling is presented as the causal condition of craving. Therefore, just as eliminating contact eliminates feeling, eliminating feeling destroys craving (97–8). Since it is only the intrinsic existence of feeling that is negated, it might seem as though craving would also continue to exist conventionally, like an illusion. In describing it as "torn asunder," Śāntideva suggests that this is not the case. This is because the pathological emotions are forms of delusion which arise from the superimposition of intrinsic existence upon conventional phenomena. Recognizing phenomena's empty nature, therefore, destroys them.

Śāntideva then suggests that recognizing the emptiness of painful feelings shows that no one is really hurt (9:101). The idea seems to be that although pain is still experienced, the recognition of its illusion-like nature strips it of its badness for the bodhisattva. This verse continues the work begun in the patience chapter, in which the bodhisattva averted anger by altering her perspective on painful feeling, in seeing it as not really harmful.[23] Using emptiness as the antidote to pathological emotions, however, is much more powerful than the piecemeal strategy deployed in the *Guide*'s sixth chapter. There, the bodhisattva was restricted to targeting specific desires as a way of eliminating particular vulnerabilities to pain. Since all phenomena are empty, however, recognizing the emptiness of pain alters the bodhisattva's attitude to all of it at once. This is one of the ways the wisdom chapter completes the work that was begun earlier in the text by developing the other perfections.

These verses in which Śāntideva explores the psychological effects of realizing the emptiness of feeling are among the most important in the *Guide*. Throughout this study we have seen him give careful attention to pleasure and pain as potential causal conditions for the pathological emotions of craving and anger, respectively. Recognizing the emptiness of feelings of pleasure and pain, therefore, enables Śāntideva to develop powerful antidotes to both craving (9:98) and anger (9:101). Notice again the contrast with the earlier sections of the text, where various meditational strategies were employed to generate distinct perfections to eliminate certain pathological emotions in particular situations. In the ninth chapter, recognizing the emptiness of the causes of the pathological emotions becomes a master tool to destroy them all.

Śāntideva's treatment of the third foundation, mind, is brief. He emphasizes the unfindability of mind, using parallel arguments to those about the unfindability of the body: the mind is not located in the sense faculties, nor in the sense objects, nor separate from them (9:102–3). He also presents a version of Nāgārjuna's three times argument, reasoning that the temporal relation between a cognition and the object which causes it cannot be specified.[24] If a cognition arises before its object comes into existence, then it originates without depending on that object (9:104). Keeping in mind that objects of cognition are momentary, the cognition also cannot arise after its object, since the object will have already gone out of existence and therefore cannot exert any causal influence (9:105). The causal relation cannot be simultaneous, however, since then the object would not be acting as the cognition's cause (9:104).

The arguments against all three of these foundations of mindfulness can be applied, with minor modifications, to any item not explicitly referenced. This is implied in Śāntideva's treatment of the fourth foundation of mindfulness, *dharmas*, where he extends his conclusions to all phenomena whatsoever (9:105cd). All entities could be subjected to one or another of the argument patterns given in this section of the text, and therefore all must be understood as empty of intrinsic existence.

6.4. The benefits of wisdom

We have seen thus far that the bodhisattva's development of wisdom enables her to continue to interact with the ordinary commonsense world of objects, persons, and social relations, but to relate to these items differently; by seeing them as empty of intrinsic existence, she does not crave them, nor become angry when they are lost and so on. Moreover, as Śāntideva's presentation of the four foundations of mindfulness shows, this transformation of experience is global, purifying the bodhisattva's interactions with all objects whatsoever, and thereby eliminating all pathological emotions. Śāntideva also describes its total efficacy in a series of verses examining the benefits of realizing emptiness:

> Since emptiness is the antidote to the mental darkness of the emotional and cognitive obscurations, why would one longing for omniscience not swiftly cultivate its realization? (BCA 9:54)

The reference to cognitive obscuration (*jñeya-āvṛti*) indicates the delusion of intrinsic existence, but it also alludes to a common Mahāyāna position that a fully enlightened buddha gains a kind of limited omniscience which enables effective intervention on behalf of sentient beings.[25] The emotional obscurations (*kleśa-āvṛti*) are all the pathological emotions other than delusion, including craving and anger. As developed by Śāntideva in chapter nine, wisdom functions as an antidote to these negative mental states in two ways. First, it can be deployed as an antidote to all instances of a single pathological emotion, as we saw Śāntideva do with craving above (9:98). Second, as we have seen in verse 9:5, and in his presentation of the four foundations of mindfulness, insight into emptiness facilitates taking a new perspective toward conventional reality as a whole, so that it is experienced as empty of intrinsic existence. As a result, all adverse psychological reactions are eliminated.

Moreover, we saw in my opening chapter that Śāntideva takes the pathological emotions to constitute suffering. Therefore, a consequence of this global transformation of perception is that the bodhisattva can remain in the realm of rebirth without suffering. We have seen Śāntideva allude to this possibility several times before in the *Guide*, but his clearest presentation of this position comes in the wisdom chapter:

> Fear should arise toward a thing which produces suffering. Emptiness extinguishes suffering. Therefore, why would one fear it? (BCA 9:55)

> If something named "I" existed, then fear might arise from any direction. If "I" does not exist, then who will fear belong to? (BCA 9:56)

These verses examine the psychological benefits of realizing emptiness for the bodhisattva. Since doing so destroys the pathological emotions, it eliminates her own suffering (9:55). Moreover, since fear is caused by grasping at the well-being of a falsely conceived intrinsically existent self, realizing emptiness eliminates fear (9:56). The verses contrast with much of Śāntideva's language in earlier chapters in the *Guide*, which stimulated fear by drawing attention to the faults of saṃsāra (e.g. 2:28–46; 7:3–14). This suggests that these past descriptions were strategic, a way of inspiring low-level bodhisattvas to develop the virtues, including wisdom, which when perfected will eliminate all fear.[26] Realizing emptiness strips saṃsāra of its terrors, purifying experience of the pathological emotions without dissolving conventional reality.

The bodhisattva, therefore, can continue to interact with conventional reality without suffering. Śāntideva, here, can be understood as developing the psychological and soteriological implications of Nāgārjuna's ontological equation of saṃsāra and nirvāṇa (MMK 25:19). Moreover, Śāntideva also argues for the incoherence of the early Buddhist strategy of attempting to escape suffering through leaving the realm of rebirth. His critique is given in a response to an objection by an early Buddhist opponent who claims that realizing emptiness is not necessary for salvation from saṃsāra:

> [Objection]: Liberation comes from insight into the (Four Noble) Truths, so what is achieved by realizing emptiness?
> [Response]: Because Buddhist scripture says that there is no awakening without this method. (BCA 9:40)

In the early Buddhist path, realizing the four noble truths, as well as related tenets like metaphysical selflessness and dependent origination, are sufficient for attaining liberation from saṃsāra. The opponent here points out that since Śāntideva also accepts these tenets, he should recognize that their realization causes liberation, making the Madhyamaka doctrine of emptiness superfluous. In the above verse, Śāntideva responds by appealing to Mahāyāna scriptures which emphasize the necessity of realizing emptiness. This is followed a few verses later with an argument that the early Buddhist strategy is psychologically impossible. The explicit reason given is that until entities are experienced as empty, craving toward them will persist. Śāntideva's response also suggests that the early Buddhist approach is incoherent, since prioritizing one's own liberation is an instance of craving, which is the cause of rebirth and suffering. The sequence is introduced when an opponent suggests that early Buddhist disciples who have eliminated craving will also be free of grasping, and therefore rebirth and all other suffering:

> [Objection]: As long as craving (*tṛṣṇā*) does not exist, grasping (*upādānaṁ*) also will not exist.
> [Response]: Why cannot their craving, even if undefiled (*akliṣṭa*), exist like a delusion? (BCA 9:46)
>
> Craving has as causal condition feeling (*vedanā*), and they experience feeling. A mind with an object must rest somewhere or other. (BCA 9:47)
>
> Without emptiness, the mind is bound and arises again, just as in non-cognitive meditative absorption. Therefore, one should cultivate the realization of emptiness. (BCA 9:48)

The psychological framework Śāntideva employs is once again the twelve links of dependent origination, where feeling (*vedanā*) is said to cause craving (*tṛṣṇā*), which causes grasping (*upādānaṁ*), and from there rebirth and all of the sufferings of saṃsāra. We have already examined Śāntideva's arguments that realizing the emptiness of feeling eliminates craving (9:93–8). The high-level bodhisattva then remains in conventional reality as a choice, through deliberate use of conceptualization to continue to interact with conventional objects and persons (9:52). Verses 9:46–8 consider the case of the early Buddhist practitioner who has realized the four noble truths (see 9:40), and early Buddhist insights like impermanence and metaphysical selflessness, but has not realized the emptiness of entities. Śāntideva argues that since these practitioners have not realized the emptiness of feeling, they still experience a subtle kind of craving (9:46). Therefore, their minds continue to become attached to objects, preventing the attainment of nirvāṇa (9:47–8; see also 9:44).

Śāntideva's claim that highly advanced early Buddhists are susceptible to a kind of undefiled (*akliṣṭa)* craving (*tṛṣṇā*) is puzzling. Given that craving *is* a mental defilement, it is unclear what undefiled craving could be. One way to understand the passage is to take Śāntideva to be referencing the three traditional objects of craving, listed frequently in early Buddhist texts: craving for sense pleasures, existence, and non-existence.[27] Defiled craving then would be craving for sense pleasures, while craving for existence and non-existence would be craving that is undefiled by sensual lust. Craving for existence references the fault of the Brahmanical schools who accept an eternal self which takes rebirth after death. Craving for non-existence refers to early Buddhist disciples, who want to escape from the realm of rebirth completely. They therefore possess a kind of "undefiled craving." Moreover, craving is the cause of rebirth in saṃsāra. Therefore, ironically, the early Buddhist practitioner is trapped in saṃsāra by his very desire to leave it.

The bodhisattva, by contrast, eliminates all three forms of craving through realizing emptiness, a point Śāntideva makes a few verses later:

> By being liberated from attachment and fear, the bodhisattva is able to remain in saṃsāra for the sake of those suffering because of delusion. This is a fruit of emptiness. (BCA 9:52)[2829]

Through transforming his perception of conventional reality so that he experiences it as empty of intrinsic existence, the bodhisattva eliminates craving for conventionally existing objects. In doing so, he eliminates the first kind of craving, for sensual pleasure. Moreover, by seeing the whole world and himself as empty of self, he also eliminates the second kind of craving, for existence, given that this kind of craving refers to the desire for an inherently existent self to be reborn. The verse references these two benefits of realizing emptiness through its claim that emptiness eliminates attachment (*sakti*), here meaning attachment to sense objects and existence. Finally, realizing emptiness frees the bodhisattva from aversion to the supposed calamities of saṃsāra, such as painful circumstances, loss of saṃsāric goods, and negative rebirths. As we saw above, fear is eliminated when wisdom realizes that the illusion-like self cannot really be hurt (9:55–6). Therefore, the bodhisattva who realizes emptiness also eliminates the craving for non-existence which afflicts even *arhats*, who desire permanent entry into nirvāṇa. This is referenced in the verse through its claim that realizing emptiness eliminates fear (*trāsa*). This verse, then, presents one of the great inversions of the *Guide*. Rather than destabilize the bodhisattva's compassionate commitment by undercutting conventional reality, understood correctly as insight into the conventional nature of entities, realizing emptiness enables the bodhisattva to remain in saṃsāra and flourish.[30]

6.5. Conclusion: Why is saṃsāra bad?

We have at this point concluded our discussion of the three questions introduced at the beginning of this chapter. The question of efficacy asked how wisdom was effective at eliminating suffering. The question of completion asked how wisdom completes the work of the other perfections. The question of compatibility asked why the acceptance of emptiness does not undercut the bodhisattva path by negating the conventional world. Śāntideva's response to all three questions depends on the global transformation of experience, in which the bodhisattva sees conventionally existing objects accurately, as empty of intrinsic existence. This is itself how the bodhisattva's pathological emotions, and therefore suffering, are eliminated, thereby providing the answer to the question of efficacy. It likewise completes the work of the other perfections, whose purpose was to eliminate pathological emotions and suffering, but who could only do so piecemeal. It also provides Śāntideva's response to the metaphysical nihilism objection and therefore solves the problem of compatibility, since seeing conventional reality as like an illusion in being empty of intrinsic existence does not wholly negate it. Conventionally existing objects continue to function in reliable causal patterns, enabling the bodhisattva to continue to interact with society, and to train in the bodhisattva path. Moreover, conventional beings can act as the intentional objects of the bodhisattva's compassion.

This global transformation of experience destabilizes the early Buddhist dichotomy between saṃsāra and nirvāṇa. For early Buddhists, saṃsāra encompasses all of conventional reality, and their soteriological strategy is to escape them together by ending rebirth. Realization of emptiness, however, purifies conventional reality of its ability to generate pathological emotions and thereby suffering. The bodhisattva advanced in wisdom, therefore, transitions from a saṃsāric to a nirvāṇic mode of experiencing the conventional world.

It is however possible to reformulate the nihilism objection in such a way that it still applies to the bodhisattva who has transformed experience through wisdom. We have above seen Śāntideva argue for the emptiness of painful feeling (9:97–101) and the pathological emotions themselves (4:46–7). One can argue, therefore, that given suffering does not intrinsically exist, it cannot be bad. Therefore, it is not clear why it needs to be removed.[31] Notice that this is not merely a repetition of the metaphysical nihilism objection; it is not the claim that pain and the pathological emotions do not (conventionally) exist. Rather, it is what we can call the "value nihilism objection": given its insubstantial nature, why be concerned about the occurrence of illusionary suffering? This can be asked both in relation to the bodhisattva's own suffering, and toward the suffering of those he has vowed to save.

Śāntideva himself has raised a version of the value nihilism objection in the eighth chapter. Following his appeal to the negation of the self in his defense of impartial altruism, Śāntideva has an opponent question why suffering needs to be removed, given that there is no one who suffers:

> If one asks why suffering should be prevented, it is because there is no disagreement from anyone in this matter. If it is to be prevented, then all of it must be treated in the same way. If not, then this applies to oneself as much as to other sentient beings. (BCA 8:103)

The objection in chapter eight focuses on the non-existence of an intrinsically existing subject who suffers, rather than the emptiness of pain and the pathological emotions. Nevertheless, Śāntideva's response to this version of the objection appears relatively muted. Although it may be true that no one would question the badness of suffering, we can wonder whether this consensus itself depends on the mistaken belief that the self is real, and therefore really experiences it.

Likewise, in the ninth chapter an opponent might claim that the belief in the badness of (empty) suffering and the motivation to remove it might themself be products of the delusive belief in suffering's intrinsic existence. This does not of itself entail that it is irrational to remove empty suffering, but it raises the question of why it should be removed. Śāntideva does not explicitly raise and respond to this concern, but he does not shy away from the conclusion that suffering does not (truly) exist, and that therefore no one (really) suffers.[32] We have already seen him state this in 9:101, and he reemphasizes it toward the conclusion of the chapter:

> When things are empty in this way, what can be gained and what can be taken away?
> Who will be praised or despised by whom? (BCA 9:151)
>
> Where would happiness or suffering come from?
> What can be liked and what can be disliked?
> What is craving? Where is this craving, when being examined from its own nature? (BCA 9:152)

> Upon reflection, what is the world of living beings?
> Who will really die in this place?
> Who will come into being, and who has passed away?
> Who is a relative and who is a friend of whom? (BCA 9:153)

Śāntideva uses this series of rhetorical questions to reject the intrinsic existence of both saṃsāra's good fortune and its calamities: gaining and losing wealth and reputation; experiencing physical pleasure and pain; developing relationships and losing friends, all are illusion-like, lacking intrinsic reality. One might expect at this point some explanation of why it is nevertheless worth removing (ultimately) non-existent suffering. Śāntideva, however, does not do this; there is not even an explicit repetition of his earlier allusion to the common agreement that suffering is bad. Instead, after acknowledging the tension, he simply restates his commitment to ending suffering. He does this by first offering an emotionally sweeping reflection on saṃsāra's miseries, stressing the frequency of violence and depression (9:155), the recurrence of negative rebirths (9:156), the shortness of life and prevalence of pain (9:158), hunger, fatigue, bad companions (9:159), and the difficulty of practicing Buddhist teachings and eliminating the pathological emotions (9:160–2). Then the chapter concludes by entreating the bodhisattva to develop compassion toward suffering beings:

> Alas, the excessive sorrow of those living in a flood of suffering! Despite abiding in misery, they are not aware of their own wretched condition! (BCA 9:163)

> Just like a madman who submerges in water over and over, only to enter into fire again and again, even though abiding in misery they think they are well-situated! (BCA 9:164)

> While these beings live this way, pretending that death and rebirth do not exist, terrible misfortunes approach the foremost of which is death! (BCA 9:165)

This evocative sequence of verses, stressing the terrors of saṃsāra, leaves no doubt as to Śāntideva's position about the badness of suffering for ordinary persons. There is, however, something of a tension in Śāntideva's positions expressed at the end of chapter nine. He is clear that suffering is bad, and relies upon common agreement that it should be removed, but in these verses he is also adamant that ordinary people are deluded about the nature of suffering and happiness. This is because, as we have seen him argue throughout the text, suffering is most essentially the condition of being dominated by the pathological emotions. By contrast, pursing what ordinary people take well-being to consist in, such as wealth and reputation, stimulates craving, anger and so on, and therefore increases suffering. This leaves us with three questions about Śāntideva's attitude toward empty suffering. First, why is conventionally existing suffering bad for ordinary people, given that it is not ultimately existent? Second, given that Śāntideva cannot appeal to the intrinsic existence of suffering in determining what experiences are bad, how is he able to argue that ordinary people are deluded in their conceptions of well-being? Third, given that suffering is bad, why does it not afflict the high-level bodhisattva, given that she continues to experience the conventional world?

Providing an answer to the last of these questions is a central theme of the entire *Guide* and has been an explicit focus of this book. We have seen Śāntideva articulate throughout the text the beneficial properties of the perfections, and the harmful nature of the pathological emotions. Likewise, we have examined his arguments that physical pain and loss of material goods are not harmful for virtuous persons.[33] High-level bodhisattvas will not suffer, therefore, when experiencing these apparent misfortunes, so long as they prevent the pathological emotions from arising. This is done by developing the virtues of the bodhisattva path, and the process is completed by viewing pleasure, pain, and all apparent misfortunates as empty of intrinsic existence.

Since ordinary people have not realized emptiness, however, they suffer from the pathological emotions. The solution is not to eliminate physical pain, nor to prevent the loss of material goods and so on, but to train them to radically alter their perspective on the conventional world, and this is precisely what happens upon realizing emptiness. This explains Śāntideva's claim, made in the first chapter of the *Guide*, that the bodhisattva path should be taken up by those desiring to escape saṃsāra (1:8). One leaves saṃsāra, not by eliminating rebirth, but by altering one's perspective on conventional reality to see it as empty, and thereby eliminate all pathological emotions. This also explains why, in the concluding verses of the chapter, Śāntideva takes teaching the doctrine of emptiness to sentient beings as central to his goal of eliminating suffering:

> Let those who are like me understand everything as resembling space. (BCA 9:154ab)

> Thus, when would I bring peace to those tormented by the fires of suffering, through acts in the service of happiness generated by the clouds of my merit? (BCA 9:166)
>
> When will I respectfully teach emptiness and the collection of merit by means of conventions and non-conceptual truth to those whose views are based on attachment? (BCA 9:167)

The reference to the accumulation of merit in 9:167 refers to all the bodhisattva's trainings, which increase positive karmic potentials and develop virtue. Most central in these verses, however, is Śāntideva's claim that it is teaching emptiness which, ultimately, will eliminate the suffering of sentient beings. He makes this claim twice; once in verse 154, just prior to beginning his long invocation of the terrors of saṃsāra, and again in 167, after he has completed it. It is not possible to extinguish suffering by escaping rebirth; even the arhats who have eliminated craving for sense pleasures are still trapped in it. Likewise, none of the supposed calamities of saṃsāra need be avoided, for one developed in virtue can bear them with ease. Rather, the antidote to all suffering is to experience reality as it truly is, as impermanent, lacking unity, and empty of intrinsic existence. As a result, nihilism is avoided, since the conventional world is not negated, and suffering is ended, since the pathological emotions are vanquished. And then saṃsāra becomes nirvāṇa.

Nevertheless, this does not yet provide an answer to the other two questions posed above. It does not explain why conventionally existing suffering is bad in the first place. Is there anything Śāntideva can say to the moral skeptic who questions why suffering need be removed?[34] Likewise, it does not explain why Śāntideva is justified in arguing that ordinary people's conceptions of well-being are misguided, given that he cannot appeal to the intrinsic badness of suffering in defending his account of well-being.

Some Abhidharma Buddhists can respond to these questions about the ontological ground of value by referencing the evaluative status of ultimately real *dharmas* of feeling, a category which includes both pleasure and pain, as well as ultimately real pathological emotions, and virtuous mental states. These Abhidharma schools are metaethical realists, in holding that value is a constitutive part of reality, independent of human conceptual schemes. Progress on the bodhisattva path, therefore, is constituted by the reduction of harmful mental states which are intrinsically bad, and the production of virtuous mental states, which are intrinsically good.[35] Not only has Śāntideva rejected this realist ontology, but he has claimed that it is recognizing its emptiness that perfects virtue and eliminates suffering. To achieve his goal, therefore, the bodhisattva must realize that claims about value and disvalue themselves can only be grounded in conventions. And the value nihilism objection asks whether these conventional distinctions are sufficient to warrant robust ethical commitment and enable the critique of mistaken moral positions. The tension is heightened in Śāntideva's bodhisattva path, given that the ethical commitment of the bodhisattva is infinite, a vow to save all beings from suffering.

This book is a study of Śāntideva's ethical thought as presented in the *Guide*, and it is simply a fact that he does not give an extended metaethical response to the value nihilism objection. Part of the reason for this may be his belief that any justification appealing to ultimately real metaphysical entities will fall prey to the Madhyamaka arguments for the emptiness of intrinsic existence. Moreover, central to early Madhyamaka metaphysics is the claim that to recognize something as conventionally real does not make it any less metaphysically robust, given that it continues to function reliably in causal patterns.[36] Like Nāgārjuna and Candrakīrti, Śāntideva also accepts the epistemic corollary of this position, and adopts a distinction between conventional truth and conventional falsity:

> How a thing is seen, heard, and cognized is not refuted here in any way. Only the conceptualization of it as truly existing, which is the cause of suffering, is negated in this matter. (BCA 9:25)

In this verse, Śāntideva follows Candrakīrti in accepting the conventional validity of properly functioning senses, as well as correct reasoning.[37] The resulting conventionally true claims are valid for all persons, and according to Candrakīrti and Śāntideva, this is compatible with the empty nature of both epistemic instruments, as well as the entities perceived and reasoned about.[38] In his reference to universal agreement regarding the badness of suffering, Śāntideva can be seen as relying on this epistemic distinction between conventional truth and falsity. It is simply a fact that living beings directly experience the badness of suffering, and that there can be no reasonable disagreement about this (8:95–6; 8:103).[39] This is the basis on which he builds his ethics. It is attention to one's own suffering which motivates the initial commitment to the bodhisattva path. He then argues that limiting concern to oneself is irrational and offers trainings to expand self-centered concern into compassion for all.

This leaves us with the question of why Śāntideva believes he is justified in critiquing common conceptions of well-being, given that he appeals to the universal agreement of ordinary people in grounding the commitment to remove suffering in the first place. This concern parallels a frequent objection raised against Madhyamaka metaphysics, where it is often argued that an ontology of emptiness entails a relativism in which problematic commonly held positions cannot be adequately criticized.[40] Śāntideva does not provide an explicit response to these concerns in the *Guide*, and I am not able to address them in detail here. Nevertheless, in chapter nine Śāntideva does give us some indication of how a response would need to be developed. As is common for Madhyamaka philosophers, Śāntideva's method in argumentation is to appeal to premises agreed on by both parties (9:4) as a way of arguing for his position. This is why he appeals to the universal agreement that suffering is bad as a justification for the bodhisattva's commitment.

There is not universal agreement as to what well-being is, however. Some people believe it is pleasure, others emphasize material success or reputation or family relations and so on.[41] This disagreement over the nature of happiness and suffering then explains why so many of Śāntideva's arguments take the form of phenomenological description. Upon close inspection of our experience, Śāntideva thinks, ordinary people will also agree that an angry mind is one that is suffering, that craving is destructive and so on. Just as one can mistake a pillar for a person walking in the dim twilight, an unfocused and chaotic mind can misperceive the true nature of our suffering and its causes. Careful attention, combined with trainings to calm the mind, and repeated reflection on good arguments, will rectify these errors.[42]

We should conclude therefore that Śāntideva is aware of what I am calling the value nihilism objection, which raises the question of the validity of his groundless ethics. The only explicit response that he gives to this concern is his appeal to human agreement about the badness of suffering in 8:103. What my comments above suggest is that, given his Madhyamaka metaphysical and epistemic commitments, this may be the only response that he thinks can or need be given. There is no real disagreement that suffering is bad and that we are better off if it is removed. And moreover, it is also uncontroversial that there are oceans of it, and limitless sentient beings in need of salvation. This provides all the motivation and justification the bodhisattva needs to commit to his infinite task.

Suggestions for further study

Oldmeadow 1994 provides a translation of Prajñākaramati's commentary on the *Guide*'s wisdom chapter. Sweet 1977 gives an explanation of the entire chapter, which also takes into account Prajñākaramati's commentary. Tillemans 2010/11 offers a sensitive treatment of the question of whether Madhyamaka ethical commitments are compatible with their account of emptiness. Cowherds 2015 offers an insightful collection of collaborative essays by a collective of leading scholars centered around this same topic. Within this collection, see in particular Jenkins 2015a for a treatment of the compatibility of emptiness and compassion, which engages with Śāntideva and Prajñākaramati.

Questions for reflection

1. Śāntideva says that all of the trainings of the bodhisattva path are done for the sake of wisdom (BCA 9:1). What do you think he means by this? What is the relation between wisdom and the other virtuous qualities studied in this book?
2. How does an acceptance of emptiness raise the risk of nihilism? How does Śāntideva address this concern? Is his response successful?
3. How and to what extent are compassion and emptiness in tension? Is Śāntideva able to resolve this tension in his treatment of wisdom in the *Guide*'s ninth chapter?

Chapter 7

DEDICATION: UNTIL THE END OF SPACE AND TIME

7.1. Introduction

In the tenth chapter, Śāntideva concludes the *Guide* with the dedication of progress made on the bodhisattva path for the benefit of all sentient beings. Commentators frequently take the purpose of this dedication to be redirecting positive karmic potencies, so that instead of ripening into pleasant results for the bodhisattva, they benefit other sentient beings, or create conducive conditions for the bodhisattva's future practice like access to teachers and monastic ordination in future lives. Although this is a central purpose of these passages, in this short chapter I will argue that we should also understand the dedicatory verses as continuing the *Guide*'s work of training the bodhisattva's mind and developing his character.

An important aspect of this continued training is deepening *bodhicitta* and commitment to the bodhisattva path. We find something of a shift in these verses; the eudaimonistic aspects of the text recede, replaced by intense and elegantly phrased expressions of universal altruistic concern. Up until this point, much of the text, including even the wisdom chapter, emphasized self-benefiting qualities of altruistic behavior and virtue. Now at the text's end, having realized the interrelatedness of the happiness of self and other, and having protected his own well-being through the trainings of the first nine chapters, the bodhisattva can focus more intensely on the well-being of others.[1]

The chapter progresses through the dedication of a series of visualized gifts to beings of various kinds, matched with aspirations for their happiness and freedom from suffering. Making these mental offerings, therefore, continues the bodhisattva's training in the virtues of compassion and generosity. Śāntideva's characterization of these virtues is expansive: all beings are benefited in all places at all times, and they receive every imaginable kind of gift, both spiritual requisites and material comforts. Chapter ten, therefore, develops these virtues to their maximal form, while infusing them with equanimity, the equal concern for all beings.

I open my treatment of the chapter by commenting on its first three verses, where the above themes are introduced. I then examine Śāntideva's use of cosmological imagery, and show how invoking the realms of rebirth, and the hell realms in particular, lets him articulate the unlimited nature of compassion, generosity, and *bodhicitta*.

7.2. Infinite compassion, infinite giving

Śāntideva begins the chapter by dedicating the bodhisattva's accumulated positive karmic merit to all sentient beings:

> Through the merit (*śubha*) that I have gained by reflecting on the *Guide to the Practices of Awakening*, may all beings be adorned with the conduct of a bodhisattva! (BCA 10:1)
>
> Let all those in all directions who are tormented by bodily or mental pain obtain oceans of pleasure and joy because of my merit (*puṇya*)! (BCA 10:2)
>
> As long as saṃsāra lasts, let there be no loss of happiness! Let the world attain the uninterrupted happiness of the bodhisattvas! (BCA 10:3)

The central gift the bodhisattva offers in this chapter is his karmic merit (*puṇya/śubha*), indicating positive karmic potentials which ripen into worldly or spiritual auspicious conditions. For Buddhists, contemplation is itself a mental action, and therefore the various trainings, meditations, and reflections conducted throughout the text will have created positive karmic potentials for the bodhisattva. We can recall that in his treatment of giving in BCA 3:10 as well as SS 4, Śāntideva lists three kinds of items which the bodhisattva gives to sentient beings: his person (*ātmabhāva*), physical possessions (*bhoga*), and good karmic merit (*śubha*).[2] In the dedication chapter, the bodhisattva focuses on the last of these items, offering his accumulated positive karmic potentials to all beings. There is some disagreement among scholars as to whether Śāntideva believes making these aspirations can literally transfer good karma to others; one possibility is that they are intended to redirect karma, so that it ripens into auspicious conditions for continuing the bodhisattva's own practice in future lives, rather than providing him material benefits.[3] I will not take a position on this issue, since my interest is in showing how these verses continue the *Guide*'s work of deepening the bodhisattva's development of generosity, compassion, and *bodhicitta*.

Throughout the chapter, the bodhisattva imagines the gift of good karma ripening into positive effects of various kinds for the benefit of different sorts of beings. This begins in the first verse, quoted above, in which she aspires for all beings to enter the bodhisattva path. By making bodhisattva practice itself the first offering given to sentient beings, Śāntideva reinforces the *Guide*'s central claim that well-being is achieved by developing the bodhisattva's virtues. The second verse expands the kinds of benefits offered to sentient beings. Karmic potentials are imagined as ripening into two pairs of items: the removal of bodily (*kaya*) and mental (*citta*) pain (*vyatha*); and the experience of pleasure (*sukha*) and joy (*prāmodya*). This attention to the well-being of others suggests that not only generosity but also compassion is being trained by giving this series of mental offerings. Compassion, here and in the *Guide*'s eighth chapter, is represented as both the wish to remove sentient beings' suffering and the wish for them to be happy. Śāntideva will alternate between offerings which remove suffering and those which generate happiness throughout the chapter.

We also find in these opening verses the introduction of a central theme of the chapter, the intensification and expansion of these virtuous mental states. Verse 1 opens with an expression of universal giving and compassion, through imaginatively granting the bodhisattva path to all beings. The gift of positive karmic potencies in verse 2 is also universal in scope, but Śāntideva strengthens the imagery by introducing a spatial dimension, in bestowing this offering to beings in all directions. The third verse then temporalizes the bodhisattva's commitment, who aspires to bring happiness "as long as saṃsāra lasts." The effect is to broaden the bodhisattva's commitment, thereby also expressing equanimity.

In the chapter, Śāntideva uses several techniques to deepen and universalize the bodhisattva's compassion and generosity. First, the bodhisattva feels compassion for and aspires to save every kind of being. Second, he imagines offering a wide variety of gifts, both worldly and spiritual, to satisfy their needs. As we have seen in the first three verses, he offers joy and freedom from suffering, as well as access to the bodhisattva's way of life, to all beings. Much of the rest of the chapter presents more specific gifts to subclasses of beings. Freedom from various torments is offered to those taking rebirth in hells and other unfortunate rebirths (10:4–18). Persons with visual and audible disabilities are offered healing of the damaged senses (10:19). Women are offered painless childbirth (10:19), and, in an allusion to a sexist aspect of many depictions of the bodhisattva path, rebirth as a male to aid in advancement in practice (10:30). Beings are offered innumerable desired physical goods: clothing, food, drink, flowers, perfume, and jewelry (10:20), as well as freedom from fear (10:21), good health (10:22), safe travels (10:23-25), an attractive appearance (10:29), long life (10:33), pleasant environments (10:34–5) and so on. As the chapter continues, attention turns from worldly gifts to spiritual requisites. Beings are offered *bodhicitta*, proximity to the buddhas, and entry to the bodhisattva way of life (10:32; 10:34; 10:36). Buddhist practitioners are given auspicious monasteries and harmony in the monastic community (10:42), as well as conducive conditions of practice such as solitude (10:43) and good alms (10:46). The bodhisattva offers himself ordination in future lives and recollection of past lives (10:51) as well as conducive places of practice (10:52).

The early verses of the chapter usually focus on worldly gifts, while later verses more frequently reference requisites of religious practice. It is significant, however, that Śāntideva begins and ends the chapter by granting all beings access to bodhisattva training (10:1, 10:57), reaffirming his claim that only the practices of the bodhisattva path can wholly liberate a person from suffering (BCA 1:6–8). Nevertheless, since more than half the verses reference material rather than spiritual benefits, we can wonder why the bodhisattva imagines giving these items, since she knows that they may stimulate pathological emotions like craving when received by non-virtuous persons.[4] A possible response is that Śāntideva considers it better for unadvanced beings to satisfy at least a subset of their sensual and worldly desires, since this will temporally lessen anger and frustration. Many of the verses also reference basic material conditions or emotional stability which would be needed to focus on spiritual trainings. We can also remember, however, that the tenth chapter is composed of mental aspirations, rather than descriptions of actual material gifts; it should still be viewed as a training activity to refine the bodhisattva's own mind. Expanding the kinds of gifts that are imaginatively given increases the varieties of beings who are imagined receiving them, and this in turn deepens the bodhisattva's feelings of compassion while weakening tendencies to partiality. We need not therefore read every line of the chapter as intending that deluded beings receive the imagined items in question.

The expansive and joyful quality of chapter ten's mental offerings should remind us of the similar list of imaginative gifts presented to buddhas and high-level bodhisattvas, just prior to taking the bodhisattva vow (BCA 2:6–22). As we have seen, giving for Śāntideva is itself the mental state of wishing to offer all one's possessions to sentient beings (BCA 3:11), where possession is interpreted expansively to include all mental experience and positive karmic potencies (BCA 3:10). This suggests that the series of mental offerings made by the bodhisattva in both chapters are themselves examples of real generosity.[5] This is one reason it is important to recognize chapter ten as not *merely* shaping the results of previously accumulated karmic potencies, but as also continuing the bodhisattva's training in developing virtue. Nevertheless, there are two important differences between Śāntideva's presentation of gift-giving in chapter two and in chapter ten. First, in the second chapter, the gifts are made upward, to the buddhas and high-level bodhisattvas, in whom the new bodhisattva takes refuge. In contrast, in the tenth chapter, the gifts are made downward, to all sentient beings. Second, in the second chapter, the beginning bodhisattva is primarily motivated by his own well-being; he makes offerings as a way of enlivening his mind to enter the bodhisattva path and eliminate his own suffering. Now, at the *Guide*'s conclusion, having progressed through seven additional chapters of training and development, the matured bodhisattva is well-protected by his virtuous character. As a result, he is now able to turn his attention to fully developing his commitment to benefit others.

This progression from an initially egoistic to an increasingly altruistic motivation for engaging in bodhisattva practice, which culminates in the tenth chapter, illustrates a key facet of Śāntideva's soteriological therapeutic pedagogy. The early chapters suggest that Śāntideva recognizes self-directed concern as being a limited but authentic form of compassion, which is artificially narrowed in scope by processes of reification of the self and the resulting pathological emotions. Śāntideva's strategy throughout much of the *Guide* is to nurture this self-centered concern, both stimulating and refining it through practices to purify partiality and broaden motivation to encompass others. At the beginning of the *Guide* the bodhisattva already offers a series of universal aspirations for others' well-being (BCA 3:6–21), prior to taking the bodhisattva vow which is itself universal in scope (BCA 3:22–3); nevertheless, many of the encouragements to the bodhisattva that Śāntideva gives in these opening chapters, and indeed for most of the text, continue to focus on the bodhisattva's own benefit. Now, in the tenth chapter, the bodhisattva has finally aligned her inner motivation with the universally altruistic language with which the bodhisattva vow was expressed.

Jay Garfield also makes the interesting suggestion that the form of the expressions of *bodhicitta* given in chapter ten are importantly different than those made earlier in the text. In the third chapter, these aspirations are given in the first person, with the bodhisattva committing *himself* to the liberation of all beings. In the tenth chapter, by contrast, most of the aspirations take third-person form, expressing without explicit subject the hope that all beings will achieve happiness and so on. Garfield suggests that this change in voice is significant, representing the elimination of egocentricity resulting from the bodhisattva's development of the realization of the emptiness of the self (Garfield 2010, 343–5). Śāntideva does on occasion use the first-person voice in the tenth chapter, but this can be understood as a recognition that conventional identity remains important to a multi-lifetime commitment to save all beings. Garfield's suggested reading, therefore, illustrates one of the ways Śāntideva represents the integration of wisdom and compassion as required by the bodhisattva path.

We have thus far introduced two important aspects of the tenth chapter. First, it shows Śāntideva's concern with shaping karmic causality into creating the conditions for continuing progress on the bodhisattva path in future lives. Second, it continues the work of training the bodhisattva's mind, through intensifying and purifying *bodhicitta*, compassion, and generosity, with each now represented as infinite in scope, directed toward all beings in all places for all times. Another central theme of the chapter, therefore, is the development of equanimity.

A prominent and striking way Śāntideva further intensifies and universalizes compassion and generosity in the chapter is through his use of cosmological language. Most of the chapter presents the bodhisattva aspiring to aid beings trapped in various realms of rebirth. The hell realms are given detailed attention (10:4–16) followed by brief reference to animal and *preta* rebirth (10:17–18), with the rest of the chapter focusing on the needs of human beings.[6] Śāntideva's use of cosmological imagery strengthens both the spatial and temporal extension of compassion and generosity that was begun in the opening verses. Spatially, the realms of rebirth constitute the entire physical universe, and so referencing multiple realms suggests that the bodhisattva's compassion reaches to the limits of the cosmos. Referencing realms of rebirth also has temporal resonances, given that saṃsāra as the cycle of rebirth is without beginning or end. A promise to save all the beings in every realm of rebirth, therefore, implies a temporally limitless commitment to taking rebirth in saṃsāra.

Arguably the most striking element of Śāntideva's use of cosmological language is the attention he gives to the various hell realms. I quote a selection of these verses below:

> Let the beings existing in as many hells as are found in all the world realms rejoice with the joy and delight of the pure land of Sukhāvatī! (BCA 10:4)
>
> May the forest of razor-leaves attain for them the splendor of a pleasure grove! May the thorn-filled śālmali trees arise as wish-granting trees! (BCA 10:6)
>
> Let the regions of hell become pleasing, with lakes filled with fragrant lotuses, lovely and delightful with the chatter of birds such as swans, waterfowl, ducks, and geese. (BCA 10:7)
>
> Through my skillful acts, may the hell-beings rejoice when they see the unconcealed clouds of bodhisattvas, led by Samantabhadra, from which fall rains whose breezes are sweet-smelling, cool, and pleasant. (BCA 10:15)

In addition to the general points made above which apply to all of the chapter's cosmological imagery, there are several particular themes which emerge in Śāntideva's attention to the hell realms. First, visiting hells shows the strength of the bodhisattva's compassion, given that they are the worst places in the universe. We should also keep in mind the close connection between cosmology and psychology in Buddhist texts. As I argued earlier, Śāntideva and his Buddhist audience would have conceived of the hells as physical sites of graphic torture where beings are reborn; however, they also function as psychological descriptions of minds tormented by anger and mental pain.[7] In this psychological reading, the bodhisattva ministering to the hell realms represents willingness to serve the most difficult and emotionally damaged human beings: the ones overcome with anger, but also perhaps persons who suffer terribly but are adept at hiding their emotional pain. The bodhisattva appearing in the hell realms in such a reading represents successful communication with and therapeutic intervention on behalf of such persons, which itself may require imaginative appreciation of their pain and paranoia. Depicting the ability to successfully intervene in the hells, therefore, is one of the ways Śāntideva represents the bodhisattva's skillful means.

Śāntideva's depictions of the purification of the hell realms, as presented in these verses, illustrates another reoccurring theme of the *Guide*: the transformation of experience. We have seen throughout this book that every bodhisattva virtue, as characterized by Śāntideva, enables its possessor to maintain their own well-being in situations of distress: patience protects from anger and mental pain; giving and compassion protect from self-centered craving; compassion eliminates arrogant pride and envy in socially competitive situations and so on. The virtuous bodhisattva flourishes in any situation, whether cosmological, social, emotional, or financial. But Śāntideva's depiction of bodhisattvas visiting the hell realms in the tenth chapter shows them transforming not merely their own experience, but the experience of hell-denizens as well. Verse 10:15 quoted above references Samantabhadra, but other bodhisattvas including Manjushri (10:14) and Avalokiteśvara (10:18) are portrayed in this section transforming the hells into regions of delight filled with lotus ponds (10:7) and gentle rain (10:15) and so on.[8] This *can* be read as religious soteriology, in which bodhisattvas intervene with wonderous powers in alternative cosmological dimensions to aid others who rely on their grace. But a reading of these passages in keeping with much of the *Guide* is that this purification of the experience of the hell-beings is brought about by the recipients' own entry into the bodhisattva path and corresponding development of virtue. Depicting the transformation of the hell realms, therefore, is a way for Śāntideva to praise the pedagogical skill of the teachers of the past who were able to take as students dysfunctional and emotionally disturbed beings and train them to pacify their pathological emotions. Taking this reading of the hell realm passages reinforces the chapter's opening claim that trainings in the bodhisattva path are the ultimate gift which will eliminate the suffering of the world.

7.3. Conclusion

It is important to recognize the significance that karmic causality plays in Śāntideva's thought, and chapter ten is one of the places in which this interest is most clearly expressed. Plausibly, a central purpose of the chapter is to redirect the bodhisattva's positive karmic potencies so that they create the conditions to continue bodhisattva practice in future lives. Other scholars understand Śāntideva to be transferring his accumulated merit directly to benefit other beings. Nevertheless, I have argued that we need not be reductive in our reading of the chapter. Śāntideva's astonishingly beautiful sequence of mental offerings should also be understood as a continuation of the bodhisattva's trainings in developing the virtues of generosity, compassion, and *bodhicitta*. I have shown how Śāntideva's descriptions of various offerings, made to all kinds of beings, and his use of spatial, temporal, and cosmological language, let him present infinitely extended depictions of these virtues and motivations. The conclusion of the *Guide*, therefore, also acts as a continuation and intensification of many of its central themes.

I will close my exploration of Śāntideva's *Guide* with an invocation of two of its most famous verses, in which we find many of the themes of the chapter, as well as the text as a whole, succinctly expressed:

> As long as space lasts and as long as the world lasts, may I remain to destroy the suffering of the world! (BCA 10:55)
>
> All the suffering belonging to the world, let it ripen upon me! Let the world gain happiness through all the good acts of the bodhisattvas! (BCA 10:56)

Verse 55 expresses the bodhisattva's aspiration to remain in saṃsāra, suggesting an infinite commitment which stretches across lives. It embeds both spatial and temporal extension into the bodhisattva's dedication: she aspires to save all beings to the limits of space—that is, anyplace whatsoever, forever. In its reference to dispelling all suffering, it expresses both equanimity and compassion. Moreover, the reference to space (*ākāśa*) is also significant, given that this is an image used by Śāntideva to indicate recognition of the empty nature of conventual reality (BCA 9:154). Vowing to remove suffering in a world conceived of like space, therefore, suggests the union of wisdom and compassion.

Verse 10:56 restates a central theme of Śāntideva's text, linking the happiness of the world to the activities of the bodhisattva. The reference to the bodhisattva's wish to take on the suffering of others is an expression of compassion, but it is also an inverse form of generosity—not giving happiness to others, but offering the "gift" of taking their suffering from them. The verse appears demanding and can be misread as a sacrifice of the bodhisattva's own happiness, but at this point in the text we known that this is impossible. Compassion, generosity, and patience protect the bodhisattva from harm; therefore, the only damage this aspiration can do is to self-grasping, the ultimate cause of the bodhisattva's own suffering.

We will leave Śāntideva's bodhisattva here, joyfully expanding his mind toward perfection for the sake of all beings.

Suggestions for further study

Basham 1981, Clayton 2006, and Kajiyama 1989 provide good treatments of the Mahāyāna practice of merit transfer. Leighton's 2012 study of bodhisattvas includes characterizations of many of the bodhisattvas who appear in the *Guide*'s tenth chapter, such as Mañjuśrī and Samantabhadra. Huntington 2018 provides an excellent introduction to Buddhist cosmology.

Questions for reflection

1. What do you think Śāntideva was trying to achieve in the *Guide*'s tenth chapter? What is the relation between this chapter and the rest of the text?
2. In the tenth chapter, the bodhisattva aspires to remain in the realm of rebirth for all time to benefit all sentient beings (BCA 10:55–6). How have the virtuous qualities developed throughout the text prepared her for this commitment?
3. A central theme in the *Guide* is that altruistic commitment to the well-being of others, and the development of virtue, are the most effective methods of eliminating one's own suffering. How did Śāntideva argue for this position? How successful is his argument?

CONCLUSION

1. *Virtue and well-being in the* Guide

Many of us will agree that moderate compassion, concern for our children and those close to us, and some degree of caring for strangers is important to a happy life. Nevertheless, we may think that the universal compassion promoted in Mahāyāna Buddhism would decrease the altruistic person's well-being by disrupting ordinary life-plans and causing excessive empathetic suffering, leading to burn-out and depression. In this book, I have shown Śāntideva's reasons for holding that deep compassion and total altruistic commitment benefit their possessor. Central to his position is the relation between two sets of terms. The pathological emotions are mental states which distort the mind, producing psychological pain and causing harmful behavior which disrupts social relationships. They arise from selfish desire, which is itself caused by the inaccurate perception of reality. The perfections, and closely related virtuous mental states like compassion, mindfulness, and introspection, are produced by wisdom, the accurate perception of the world as empty, radically impermanent, and dependently arisen. They eliminate the pathological emotions and the selfish desires from which they arise, thereby stabilizing the mind, preventing harmful actions, and harmonizing social relationships.

Śāntideva's belief in the self-benefiting nature of altruistic commitment, therefore, follows from his position that virtue deeply benefits its possessor. The loss of external goods, such as possessions, reputation, and even bodily health, does not harm the individual, so long as virtuous character prevents the pathological emotions and mental pain from arising. Throughout the text, we have seen Śāntideva give trainings to develop this psychological possibility, resulting in the unassailable happiness of the high-level bodhisattva. Likewise, we have seen that the other-regarding virtues of compassion and generosity are two of the most important virtuous mental states which benefit the bodhisattva by eliminating the pathological emotions. Moreover, all the virtues of the bodhisattva path prepare her to work effectively for the benefit of others. Their development, therefore, explains the self and other benefiting structure of Śāntideva's moral thought.

Each of the chapters of this study developed in more detail some aspect of Śāntideva's defense of the self-beneficial status of altruistic commitment and virtue. I showed how mindfulness and introspection facilitate focusing on virtuous objects and alert the bodhisattva when a pathological emotion is present. Generosity eliminates craving and prepares the bodhisattva to interact safely with material possessions. Patience keeps the bodhisattva's mind tranquil in situations of distress and enables her to interact with aggressive people. Compassion destroys the pathological emotions of envy, competitiveness, and pride, thereby harmonizing social relationships, and weakens self-grasping, the deepest form of craving. Virtuous forms of joy help prevent pathological emotions and enliven the bodhisattva's experience. Finally, wisdom transforms the bodhisattva's perception of conventional reality, eliminating the disposition to see it as intrinsically existent, thereby completing the purification of her mind of pathological emotions. The work of the *Guide* continues even after this point, however; in the dedication chapter, the bodhisattva broadens and intensifies the other-regarding virtues of generosity and compassion and strengthens her core motivation of *bodhicitta*.

There are several aspects of Śāntideva's conception of the bodhisattva path that follow from his understanding of virtue and its relation to the pathological emotions, and that deserve reemphasis in this conclusion. First, although it is difficult and takes great dedication to complete, Śāntideva's conception of the bodhisattva path is not demanding, in the sense that it does not decrease the bodhisattva's well-being. This is initially surprising, given that the bodhisattva commits to taking infinite rebirths, visits unfortunate realms, and offers her body and life for others. It would therefore be easy to understand the bodhisattva path as requiring the sacrifice of one's own happiness. Nevertheless, attention to the protective power of the bodhisattva's virtues, as just summarized, shows why this is a misunderstanding of the *Guide*. Perfect generosity, in Śāntideva's worldview, protects the bodhisattva's well-being no matter how great the gift, and all the virtues contribute to enabling her to flourish no matter how severe her environment. Moreover, she experiences beneficial kinds of joy which result from her efforts on behalf of others. Finally, according to Śāntideva's arguments in the wisdom chapter, there is no way to wholly eliminate one's own suffering other than the bodhisattva path; radical altruism, therefore, is the only escape from saṃsāric experience.

Second, given Śāntideva's valorization of isolated meditation in the first half of chapter eight, it is easy to misunderstand his position as one which deemphasizes the importance of human relations in its conception of well-being. It is a mistake, however, to draw too strong a contrast between Śāntideva's ethics and the portrayals of virtuous exemplars of authors such as Aristotle and Confucius, for whom human flourishing is intimately connected to the richness of social relations. Certainly, the bodhisattva maintains his happiness in any situation, including one of social isolation. Nevertheless, attention to the manner in which Śāntideva develops each of the perfections shows that they play an integral role in achieving conducive relationships. Since possessions cause strife between human beings, the bodhisattva needs perfect generosity to interact with material goods in a socially beneficial way. Some level of discord is inevitable in associations with non-liberated persons, and so patience will be essential to maintaining tranquility as the bodhisattva interacts with others. Likewise, distinctive to Śāntideva's account of compassion is its ability to eliminate afflictive social emotions, thereby harmonizing human relationships. Finally, Śāntideva develops wisdom in such a way that it enables the bodhisattva to successfully interact with the objects of his compassion, suffering sentient beings. Wisdom does not isolate the bodhisattva from the world, but rather allows him to effectively engage with it.

Finally, my analysis shows the central role reasoning plays in Śāntideva's account of how virtue is developed. Although his most technical arguments are reserved for the wisdom chapter (BCA chapter nine), we see Śāntideva appeal to rational consistency repeatedly throughout the *Guide* as a way of developing virtue and abandoning vice.[1] A repeated strategy is to emphasize the universal wish for happiness: since virtue protects happiness, it should be developed, and since the pathological emotions destroy it, they should be eliminated. Moreover, in chapter eight, Śāntideva's appeal to rational consistency is expanded to focus on the needs of others; given the non-existence of an enduring unified self, and the universality of suffering, the bodhisattva has no justification for special prioritization of his own well-being, and so should commit to removing the suffering of all. These arguments are complemented by Śāntideva's repeated insistence that pathological emotions are irrational, arising out of inaccurate ways of perceiving the world. This is true of anger, which arises out of the false belief in an independent autonomous harm-doer, but also of craving, which is caused by an erroneous conception of the object as enduring, and capable of bringing lasting satisfaction.

All of these features of Śāntideva's bodhisattva path, which have been emphasized throughout this study, illustrate a core position of this book: that philosophical analysis of Śāntideva's conception of virtuous character and mental states, as well as his emphasis on the refinement and transformation of desire, is essential to understanding his moral thought. I have strived to show that this is not in opposition to phenomenologically oriented approaches to the text, nor to studies focused on Śāntideva's emphasis on the consequence of ending suffering; to the contrary, the moral quality of experience and the lessening of suffering are key components of Śāntideva's characterization of virtuous response. I have characterized my study as a work of virtue theory, rather than virtue ethics, as a way of avoiding unnecessary oppositions with consequentialist and phenomenological readings of the *Guide*. Real differences in interpretation of Śāntideva's fundamental moral commitments are, of course, possible, but any approach can and should recognize the role virtuous character plays in his thought.

In the remainder of this conclusion, I turn to a few of the remaining questions related to my study.

2. *Wisdom and the perfection of virtue*

In my sixth chapter I raised and developed a partial response to the question of the relation between wisdom and the other perfections in the *Guide*. There, I showed that Śāntideva conceives of wisdom as completing the work of the other perfections, by wholly eliminating the pathological emotions. Nevertheless, I have not yet considered the extent to which Śāntideva believes wisdom is integrated into the functioning of the other virtues. Mahāyāna authors often claim that the other perfections cannot be theorized without reference to wisdom; in fact, the perfections themselves gain the title of "perfection" because they are "perfected" by it. For example, giving, according to Candrakīrti, becomes the perfection of generosity when the giver, gift and receiver are conceived of as empty of intrinsic existence (Candrakīrti 2004, 61).[2] In the *Guide*, Śāntideva does not offer such explicit analysis of the relation between wisdom and the other virtues; nevertheless, he appeals to various grades of wisdom in his development of them throughout the text. In this section, I offer some suggestions about what he takes their relationship to be.

We can begin to approach this question by recalling that Śāntideva presents wisdom and the other virtues as the antidotes to delusion and the other pathological emotions. This suggests that the relation between wisdom and the perfections may be analogous to that between delusion and the psychopathologies. Delusion is the false superimposition of intrinsic existence, permanence, unity, and self-sufficiency upon empty, dependently arisen, and radically impermanent entities. As a result of these superimpositions, we crave reified external objects, become angry when they are lost, become proud of the reputation of the reified subject and so on. The pathological emotions, therefore, not only arise from delusion, but are partly constituted by these erroneous ways of viewing reality. They are the affective complements to delusion. Wisdom, as the opposite of delusion, is the elimination of these inaccurate ways of perceiving the world; the wise bodhisattva views reality as it is, composed of empty, fragmentary, dependently arisen, radically impermanent, and unsatisfactory phenomena. The other virtuous mental states, therefore, have the same relation to wisdom, as do the pathological emotions to delusion; they are not only caused by wisdom, but are partly constituted by it, and can be understood as its affective complements.

Wisdom, therefore, is not merely supported by the other virtues, in a way that lets us conceive of them as independent from it; rather, wisdom is integral to the development and functioning of each perfection. In the moral psychology of the *Guide*, this is the case in two ways. First, we have seen Śāntideva appeal to various grades of wisdom throughout the text in his development of the virtues. Generosity is perfected when the body and possessions are seen as empty, enabling them to be given freely to sentient beings (BCA 7:25–6). Patience is perfected when we realize the unsatisfactory nature of ordinary motivations (BCA 6:7–21; BCA 6:53–133), as well as the radically dependent nature of events (BCA 6:22–51). Compassion is perfected when the bodhisattva realizes the non-existence of a metaphysically unified self, and the universality of social and psychological suffering (BCA 8:90–154).

There is, however, a second and even more basic way in which wisdom, in its form of insight into the selfless nature of persons, is incorporated into Śāntideva's account of each of the virtues analyzed in this study. The core insight Śāntideva draws upon is that given metaphysical selflessness, the boundaries between different persons, as well as between temporal segments of the same person, are conceptually constructed. This does not mean that these distinctions are arbitrary, but it suggests that there is some flexibility in how we conceive of our present self in relation to our future self, as well as in relation to contemporary others. We can give intuitive examples to illustrate the basic point behind this insight. I can think of my 4-year-old self as the same person as me now, or as a different person with an intimate relationship to my present self. Likewise, we can conceive of friends or children as extensions of ourselves and so on. Śāntideva has appealed to these kinds of insights in his development of the equalizing self and other argument (BCA 8:90–107) and exchanging self and other meditations (BCA 8:111–15; BCA 8:140–54).

However, it is not merely the spatial and temporal boundaries of persons which are conceptually constructed, according to a metaphysics of emptiness. In addition, the supposedly basic structures of consciousness and subjectivity, and in particular the distinction between subject and object, are themselves conceptual constructs, in the sense of being ways the stream of experience is interpreted. Contemporary studies of Madhyamaka's sister school Yogācāra have analyzed this feature of their phenomenological thought carefully.[3] Moreover, just as for Yogācāra, Madhyamaka metaphysics also entails that the distinction between the subject and object is not a ridged metaphysical boundary, and I think we can see Śāntideva manipulate this feature of human experience in his development of generosity, patience, and compassion. His basic insight is that the conceptually constructed nature of the division between subject and object entails some fluidity as to what elements are conceived of as on the subject side of experience, and which are conceptualized as objects, from any given perspective. Śāntideva's strategy is to narrow or widen the subject and object divisions of awareness strategically, as a way of enabling the relevant virtue to purify experience of craving, aggression, and delusion more effectively. Again, I can offer intuitive commonsense examples to give an idea of how this strategy works. In a sudden fit of anger, I can think to myself that this aggression is not who I really am—that is, I can externalize it.[4] Likewise, sometimes I identify strongly with my body, while at other times—when recovering from illness, for instance—I might conceive of some bodily experience as external to my identity.

In his explanation of the perfection of generosity, we saw Śāntideva employ an expansive account of the objects that are given, to include not merely physical possessions, but also good karmic potentials, and even the body and mental experience of the bodhisattva. The perfection of giving, therefore, narrows the subject position and widens the objective sphere, which is then mentally offered to all beings. This provides the strategic benefit of expanding the collection of items which the bodhisattva can give; in contrast to Aristotle, lack of wealth is no impediment to developing generosity, since the bodhisattva's most basic gift is his entire physical and mental being.[5] Likewise, epistemically, it widens the scope of analysis regarding the pernicious effects of craving in relation to possessions. In ordinary giving, one can only observe the way physical possessions are appropriated and desired. In the perfection of giving, by contrast, the bodhisattva can analyze the reification and appropriation of experience itself and thereby take the intimate processes through which subjectivity is constructed as objects for purification of craving.

We find a partial contrast when we turn to Śāntideva's approach to subjectivity in his characterization of the perfection of patience. In the patience chapter, he uses a sharper distinction between the subject and the objects of experience, remaining within the commonsense perspective of persons standing out against an external realm of objects and other beings. This provides strategic benefits that are more difficult to access in the narrowed subjective sphere of perfect giving. A widened subjective domain allows Śāntideva to employ fairly standard psychological treatments, which analyze the subject's mental experience, identify the causes of anger (mental pain and frustrated desire), and provide therapeutic techniques to eliminate them. Likewise, the fact that the objective domain is conceived of as a realm of externally existing conventional entities facilitates the bodhisattva's analysis of their causal conditions, and his subsequent realization of the dependently originated nature of harm.

This preliminary analysis lets us begin to draw a contrast in the basic experiential attitude manifested in these two virtues. Generosity, in its radicalized offering of the expanded objective domain, can be seen as a mode of opening toward the world. Patience, in partial contrast, is largely a defensive response; it ensures the bodhisattva, conceived of as possessing a (conventionally) fixed subjective domain, remains tranquil in hostile circumstances. Giving manifests in situations calling forth an attitude of plenty; it motivates intervention and a commitment to improving the world. Patience, by contrast, withstands the attacks of a world that manifests as hostile, ensuring no harm is done to or by the subject.

Compassion, in contrast to these other two virtues, adopts no fixed position between the subject and the world; its manifestation for Śāntideva depends on the deep recognition of the fluidity of both social location and subjective standpoint. Subjectivity is expanded during the equalizing argument, where the bodhisattva temporarily takes on the perspective of the entire world (BCA 8:91; BCA 8:114); in fact, we can view these passages as the complement of the giving meditations, in which the subject position is narrowed. Likewise, we also find passages in the equalizing argument that briefly adopt the strategy of subjective disintegration, and subsequent analysis at the sub-personal level of *dharmas* (BCA 8:101–3). Finally, as the chapter moves to its conclusion, Śāntideva uses rapid alteration of perspectives and blurring of subjectivities during the exchanging self and other meditations (BCA 8:140–54). Subjectivity, Śāntideva teaches the bodhisattva, is contingent and constructed and can be dissolved for strategic benefit, as a way of disrupting habitual patterns of reification and harmful self-centered narratives.

The root insight manifested in Śāntideva's development of all three virtues is that not just the conventional person and continuity of identity, but the basic divisions of experience itself, are conceptual constructs. This enables strategic expansion and contraction of the subject and object poles of experience and facilitates imaginative exchange of one's own perspective with the perspective of others. It results from the realization of the emptiness of the person, and the corresponding realization of the contingent nature of the boundary between the subject and the object. There is no fixed inside or outside of the subject, no metaphysical demarcation between personal experience and the external world. All experience is fluid, constructed, and momentarily organized into dissolvable structures which constitute conventional reality. The bodhisattva's development of wisdom enables her to manipulate and reinterpret these conventional boundaries to her benefit.

3. *Early Buddhism and Śāntideva's gradated path*

A reoccurring feature that we have found in multiple chapters of the *Guide* is that of the gradated path, in which trainings to develop virtue are presented so as to be accessible to persons outside or at the beginning of bodhisattva practice. Śāntideva offers the gentle training of giving vegetables as a way of beginning the practice of generosity (BCA 7:25). He suggests that bodhisattvas endure minor pains associated with bug bites and bad weather when starting to develop patience (BCA 6:14–16). He also offers a period of seclusion during which calming meditations to reduce craving are performed prior to developing the radical altruism of the bodhisattva (BCA 8:26–88).

One of Śāntideva's psychological insights that is relevant to this approach is that there is a salvageable core to afflicted energy, which is associated with the pathological emotions, that can be purified and channeled into liberative practices.[6] The clearest use of this strategy is found in the first chapter of the *Guide* where Śāntideva appeals to the self-interest of the bodhisattva to motivate her to embark on the bodhisattva path. This is not merely a strategic and provisional tactic, however; rather, Śāntideva recognizes that concern for oneself is itself compassion, artificially narrowed by the constraining and distorting grip of the pathological emotions. Eventually, compassion must be universalized, most explicitly through the equalizing and exchanging self and other practices in the second half of the chapter on meditation. In the beginning of the path, however, this nascent compassion manifesting primarily as concern for oneself can be used as the initial moral motivation to enter and begin progressing on the path.

A related aspect of the strategy of gradated trainings is the incorporation of early Buddhist practices and insights into the bodhisattva path. We have seen that in the *Training Anthology*, Śāntideva supports the development of the perfection of generosity with the four right strivings, through which pathological emotions are prevented or eliminated, and virtuous mental states are developed. In the *Guide*'s chapter on patience, Śāntideva draws on the early Buddhist tenet of dependent origination to argue that anger toward the enemy who harms us is irrational. Likewise, he appeals to early Buddhist conceptions of suffering and the pernicious nature of craving to eliminate self-centered motivations whose frustration results in mental pain and anger. Finally, in his treatment of compassion, we found Śāntideva employ long sequences of meditations on the dissatisfactory nature of saṃsāric society, and the fragility of the human body, as preparatory practices to develop compassion.

Nevertheless, in all these cases, Śāntideva incorporates these early Buddhist techniques and insights into a Mahāyāna framework, as a way of strengthening the bodhisattva's compassion and altruistic commitment. In developing perfect generosity, the bodhisattva does not simply abandon craving toward all possessions, but mentally offers them to all sentient beings. In the chapter on patience, pernicious self-centered desire is not merely removed, but is transformed into compassion and *bodhicitta*. Likewise, in the meditation chapter, Śāntideva does not allow the bodhisattva to remain in the state of seclusion, but obligates her to purify partiality, strengthen universal compassion and return to society to benefit all beings.

Moreover, in the eighth and ninth chapters of the *Guide*, Śāntideva develops a more explicit critique of early Buddhist attitudes toward liberation for one's own sake, even while continuing to incorporate their insights into his conception of the bodhisattva path. Between the two chapters, we can distinguish four arguments in total. During the equalizing self and other argument in the meditation chapter, Śāntideva argues for the irrationality of anything less than the full bodhisattva commitment to eliminate the suffering of all beings, taking as his key premises the universal vulnerability to suffering, and the non-existence of an enduring self. In the exchanging self and other meditations which follow, he offers prudential reasons to develop impartial benevolence, arguing that this, rather than the early Buddhist path, eliminates the suffering which is caused by selfish motivations. In the wisdom chapter, he argues that until experience is conceived of as empty of intrinsic existence, feeling will continue to give rise to subtle forms of craving, resulting in the continuation of rebirth and suffering. Finally, he argues that the early Buddhist psycho-soteriological strategy of eliminating craving as an instrumental means to liberate oneself from suffering and rebirth is incoherent, given that prioritizing one's own release from saṃsāra is itself a form of craving. For Śāntideva, altruism, rather than egoistic motivations, no matter how refined, is the only way to escape saṃsāric experience.

4. *Śāntideva and global philosophy*

The last thirty years have seen a welcome increase of interest in Indian Buddhist ethics in academic scholarship, with particular attention paid to Śāntideva's moral thought. Nevertheless, a potential barrier to taking Buddhist ethics seriously as relevant to contemporary philosophical theorizing remains its emphasis on ethical karmic causality. The concern is that if the main reason provided by an ethical system to be moral is to escape negative karmic consequences, including bad rebirths, then we are not engaging with a philosophical position that provides reasons open to rational scrutiny by those who do not share Buddhist presuppositions.

In this study I have acknowledged the importance of karmic causality in Śāntideva's moral thought, while arguing that this should not prevent us from taking his insights as philosophically important. Śāntideva's frequent descriptions of the hell realms should be understood both as references to cosmological places of rebirth, and as phenomenological descriptions of human moods, which characterize a mind obsessed with anger and overwhelmed with emotional pain. They therefore provide introspective evidence for Śāntideva's positions about the badness of the pathological emotions, and other elements of his theory of value. Likewise, his emphasis on karmic consequence can be profitably read as analyzing the relevance of past actions to present situations, with the consequences emphasized in no way limited to the results of non-natural karmic causation, but also including social harmony or dysfunction, psychological tranquility or instability, and emotional well-being.

Throughout this book, I have tried to show that many of Śāntideva's ethical insights do not centrally depend on a conception of Buddhist karmic causation that is irreducible to ordinary physical and psychological regularities. We have examined Śāntideva's analysis of the ethical implications of metaphysical selflessness; his distinction between impoverished and morally conducive forms of motivation; his arguments for the moral importance of joy, and categorization of virtuous and impoverished varieties of pleasure; his challenging but insightful conception of the vast potential for human development, matched with training programs for the development of moral emotions; his alternation between syllogistic and phenomenological argumentation; and finally, his analysis of the virtues of generosity, patience, compassion, and wisdom and their conduciveness to well-being. Every one of these elements can be taken seriously as a contribution to contemporary moral theorizing. And of course, I have not provided a full study of Śāntideva's ethical thought, nor done more than make occasional references to the other giants of the Buddhist moral tradition, such as Candrakīrti, Āryaśūra, Buddhaghosa, Asaṅga, Vasubandhu, as well as the historical Buddha and the authors of the early Buddhist canons.

I hope, therefore, to have made a little progress toward providing support for my belief that the Indian Buddhist tradition of moral philosophy is a great intellectual resource for contemporary ethical theorizing. I look forward to a time when academic philosophers will conceive of it as an inexhaustible reserve to be repeatedly consulted in developing their ideas.

NOTES

Introduction

1 I limit my attention in this study to Indian Buddhist sources, but to save space I will often omit the word "Indian."

2 Śāntideva's *Guide* provides numerous trainings to facilitate the reliable occurrence of virtuous mental states, and weaken the propensities for the arising of afflictive mental states. It is naturally described, therefore, as developing both a moral psychology and an account of virtue. The key point to recognize is that virtuous response is not here limited to virtuous *actions*, but includes appropriate mental responses, such as the feeling of compassion when perceiving another's suffering. I develop this point in greater detail in my first chapter.

3 I use the term "altruism" throughout this study to mean behavior which intentionally benefits others. It does not imply that such behavior decreases one's own well-being.

4 In Buddhism, saṃsāra is the endless cycle of suffering and rebirth which beings experience until they are liberated from craving and delusion.

5 Good introductions to Buddhist philosophical thought include Gethin 1998, Williams and Tribe 2000, and Westerhoff 2018. See Goodman 2016b, Heim 2020, chapter three, and Harris 2022 for introductions to Śāntideva's thought and Harris 2021 for an introduction to the *Guide*. A helpful presentation of basic Buddhist tenets with emphasis on their relevance for moral philosophy is provided by Gowans 2014, chapters one and two. Important studies of Indian Buddhist ethics which provide relevant background for appreciating Śāntideva's moral thought include Keown 1992, Harvey 2000, Gowans 2014, and Garfield 2021.

6 Although my study will primarily focus on Śāntideva, the self-benefiting nature of compassion and altruistic commitment is one of the central themes of many Mahāyāna texts. As Jenkins 1999 argues, it is also stressed by many early Buddhist authors. See Jenkins 1999, 2015b, and 2021 for wide-ranging studies of early Buddhist and Mahāyāna sources emphasizing this theme. Benefits emphasized by Jenkins which are not analyzed in detail in my own study include good rebirth, good karmic consequences, and protection by deities. Jenkins's work has done much to inspire my own interest in the self-benefiting nature of compassion and the other virtues in Śāntideva's thought.

7 All translations from Śāntideva are my own, unless otherwise noted.

8 I use the term "well-being" throughout this book in the philosophical sense of how well the individual's life is going for that individual themself. Well-being, here, has a similar meaning to *eudaimonia* in early Greek

philosophy. See Crisp 2021 for a succinct and skillful introduction to this philosophical conception of well-being.

9 The apparently demanding nature of the bodhisattva path includes a willingness to renounce all possessions and wealth; sacrifice one's body and life for others; delay escape from rebirth to continue bodhisattva trainings; and visit unfortunate realms such as hells to work for others' benefit. We will examine references by Śāntideva to all these apparent hardships during this study. We will see, however, that he holds that these items do not really decrease the bodhisattva's well-being. See Harris 2014b, 9–13 for a summary of the apparent hardships of the bodhisattva path. See Ohnuma 2006 for an in-depth study of the bodhisattva's gift of his body and life.

10 One of Śāntideva's clearest arguments for this position comes at BCA 8:90–103, in which he argues that to do anything less than commit to eliminating all suffering would be inconsistent. I analyze this argument in my fourth chapter. At other times, Śāntideva argues that developing bodhisattva qualities is in one's best interest (e.g., BCA chapters 5–9), or that compassion is the only rational response to the suffering of others (e.g., BCA 6:38–40).

11 See Brassard 2000 for a study of the concept of *bodhicitta* in Śāntideva's *Guide*, and Wangchuk 2007 for a broader study of *bodhicitta* in the Indo-Tibetan Buddhist tradition.

12 Influential descriptions of the hell realms include Vasubandhu 1988, 456–7 and Tsong-Kha-Pa 2000, 162–9. Rebirths in hell, like all rebirths in Buddhist cosmology, are temporary and all non-liberated beings cycle through all the realms of rebirth.

13 I develop this interpretation in more depth in Harris 2018a.

14 See Annas 1993, 388–411 for an explanation of Stoic conceptions of well-being.

15 Śāntideva differs from ancient Greek eudaimonisms, however, in that he does not claim that all rational action aims at one's own benefit (see Irwin 1995). As we have already seen, Śāntideva frequently emphasizes the importance of other-regarding motivations, which are themselves conducive to one's own well-being. See Annas 2006, esp. 519–23 and Hursthouse 1999, chapter eight for influential accounts of virtue which stress its centrality to well-being.

16 Following Garfield 2021, I use "pathological" in my translation of *kleśa*, given that the Greek term *pathos* means suffering. A pathological emotion, therefore, is an emotion which causes or constitutes suffering. This is exactly what Śāntideva means by *kleśa*. Thanks to Jay Garfield for discussion on this point.

17 Patience is the antidote to anger, wisdom eliminates delusion, and generosity eliminates craving. Compassion, as developed by Śāntideva in the *Guide*, primarily targets craving, but also eliminates certain forms of aggression. I return to each of these virtues in the chapters to come.

18 See Gómez 1999 for a list of existing translations of the *Guide* into modern languages.
19 See Harrison 2007 for an argument that the canonical version of the *Guide* is Śāntideva's own revision of an earlier version of his text, primarily made by incorporating additional material from the *Training Anthology*.
20 See Crosby and Skilton's introduction to their translation of *Guide* chapter five in Śāntideva 1995, 30–3.
21 As we will see in the fourth chapter of this study, the *Guide*'s eighth chapter takes the development of compassion and *bodhicitta* as its central aims.
22 See Mahoney 2002 and Clayton 2006 for good explanations of the structure of the *Training Anthology*.
23 There is also a rich collection of commentarial works on the *Guide* composed by the Tibetan tradition. Because of limitations of time and space, and the relative rarity of English translation, I make limited use of this exceptional body of literature in this study. See Williams 1998, 4–5 for a listing of the most influential of the premodern Tibetan commentaries. See Pelden 2010 for an English translation of an influential early-twentieth-century commentary. See Sonam 2019 for an English translation of the extended commentary on the *Guide*'s ninth chapter by Künzang Sönam.
24 Since the *Guide*, which is the focus of this study, is written in Sanskrit, I will generally provide the Sanskrit of translated terms from the Buddhist tradition. Sometimes, when dealing with ideas from the early Buddhist tradition, I provide the Pali term followed by the Sanskrit, as I have done here.
25 See Nattier 2003, especially 172–6. Also relevant are Harrison 1987, Samuels 1997, and Silk 2002.
26 The other primary Mahāyāna school of Yogācāra Buddhism takes emptiness to refer to the emptiness of subject and object duality. See Westerhoff 2018, chapter three for an introductory explanation of Yogācāra thought.
27 Certain Abhidharma philosophical systems agree with the Madhyamaka school that conventionally existent entities are empty of intrinsic existence, and therefore are dependently originated. They claim, however, that ultimately real entities called *dharmas* possess intrinsic existence. Madhyamaka Buddhists deny that anything is ultimately existent in this sense. Rather, an entity's ultimate nature is its emptiness of intrinsic existence. See Westerhoff 2009, chapter two for an excellent introduction to emptiness and intrinsic existence from the Madhyamaka perspective.
28 See Bodhi 2010.
29 See Reeves 2008 for a translation of *The Lotus Sutra*.
30 BCA 8:108, quoted above. The term *arasika* can also mean "in bad taste." It is tasteless, or in bad taste, in comparison to the achievement of the Mahāyānist, who takes great joy in liberating others from suffering. I return to this verse in my fourth and fifth chapters.

31 See BCA 8:90–107. I explore this argument in my fourth chapter.
32 See BCA 9:44–8. I analyze this argument in my sixth chapter.
33 At times, Śāntideva employs premises which would apply only to those who have taken the bodhisattva vow. See for example BCA 6:104–11, where he argues that a bodhisattva training to develop patience should welcome abuse by enemies which provides an opportunity to practice spiritual development. Even in such cases, however, the argument often can be naturally reformulated to apply more broadly. In this case, Śāntideva might argue that, given the beneficial nature of patience, all persons should welcome the opportunity to develop it afforded by enemies.
34 Śāntideva's argument for the irrationality of anger stretches throughout BCA chapter six. I focus on these passages in the third chapter of this study. The argument for the irrationality of selfishness is given most centrally in BCA 8:90–103, which I analyze in my fourth chapter.
35 See Cowherds 2011 for a recent thorough treatment of this issue.
36 Nāgārjuna makes this reply to a hypothetical opponent in his auto-commentary to the *Dispeller of Disputes (Vigrahavyāvartanī)*. See commentary to verses 7–8 and 52–6. See translation and analysis by Westerhoff 2010b, 94–104.
37 Śāntideva references common agreement that suffering is bad and should be removed at BCA 8:103.
38 See Tillemans 2010/11, Davis 2013b and 2018, Finnigan 2015, and Goodman 2015 for studies which address aspects of this question
39 A partial exception is my consideration of Śāntideva's response to what I call the "value nihilism objection," the concern that empty suffering is not bad and therefore does not need to be removed. I treat this issue at the conclusion of my sixth chapter.
40 See Gowans 2014, chapter four for a philosophically sensitive introduction to karmic causality and rebirth, in relation to Buddhist ethics.
41 They are therefore, to use Owen Flanagan's language, examples of "tame karmic causation" (Flanagan 2011, 77). In the chapters to follow, I will show that a great deal of Śāntideva's thought is already accessible to those like Flanagan who are developing a naturalized Buddhist ethics.
42 On the psychological reading of Buddhist cosmology, see Garfield 2021, 7–9. See Burley 2017 for a helpful analysis of the advantages and disadvantages of this kind of interpretation. For a study of the relation between cosmology and meditation that also has relevance to this issue, see Gethin 1997.
43 See Flanagan 2011 for an influential presentation of a naturalized Buddhist ethics. Śāntideva's *Guide* is one of the sources Flanagan draws on in developing his account. See also Segall 2020, chapter four and Garfield 2021, chapter eleven.
44 An interesting question which Śāntideva does not consider at length is whether it is plausible to ascribe continuity of identity across lives, thereby

conceiving of the bodhisattva's development as stages of a single conventional identity. See Harris 2018b for a treatment of this issue.

45 See Garfield 2006 for a characterization of enlightened experience with similarities to this position.

46 See Gómez 1999 for a critique of the Crosby and Skilton, the Wallace and Wallace, and the Padmakara Translation Group translations.

Chapter 1

1 For Buddhists like Śāntideva, virtue cannot be understood exclusively or even primarily as the disposition to *act*, as in a virtue theory like Aristotle's, since Śāntideva is most centrally concerned with virtuous mental response. Generous and compassionate feelings themselves, for instance, are virtuous responses to situations of deprivation, even when no beneficial action can be taken. Thanks to Jay Garfield and Amod Lele for suggesting I emphasize this point.

2 See Gethin 2001 for a study of the five powers and the seven factors of awakening, and Heim 2017 for a study of the four Brahmavihāras.

3 The Abhidharma schools sort phenomena into a variety of categories, and their presentation differs somewhat depending on the school in question. The distinction between virtuous and afflictive mental states is shared by all these schools, however, although terminology used differs somewhat. See Keown 1992, Waldron 2003, chapter two, and Ronkin 2005, chapter three for good introductions to Abhidharma philosophy and psychology.

4 See also Locke 2018 and Simonds 2021 for studies of Buddhist moral thought that emphasize its phenomenological dimensions.

5 Garfield agrees that moral character is important to Buddhist authors like Śāntideva but holds that their primary interests are best described as phenomenological. See Garfield 2021, chapters two and three.

6 See Bommarito 2018 for an extended study of the importance of internal virtuous response, written from the perspective of contemporary analytic ethics.

7 See Keown 1992, Whitehill 1994, Wright 2009, Flanagan 2011, part two, and Segall 2020 for studies of Buddhist ethics which emphasize the development of virtue.

8 See Ronkin 2005, 216 for an explanation of the immediately preceding condition.

9 See Snow 2020 for a useful treatment of this contrast between Buddhist moral thought and Aristotelean eudaimonism.

10 See Flanagan 2011, part two, and especially 143–52, for an influential development of this approach. Also relevant is Gowans's suggestion that we understand Buddhist ethics as offering a nature-fulfillment theory of well-being at the conventional level (2014, 117–19).

11 See chapter one, section 3.3; chapter three, section 3.3; and chapter four, sections 2.1 and 2.2.

12 I claim that virtue is only partly constitutive of flourishing for Śāntideva, given that he also holds that certain kinds of pleasure are beneficial (see chapter five). In addition, nirvāṇa without remainder (*anupadhiśeṣa-nirvāṇa*) and the non-abiding nirvāṇa (*aparatiṣṭhita-nirvāṇa*) of the highly developed bodhisattva are not given explicit analysis by Śāntideva in the *Guide*. A fuller treatment of Mahāyāna ethics would need to specify the relation between these kinds of nirvāṇa and the perfections. See Gethin 1998, 75–6 for an explanation of nirvāṇa without remainder.

13 On distinguishing these two kinds of intrinsic value, see also Korsgaard 1982. Vélez 2010 offers a useful discussion about the challenges of applying the instrumental/intrinsic distinction to Buddhist texts (221–30).

14 Goodman also claims that pleasure is an important component of well-being, for Śāntideva (2009, 110–15). I return to this issue in my fifth chapter.

15 See Hursthouse 1999, chapter one, for a virtue-centric theory of right action.

16 This paragraph is adapted from Harris 2015a.

17 For instance, see Mackenzie 2018.

18 See Engle 2009 for a translation of Vasubandhu's *Summary of the Five Heaps*, an influential presentation of these virtuous and afflictive mental states.

19 See Hayes 1996 and Tillemans 2008 for studies of Śāntideva's moral psychology emphasizing the pathological emotions' role in disrupting mental control. Carpenter 2014, chapter one argues that Buddhists conceive of lack of control as a kind of suffering.

20 Examples include BCA 2:57–8; 4:30–1; 5:7; 5:20; 5:29; 6:72–4; 7:11–12; 8:40; 8:71; 8:84.

21 See also Garfield 2021, 7–9. On the relation between psychology and cosmology in Buddhist thought, see Gethin 1997 and Burley 2017.

22 I follow the verse numbering provided by Crosby and Skilton in Śāntideva 1995, Gomez in Śāntideva 2015, and Steinkellner and Peck-Kubaczek in Śāntideva 2019 for BCA chapter two, which differs from the edition by Vaidya 1960, and the numbering provided by Wallace and Wallace in Śāntideva 1997.

23 In my fifth chapter, I argue that Śāntideva believes the empathetic pain caused by compassion benefits the virtuous bodhisattva. See 5.6 below.

24 I discuss mental pain (*daurmanasya*) in more detail in chapter three. See 3.2 and 3.3 below.

25 The arguments that pain does not damage the well-being of a virtuous person are given in BCA 6:12–21. Śāntideva's claim that this extends to pain experienced in the hell realms is given in the *Training Anthology* (see Goodman 2016a, 179–80). I explore these passages in my third chapter. We have already seen this position expressed in BCA 8:107–8, quoted at the beginning of the introduction to this book.

26 See BCA 8:5–25 for Śāntideva's arguments that self-grasping and the envy and arrogant pride which it causes are the root sources of social disfunction. He argues that these afflictive social emotions are themselves instances of suffering in 8:140–53. Seclusion is characterized as at least provisionally beneficial for the bodhisattva at BCA 8:26–9 and BCA 8:85–8. See chapter four below.

27 In Abhidharma terminology, my suggestion is that the pathological emotions (*kleśas*) and the mental pain which accompanies them (*mānasika-duḥkha-vedanā*) constitute suffering (*duḥkha*) for Śāntideva. Fear (*bhaya*) appears to have intrinsic disvalue as well, although it can be instrumentally valuable as an aid in deepening commitment to bodhisattva practice. As we will see in my third and fifth chapters, Śāntideva holds that both physical pain (*kāyika-duḥkha-vedanā*) and the mental pain which accompanies compassion do not harm a high-level bodhisattva.

28 See Wright 2009 for a study of the six Mahāyāna perfections.

29 See Crosby and Skilton's introduction to their translation of BCA chapter five in Śāntideva 1995, 30–3.

30 Like Philippa Foot's account of virtue, Śāntideva understands Buddhist virtue as having a corrective function, in the sense of resisting or eliminating non-virtuous motivations and harmful emotion. See Foot 2002, 8. I take this point from Hanner 2021, 62, 66–8.

31 See Jenkins 1999 and 2015b for excellent textually based studies of the convergence of altruism and self-interest in Buddhist moral thought.

32 Bommarito 2014 also references generosity as a mental state with intrinsic value (279), although my example here differs from his presentation.

33 I analyze Śāntideva's attitude toward pleasure and joy in my fifth chapter.

34 On Śāntideva's devaluation of material goods, see also Lele 2007, especially chapter three. See Framarin 2016 and 2017 for philosophically sensitive treatments of the relation between suffering and material success in Brahmanical sources.

35 Right effort is used as a central structuring device in the *Training Anthology*, however. I return to this point in my second chapter.

36 Right mindfulness is the seventh limb of the eightfold path, so we can understand Śāntideva as analyzing the relation between the sixth (right effort) and seventh limbs.

37 Śāntideva also utilizes other virtuous mental states as antidotes in the *Guide*, although they do not receive chapter-length focus. I analyze his employment of generosity in my second chapter, and his extended treatment of compassion in my fourth chapter.

38 For a philosophically sensitive treatment of Śāntideva's conception of mindfulness and introspection, see Garfield 2012. See Bodhi 2011 for a good introduction to mindfulness in early Buddhist texts.

39 The term *matta,* which can mean to be out of one's mind, can also connotate an animal in heat. The mind, therefore, is being compared to an elephant in heat, driven mad by sexual desire. I translate *matta* as "in

heat" in 5:2, and switch to "mad" in 5:40, in order to bring out both connotations.

40 Although Śāntideva most frequently uses the virtuous mental states to eliminate the pathological emotions, other mental states are also employed. For instance, joy prevents anger (see chapter 3.3.1 and 3.3.2), and disgust at the filthiness of bodies eliminates sensual craving (see chapter 4.2.2).

41 There is much to recommend the recent attention given to comparisons between Śāntideva's thought and Pierre Hadot's analysis of the use of philosophical argumentation by the ancient Greek traditions to develop moral character. See Kapstein 2013, Fiordallis 2018, and Gowans 2021, chapter four.

42 The five aggregates (*skandhas*) are an early Buddhist classification of experience into form (*rūpa*), feeling (*vedanā*), recognition (*samjñā*), awareness (*vijñāna*), and a fifth category of conditioned factors (*samskāra*). Both the perfections and the pathological emotions are classified as conditioned factors. The aggregates make up all human experience, and thereby constitute the conventional self. See Gethin 1998, 135–7 for a good introductory discussion.

43 See Repetti 2010, Repetti 2019, and Adam 2010 for explorations of similarities between Buddhist moral psychology and Frankfurt's compatibilist account of free will.

44 See also Gómez 1995.

45 Huntington himself does not make this latter suggestion. It is proposed by Harrison 2019, 35–7.

Chapter 2

1 The Sanskrit word *dāna*, which I am translating as "generosity," can mean giving, what is given, and the quality possessed by one who habitually gives. In the passages under consideration, the meaning will alternate between a verbal sense of giving, and generous character. Therefore, I alternate between "giving" and "generosity" as translations, depending on the context. As we will see in this chapter, however, for Śāntideva the act of giving itself is primarily a mental adjustment in one's attitude toward what one possesses, rather than a physical transfer of these possessions. The distinction between the act of giving and generous character, therefore, will be less clear-cut than in a virtue theory like that of Aristotle that conceives of generosity as the skillful transfer of material possessions.

2 See Crosby and Skilton's introduction to their translation of BCA chapter five in Śāntideva 1995, 30–3.

3 See Huntington 2019 and the introduction by Crosby and Skilton to Śāntideva 1995 (pp. 9–13) for explanations of the ritual of unexcelled worship in the *Guide*.

4 Rotman 2009, 65–150 provides a useful study of the importance of positive affect, faith, and confidence in Buddhist literature.

5 Cf. Heim 2004.

6 I use Gomez's elegant translation of these verses, and for 2:8–9 below. See Śāntideva, 2015, 1081.

7 Gomez's translation of these verses can be found in Śāntideva 2015, 1081–2.

8 See Ohnuma 2006 for an excellent study of the bodhisattva's sacrifice of his body.

9 See also BCA chapter 10, in which Śāntideva concludes his text with a long series of aspirations for the well-being of all sentient beings. I analyze some of these verses in my seventh chapter.

10 On abandonment and the pathological emotions, see for example Bodhi 2000: S II 282, and Bodhi 2000: S III 9–10. See also Harvey 1995, 58–60.

11 The significance of the equation of giving with nirvāṇa will be clearer once the equation of giving and abandonment is explained. I return to this in the following section.

12 *tyajet* is the verbal optative form derived from the verbal root *tyaj* from which *tyāga* is also formed. The meaning here is that one could, or should, give/abandon.

13 As I explained in the third section of the introduction of this book, Śāntideva's introspection chapter functions as his chapter on ethical restraint.

14 Translations from the *Training Anthology* are my own, but see also the complete translation of the text by Goodman 2016a.

15 In the body of the SS, the chapter that provides commentary and supporting sutra quotations to the first line of verse 4 is titled "generosity" (*dāna*), further strengthening the relation between generosity (*dāna*) and abandoning (*utsarga*/*tyāga*).

16 A noteworthy difference is that person (*ātmabhāva*) in BCA 3:10 is given in the plural, suggesting an emphasis on the bodhisattva's gift of his being in all future rebirths.

17 Here, I am particularly influenced by Mrozik, who takes *ātmabhāva* in the *Training Anthology* as having a broader meaning than the physical body because the sections of the text dealing with purification of *ātmabhāva* place great emphasis upon purifying the mind by eliminating negative mental factors, such as lust (*rāga*) and anger (*dveṣa*) (Mrozik 2007, 23). See also Mahoney 2002, Clayton 2006, Lele 2007, and Nelson 2021, 278 n. 3.

18 I take the translations of all the titles of the Buddhist texts quoted in the *Training Anthology* from Goodman 2016a. His translation of these two passages can be found at p. 22.

19 See Nattier 2003 for a translation and study of the *Questions of Ugra* sutra.

20 Goodman's (2016a) translation of this passage can be found at p. 23.

21 Goodman's (2016a) translation can be found at pp. 24–5.

22 Goodman's (2016a) translation can be found at p. 25.

23 As Amod Lele points out, to increase does not literally mean to obtain more of an object. This is particularly obvious in the case of external possessions (*bhoga*) which are usually characterized as being given away. The point instead is that our interaction with these objects should be free of the pathological emotions and suffused with the virtuous qualities. See Lele 2007, 42–3.

24 See section six of the introduction to this book.

Chapter 3

1 This premise is stated explicitly later in the chapter (BCA 6:34) and in chapter eight (BCA 8:95–6).

2 My understanding of what I am calling the "subject-oriented strategy" is heavily indebted to Nelson 2021.

3 This is an area where the *Guide* had an enormous impact on the Tibetan philosophical tradition, and in particular the Géluk school, which develops the Stages of the Path (*lamrim*) textual tradition to offer systematic gradated trainings to enlightenment. Śāntideva's *Guide* is frequently cited in these texts. See Powers 2007, 481–94 for an introduction to *lamrim* as developed by the Géluk school. See Jackson 2019 for an examination of Tsongkhapa's use of Śāntideva's *Guide* in his influential *lamrim* text, *The Great Treatise on the Stages of the Path to Awakening* (*Byang chub lam rim chen mo*).

4 See Chuosavasdi 2018 and Barnes 2020 for defenses of Śāntideva's claim that anger should be eliminated. See also Nussbaum 2016 for a contemporary argument for the irrationality of anger.

5 In the *Training Anthology*, Śāntideva also characterizes patience as making the mind unshakable (*akṣobhya*) when encountering hardships (Nelson 2021, 212–13).

6 In the *Training Anthology*, Śāntideva structures his patience chapter around three kinds of patience commonly referred to in Mahāyāna texts: patient endurance of physical pain, others' wrongdoings, and reflecting on the Dharma (Goodman 2016a, 177–85). Śāntideva does not use this schema in the *Guide*, however. Although he does not refer to patient endurance of physical pain, or others' wrongdoings by name in the *Guide*, he provides arguments and meditations to develop these two kinds of patience in its sixth chapter. The third kind of patience, that of reflecting on the Dharma, appears to be absent in the *Guide*. See Nelson 2021, 180–201 for a careful discussion of the three kinds of patience in relation to Śāntideva's texts.

7 See Williams 2009, chapter nine for a summary of the stages of the bodhisattva path.

8 See Nelson 2021, chapter five, especially 202–3 and 210–12.

9 Influential early Buddhist descriptions or depictions of the distinction between physical and mental pain include the *Arrow Sutta* (*Sallatha Sutta*)

(Bodhi 2000, 1263: S iv 207), the *Stone Splinter Sutta* (*Sakalika Sutta*) (Bodhi 2000, 116: S i 27) and *Questions of King Milinda* II.2.4 (Rhys Davids, 69). See Sumanacara 2019 for an explanation of the distinction in early Buddhism.

10 See Nelson 2021, chapter five.

11 The verse can more naturally be translated as: "If there is a remedy, then what's the point in becoming upset (*daurmanasya*)? Moreover, if there is no remedy, then what's the point in becoming upset (*daurmanasya*)?" I use the slightly awkward "feeling mental pain" to translate *daurmanasya*, however, to emphasize that Śāntideva is *not* referring to the pathological emotion of anger (*krodha*) in this verse, but rather its causal condition which is itself a kind of hedonic sensation (*vedanā*). "Upset," "irritation," "discontent" and so on, all of which are possible translations of *daurmanasya*, are also readily understood as referring to subtle kinds of anger, and therefore risk eliding this important distinction.

12 See Gethin 1998, chapter eight and Williams 2000 chapter four for accessible introductions to Abhidharma theory of mind, in which this distinction is made. For a more in-depth treatment, see Ronkin 2005, especially chapter two.

13 The term translated as "(physical) pain" in this verse is *duḥkha*, which often refers more broadly to both physical and emotional suffering. In the *Guide*'s chapter six, however, Śāntideva's treatment of this first unpleasant item, which comes in verses 6:12–21, shows that its meaning here is more narrowly confined. I examine these verses below.

14 A natural concern which may arise at this point is the question of whether the bodhisattva's wish to eliminate the suffering of sentient beings would also cause mental pain and anger whenever it is impeded. Śāntideva does not address this concern explicitly in chapter six. In chapter eight, however, he claims that suffering arises from egocentric attachment to one's own benefit (BCA 8:92–3), and we have already seen that he claims that the pathological emotions, which are themselves manifestations of egoistic concern, constitute suffering (see chapter 1.3.1 above). The frustration of non-egocentric motivations, such as compassion for others, does not therefore generate the kind of mental pain which stimulates anger. My own position is that Śāntideva does hold compassion is painful (see BCA 6:122–3), but that it is not an afflictive kind of pain, and thereby does not generate pathological emotions. I return to the issue of the painfulness of compassion in my fifth chapter.

15 For a portrayal of the Buddha withstanding physical pain with mental tranquility, see the *Stone Splinter Sutta* (*Sakalika Sutta*) (Bodhi 2000, 116: S i 27).

16 I am indebted here and in much of this section to Bommarito 2014, who argues convincingly for the importance of perspective in Śāntideva and other Mahāyāna Buddhist accounts of patience.

17 See also BCA 6:75.

18 See Cozort 2013 for a discussion of the religious aspect of Śāntideva's treatment of pain.
19 See BCA 4:28–47.
20 See Lele 2007, 154–61 for a useful discussion of *prasāda*.
21 See also Cozart 2013 for a treatment of Śāntideva's emphasis on the importance of finding meaning in suffering.
22 Śāntideva uses this enhanced sensitivity to the suffering of others as the basis of his equalizing self and other argument, which begins at BCA 8:90. See in particular BCA 8:90, 95, and 96. I discuss this argument in my fourth chapter.
23 For useful treatments of *saṃvega* and other virtuous uses of fear in Buddhist texts, see Brekke 2002, Garfield 2010, Giustarini 2012, and Brons 2016.
24 See BCA 7:25–8 and BCA 8:108.
25 Goodman's translation of this passage can be found at Goodman 2016a, 179–80.
26 A full translation of the passage can be found at Goodman 2016a, 180.
27 See Harris 2018a for a treatment of early Buddhist and Mahāyāna strategies to prevent physical pain from causing mental pain.
28 There is an obvious connection between ancient Greek Stoicism and Śāntideva in their shared claim that the virtuous person flourishes regardless of physical pain. See Annas 1993, 388–411 for an explanation of Stoic conceptions of *eudaimonia*.
29 The desires for esteem, praise, and fame, as the opposites of the unwanted situations of contempt, abusive speech, and disgrace, are emphasized by Śāntideva as causes of anger in his verses laying out the structure for this part of the text (BCA 6:11, 6:53). I include the desire for material possessions in this section because Śāntideva offers several arguments for its irrationality, in relation to its role in causing anger.
30 See Harris 2014a, Breyer 2015, and Sumanacara 2019 for treatments of Buddhist conceptions of suffering.
31 Schmidt-Leukel 2019 points out that envy is conceived of as a form of anger by Śāntideva (258–9).
32 Rejoicing (*muditā*) is one of the four Brahmavihāras. See Heim 2017. In BCA 6:77, Śāntideva uses the synonym *hṛṣṭi* to refer to this state of mind.
33 In his commentary on Śāntideva's patience chapter, Tsongkhapa distinguishes between the object of anger, that is the person or thing the anger is directed toward; the subject, that is the angry person; and the basis of anger, that is the subject's predisposition for anger and other pathological emotions to arise. See McRae 2012, 161–3. The first of these causes is the focus of what I am calling the object-oriented strategy, and the second and third are the focus of different aspects of the subject-oriented strategy. I am influenced by McRae's analysis of Tsongkhapa's explication of these three causes of anger in my development of this section. For a similar distinction, see Hume's treatment of the difference between the cause and

the object of a passion (Hume 2007, 182–4). Garfield 2019b notes the resemblance between Hume and Śāntideva on this issue (p. 60 n. 18).

34 Prajñākaramati connects Śāntideva's argument in these verses with Śāntideva's psychological analysis of anger's causes given in 6:7. "Just as pain, even though unintended, inevitably arises from bile and the rest, whose efficacy is produced from its own conditions, similarly anger arises from dejection etc" (Nelson 2021, 290). "Dejection" here translates *daumanasya*.

35 See Bommarito 2011 for an extended analysis of this analogy. I differ from Bommarito in that I do not take the form of Śāntideva's reasoning to be an argument by analogy. Rather, he uses the analogy with bile to emphasize the key premises in his argument, that enemies are not autonomous, and that harm occurs because of multiple causal conditions.

36 Both Sāṃkhya and Nyāya are philosophical schools who accept the existence of an eternal, unified self (an *ātman*). Some of the arguments in this section apply to any conception of an eternal self. For instance, Śāntideva argues that if an eternal self were to act, since it cannot change, it would always continue performing the action, which is absurd (6:28). He also offers specific arguments against the Nyāya conception of self, which possesses cognition, but is not intrinsically aware. If the self has no awareness, Śāntideva argues, then it cannot deliberately initiate action (6:29ab). Of course, given his acceptance of metaphysical selflessness, agent-causation at anything but a conventional level of description is not a conceptual option for Śāntideva.

37 See for instance the fifth chapter of the *Vimalakīrti Sutra* (Thurman [1976] 2003) and *The Perfection of Wisdom Sutra in Eight Thousand Lines* (Conze 1973, 259).

38 Even were anger toward sentient beings correctly perceived of as empty of intrinsic existence possible, Śāntideva would still claim it was irrational given his arguments for anger's harmfulness, and the many other arguments made in the chapter that do not use metaphysical selflessness as an explicit premise.

39 Verse 6:34 introduces the argument, by claiming that all persons desire to avoid suffering. The instances of self-harm that follow, therefore, show that these individuals are not in control of their behavior.

40 We will, however, find the bodhisattva imaginatively examining how pathological emotions distort the minds of other persons later in the text, during the exchanging self and other meditations which I analyze in my fourth chapter.

41 I am influenced here by McRae 2012.

42 See section six of the introduction to this book.

43 See chapter 1.3.3 above.

44 In my first chapter, we saw that the perfection of giving, for Śāntideva, is the elimination of craving toward all possessions, accompanied by mentally offering them to all beings, rather than the physical transfer of a gift.

Śāntideva's reference here in BCA 6:105 is to ordinary generosity, in the commonsense meaning of free transfer of possessions. This is conducive to the bodhisattva path, in that it both develops and results from the attitudinal change constituted by the perfection of generosity.

45 In more recent work, however, Nussbaum argues that anger is always an irrational response to injustice (2016).

46 See chapter 1.4.1 above.

Chapter 4

1 Although my own approach in what follows is to argue for a unified reading of the meditative concentration chapter in its canonical form, it is also possible to appeal to the *Guide*'s historical process of textual formation to provide an explanation for its initially confusing structure. As Schmidt-Leukel points out, in the shorter and (presumably) older version of the *Guide*, the verses focused on developing compassion, including the equalizing self and other argument and exchanging self and other meditations, appear in the earlier effort (*vīrya*) chapter. In this shorter version of the text, the concentration chapter deals primarily with verses praising seclusion, which can more straightforwardly be understood as aids to concentration meditation. See Schmidt-Leukel 2019, 347–9.

2 Often the title of the *Guide*'s eighth chapter, *dhyāna*, is translated into English as "meditation." Moreover, most of the contemplations given by Śāntideva in the chapter can naturally be considered meditations, in the English meaning of the term. But the Sanskrit term *dhyāna* usually has a narrower meaning in Buddhist texts, generally referencing states of deep concentration. The broader English meaning of meditation, therefore, should not be appealed to as providing an organizational principle for the chapter.

3 See Gunaratana 1980 for a useful introduction to concentration meditation in the early Buddhist tradition.

4 Contrast, for instance, the eighth chapter of the *Guide* with Āryaśūra's treatment of concentration in his bodhisattva manual, *Compendium of the Perfections* (*Pāramitāsamāsa*). Āryaśūra gives detailed instructions on how to engage in concentration meditation, including which objects to focus on and descriptions of the *dhyāna* states of concentration. See translation by Meadows 1976, 230–43.

5 I omit verse 8:4, which continues to describe the importance of developing concentration. The reflections to develop renunciation begin on 8:5, quoted below.

6 See Gunaratana 1980, 54–5.

7 See Harris 2014a for an analysis of the suffering of change.

8 Śāntideva uses the term *viveka* (seclusion) at BCA 8:2 and BCA 8:89, but also refers to solitude with a variety of synonyms throughout the first half of the chapter.

9 Temporary freedom from pathological emotions is a result of successful concentration meditation. This suggests that the bodhisattva's sojourn in the wilderness metaphorically represents an extended period of concentration. Given that the meditations and arguments given in this section are highly discursive, however, we cannot understand them as literally providing instructions for developing concentration.
10 See also Śāntideva's descriptions of the peace of the wilderness at BCA 8:85–6.
11 See Thomson 2013 for a good explanation of the collapse of meaning in Heidegger's *Being and Time*. One of Kierkegaard's most influential presentations of despair is in *The Sickness Unto Death*. See Kierkegaard 1983.
12 See chapter 1.4.2 above.
13 See chapter 1.4.1 above.
14 Goodman 2009, 92 references the equalizing self and other passages as part of his argument that Śāntideva is a consequentialist.
15 Compare John Stuart Mill's response to the objection that it is psychologically unrealistic to expect the proponent of Utilitarianism to always act from the motivation to promote the greater good (Mill 1979, 17). Mill claims that in most cases, acting from ordinary motivations to benefit specific individuals will, in the long run, maximize utility (18).
16 Compare this strategy with Buddahghosa's development of the Brahmavihāra of love (*metta*) in his *Path of Purification*, where the meditator begins by generating affection for himself and expands this feeling to all beings. See Buddhaghosa 1991, 288–306.
17 There is an interesting tenson between Śāntideva's claim here that (at least in ordinary cases) personal identity does not survive rebirth, and his phrasing of the bodhisattva's commitment as a trans-life project (e.g., BCA 10:55). In the *Guide*, he does not address or attempt to resolve this apparent inconsistency. See Harris 2018b for a treatment of this issue.
18 See Williams 1998, chapter five for an influential critique of Śāntideva's argument. For responses to Williams, see Pettit 1999, Siderits 2000, Wetlesen 2002, Harris 2011, and Harris 2018c. An excellent summary of Śāntideva's argument is provided by Garfield, Jenkins, and Priest 2015. See Finnigan 2018 for an analysis of the plausibility of the various interpretive options. See also Gómez 1973 for an earlier treatment of Śāntideva's argument, and the relation between emptiness and compassion in Mahāyāna ethics.
19 I consider the painfulness of compassion in chapter 5.6 below.
20 See chapter 3.3.2 above.
21 I am uncertain how to translate *vismaya* in verse 8:109. If we take it in the sense of dejection/dismay, this creates a natural pairing with the rest of the verse. Compassion protects against conceit (*mada*) given that high social position, when attained, is conceived of merely as a means to help others. It protects against "dismay" (*vismaya*) against taking a lower social position,

given that one is no longer attached to one's reputation, since one's goal is to benefit others. Dismay is not the primary meaning of *vismaya*, however, and so I offer these other ways to understand the verse.

22 See Harris 2017 for an exploration of Śāntideva's strategic use of afflictive mental states.

23 This occurs during the exchanging self and other meditations (BCA 8:140–54) which I explore below, but even more strongly at the conclusion of the chapter. See in particular BCA 8:166–73. For reasons of space, I do not comment on these passages.

24 See Railton 1984, 140–6 for an influential treatment of the paradox of hedonism.

25 See Frankfurt 1971 for an influential exploration of the philosophical importance of first and second order motivations.

26 My reading of 8:140 here is influenced by Pema Chödrön's commentary on this verse. See Chödrön 2005, 324. See also McRae 2015 for an exploration of Tibetan sources that use this kind of strategy.

27 For a clear statement of the disadvantages of anger, see BCA 6:2–3. Envy is treated at BCA 6:76–86.

28 In my translation and analysis, I interpret Śāntideva as presenting the bodhisattva as conducting the exchange of positions three times: once with a social inferior (8:140–6), once with a person of equal standing (8:147–50), and once with a social superior (8:151–4). This is a frequent and influential way to understand the text. See for instance Pelden 2010, 298–304 and Dalai Lama 1994, 108–12. This reading fits well with Śāntideva's emphasis in the first part of the chapter on the pathological social emotions of envy, competitiveness, and arrogant pride arising between persons of these three social positions. An alternate reading of these verses is to see the bodhisattva as making only one exchange, in verse 8:140, and for the remaining verses to be understood as representing the perspective of the social inferior as he contemplates the bodhisattva in the superior position. In Schmidt-Leukel's interpretation, verses 148–54 continue to represent this position, but now describe the thoughts of the social superior *as imagined by* the person of lower social position, the position the bodhisattva has taken up. See Schmidt-Leukel 2019, 388–402, and n. 150 (p. 394). In my view, multiple interpretations of these passages are possible. We can take this ambiguity of perspective-shift as another element of Śāntideva's representation of the mingling of subjectivities that characterizes this section of the text. See Gyatso 2019 for a sensitive treatment of the exchanging meditations which emphasize this theme.

29 See chapter 1.3.3 above.

30 See chapter 1.3.3 above.

31 This is a strategy developed in the Tibetan tradition of Mind Training (*Lojong*), whose literature takes Śāntideva's *Guide* as one of its key inspirational sources. See Jinpa 2019.

32 See Schmidt-Leukel 2019, 404–12 for an explanation of these verses.

Chapter 5

1 As I show below, Śāntideva uses the term *muditā* to refer to a joyful state of mind, rather than rejoicing in others' good fortune, as do authors like Buddhaghoṣa (1991) and much of the early Buddhist tradition. See for instance BCA 6:9. Rejoicing in others' good fortune is expressed through a variety of synonyms, including *anu-mud* (BCA 3:1, 3:3), *tuṣṭi* (BCA 5:77), and *hṛṣṭi* (BCA 6:77). See 5.5 below.

2 A full translation of the passage can be found at Goodman 2016a, 28.

3 The same claims about the benefits of the bodhisattva path are made by Nāgārjuna in his *Precious Garland*. See verses 221–3 (Nāgārjuna 1998, 123).

4 I return to the issue of the superiority of the bodhisattva path, in terms of one's own happiness, in my sixth chapter.

5 The first half of chapter seven develops antidotes to four obstructions for developing enthusiastic effort: sloth (*ālasya*), attachment to the contemptable (*āsakti-kutsita*), dejection (*viṣāda*), and self-contempt (*ātmā-avamanyanā*) (BCA 7:2). According to Crosby and Skilton, these negative factors are eliminated by application of four positive factors, one of which is joy (*rati*). The other three are aspiration (*chanda*), steadfastness (*sthāma*), and letting go (*mukti*) (BCA 7:31). This is followed in the second half of the chapter by contemplations to develop six positive factors which promote the development of effort. Joy and aspiration also appear on this list, joined by pride (*māna*), giving up (*tyāga*), dedication (*tātparya*), and control (*vaśitā*). See BCA 7:31–2, and the introduction by Crosby and Skilton at Śāntideva 1995, 63–6.

6 I follow Crosby and Skilton (Śāntideva 1995, 72) in taking *krīḍā* to refer to sexual activity, rather than the more neutral translation of "game" used by Wallace and Wallace (Śāntideva 1997, 82). This better captures Śāntideva's use of the language of addiction (*śauṇḍa*, *atṛpta*), in 7:62, and fits with the reference to sensual pleasure (*kāma*) in 7:64.

7 See chapter 4.4.2 above.

8 See chapter 1.4.1 above.

9 Many Buddhist texts use the Sanskrit term *muditā* to refer to rejoicing, in this sense. Śāntideva, however, uses this term more generally, to refer to a joyful state of mind, rather than rejoicing in others' achievements. See Heim 2017, 181–3 for a good explanation of rejoicing according to the early Buddhist commentator, Buddhaghosa. Buddhaghosa's own presentation can be found in Buddhaghosa 1991, 309–10.

10 See Lele 2007 and Mrozik 2007 for studies that emphasize the importance of the bodhisattva's ability to attract those she wishes to serve.

11 See chapter 4.4.3 above.

12 See the *Universal Vehicle Discourse Literature* (*Mahāyānasūtrālaṃkāra*) (Thurman 2004, 170–1) for additional references to the bodhisattva's immunity to suffering while caring for beings in the hell realms. See also this chapter 3.3.2 above.

13 See also the introduction to this book, section two.
14 See also chapter 2.2.2 and 2.3.2 above.
15 See chapter 3.3.2 above.
16 See Annas 1993, 388–411 for a discussion of the Stoic view that virtuous character is the only constituent of well-being.
17 See chapter 4.4.3 above.
18 See chapter 3.3.2 above.
19 Arguably, this position would open Mahāyāna ethics to concerns about the overdemandingness of morality. See Harris 2015b for an argument against this position.
20 See the introduction to this book, section seven.
21 See Williams 2010 for a study of these verses and the question of whether Śāntideva believes enlightened buddhas have mental experience. See Griffiths 1994, chapter six for a useful study of the mental experience of a buddha.

Chapter 6

1 In my translation of BCA chapter nine, I follow the numbering of the verses provided by Crosby and Skilton in Śāntideva 1995 which is followed as well by Wallace and Wallace in Śāntideva 1997. After verse 20, this numbering deviates by a single number from the Vaidya edition on which I base my translation. As Crosby and Skilton explain, the discrepancy is caused by a scribal error, reproduced in the 1890 edition by Minaev, in which a single verse is copied out twice. Vaidya, following the de La Vallée Poussin edition (1901–14), notes but does not correct the error. See their explanation in Śāntideva 1995, 113–14.
2 For influential early examples of the nihilism objection, see *Questions of King Milinda* (Rhys Davids 1890, 41–3) and Nāgārjuna MMK 24:1–6 (2013, 164–7).
3 This controversy focuses on the correct interpretation of BCA 9:2, in which Śāntideva claims the ultimate truth is not accessible to the intellect. Influential proponents of the Tibetan Buddhist Geluk school, including Tsongkhapa and Gyaltsab, argue that this verse should not be taken literally (Sweet 1979, 79). Gyaltsab, for instance, interprets Śāntideva as claiming only that dualistic awareness cannot grasp ultimate truth (Sweet 1979, 85). See Sweet 1979 and Williams 1998, chapter four for helpful treatments of this dispute.
4 See Sweet 1977 for an overview of BCA chapter nine, including a summary of Śāntideva's defense of the metaphysics of emptiness from objections of rival philosophical schools.
5 On Nāgārjuna's understanding of conventional reality, see Garfield 1995, esp. 304–8. Garfield 1995 provides an influential translation of the MMK.

See also the translation by Siderits and Katsura (Nāgārjuna 2013).

6 The idea behind Śāntideva's initial response, given in this line, is that a buddha with intrinsic existence could not benefit anyone, given that he would be permanent, and therefore could not be causally efficacious. Śāntideva's response, therefore, parallels the one given by Nāgārjuna in MMK chapter 24. See Garfield 1995, 301–21.

7 This last verse responds to the objection that if an illusionary Buddha continues to exist, then reaching enlightenment is impossible given that illusionary suffering and rebirth will continue to exist as well (BCA 9:13). The response given in 9:14 is that, just like illusions, conventionally real entities (including rebirth and suffering) can be eliminated by destroying their causes. Since this response is also relevant to the objections given in 9:9 and 9:11, I present it here.

8 See Jenkins 2015a for a translation and analysis of Prajñākaramati's commentary on these verses. As Jenkins shows, Prajñākaramati argues that compassion continues to take conventionally existing sentient beings as its object. I am indebted to Jenkins for drawing my attention to this aspect of Śāntideva's thought.

9 As Tillemans points out, Candrakīrti, Jñānagarbha, and Kamalaśīla all emphasize the importance of eliminating the false superimposition (*samāropa*) of intrinsic existence without negating conventionally existing phenomena (2007, 517–19). See also Westerhoff 2009, 48.

10 On Śāntideva's strategy of alternating between everyday and impersonal levels of reality for soteriological benefit, see Todd 2013.

11 See also Todd 2013, especially section 4.3, who argues that, for Śāntideva, realization of emptiness results in a "reorientation" of the relationship between the bodhisattva and society (95–119).

12 The transformation of the bodhisattva's experience by the perfections, and most centrally by wisdom, is emphasized in Garfield's phenomenological reading of the *Guide*. See Garfield 2010, Garfield 2019a, 192–6, and Garfield 2021, chapter two. Carpenter 2019 also emphasizes the role of wisdom in transforming the bodhisattva's perspective on reality.

13 For a good discussion of this question, see Sweet 1977.

14 For at least much of the bodhisattva path, Śāntideva believes that the bodhisattva must maintain a conventional object of awareness. It is a common Mahāyāna position, however, that fully enlightened buddhas have no objects of awareness, and respond automatically to benefit sentient beings. See Dunne 1996 for an interpretation of Candrakīrti that takes this position. BCA 9:34–9 seem to suggest that Śāntideva holds this position as well, although it seems to me that these verses are in tension with the remainder of the chapter, which emphasize maintaining a conventional object of compassion. For our purposes, it is enough to recognize that Śāntideva holds that highly developed bodhisattvas maintain a conventional object of awareness while recognizing its emptiness. For a discussion of BCA 9:34–9 on this issue, see Williams 2010.

15 Prajñākaramati uses the magician example to illustrate the way the bodhisattva relates to conventional reality in his commentary to BCA 9:5. See Oldmeadow 1994, 38 for translation.
16 There are, however, a couple deficiencies in the magician example, in which the comparison to conventional reality breaks down. First, the illusions of the magic show are not integrated with the world; a magic dragon is simply conjured and then vanishes, unable to affect anything. This differs from the causally dependent and efficacious illusion-like items of conventional reality. Likewise, the magic show cannot represent the holistic nature of the transformation of the bodhisattva's experience of conventional reality; magic shows take place in only a small part of the world. See Hirst 2005, chapter five for an excellent analysis of the use of metaphors like the magician by Advaita Vedānta that has influenced me in this section.
17 For a good translation of the *Foundations of Mindfulness* sutra in the Pali canon, see Ñānamoli and Bodhi 1995, 145–58.
18 The lists include, for example, the five aggregates, the seven enlightenment factors, and the four noble truths. See Ñānamoli and Bodhi 1995, 151–5.
19 See Tillemans 2007 for an explication of the Madhyamaka use of findability arguments.
20 See Siderits 2004 for an explication of this strategy as used in the first chapter of Nāgārjuna's *Root Verses on the Middle Way*.
21 Contact is presented as the causal condition of feeling in the forward order of the twelve links of dependent origination. See for example Ñānamoli and Bodhi 1995, 353–4: M i261.
22 See Mrozik 2007 for a careful study of the role of the body in Śāntideva's *Training Anthology*, and Ohnuma 2019 for a short insightful analysis of its role in Śāntideva's *Guide*.
23 See chapter 3.3.1 and 3.3.2 above.
24 See Nāgārjuna 2013, MMK 1:6.
25 For a discussion of omniscience in early Buddhist and Mahāyāna conceptions of Buddhahood, see Jaini 1992.
26 See also Harris 2017 and Finnigan 2019 and 2021 for explorations of Śāntideva's strategic use of fear.
27 See for instance the *Turning the Wheel of Dharma Sutta* (Bodhi 2000, 1844: SN 56.11).
28 Following Steinkellner 2019, I translate *trāsāntanirmuktyā* (because of liberation from fear), given in the Tibetan edition of the text, rather than *trāsāt tv anirmuktyā* (because of not being liberated from fear), as given in the Vaidya edition of the Sanskrit version. According to Sweet, Prajñākaramati's Sanskrit commentary considers both readings, with the second being interpreted as an objection raised by Śāntideva's opponent, in pointing out the inefficacy of emptiness. See Sweet 1977, 97–9.
29 I follow Crosby and Skilton in Śāntideva 1995 and Wallace and Wallace in Śāntideva 1997 in taking delusion (*moha*) in the instrumental case as giving the reason for sentient beings' suffering. Another natural reading of

the verse that fits well with my overall analysis of the chapter takes delusion to provide the reason for the bodhisattva's ability to remain in *saṃsāra*, presaging Śāntideva's invocation of delusion for this purpose in 9:75–6. This is one of the readings Prajñākaramati offers in his commentary on the verse, and is also given by Steinkellner 2019 in his translation. See Sweet 1977, 97–9 for a summary of Prajñākaramati's analysis of the verse.

30 This is then an analogue to the inversion of the metaphysical nihilism objection which Nāgārjuna presents in the *Root Verses on the Middle Way*, chapter twenty-four. In that text, Nāgārjuna turns the tables on his opponent by arguing that rejecting emptiness entails destruction of the Buddhist path, given that nothing can change or be causally influenced. See translation and commentary by Garfield 1995, 293–321. In the *Guide*, Śāntideva crafts a more psychologically focused formulation of this inversion. Rather than destabilize the conventional world, emptiness, properly understood, allows the bodhisattva to remain within the realm of rebirth without suffering.

31 The point of this objection is to emphasize the unreality of suffering; that is, its illusion-like nature in being merely a conceptual construct, thereby questioning its badness. It is not the claim that, by definition, an object lacking intrinsic existence (*svabhāva*) cannot be non-relationally bad. As Shelly Kagan argues, we can distinguish between intrinsic value, in the sense of having value depending only on non-relational properties, and intrinsic value in the sense of being valued non-instrumentally; that is, for its own sake, or as an end (Kagan 1998, 278–9). Only the first meaning of intrinsic existence is by definition incompatible with a Madhyamaka metaphysics of emptiness. The value nihilism objection focuses on the second sense of intrinsic existence. See also my discussion in chapter 1.2 above.

32 In the auto-commentary to verses seven and eight of his *Dispeller of Disputes (Vigrahavyāvartanī)*, Nāgārjuna has an opponent object that the Madhyamaka doctrine of emptiness is incompatible with the Buddhist claim that certain phenomena like the virtues are by nature auspicious, and that the intrinsic badness of the nature of negative phenomena like suffering accounts for the necessity of removing it (see translation and commentary by Westerhoff 2010b, 94–9). Nāgārjuna responds in his auto-commentary to verses 52–6 (Westerhoff 2010b, 99–104) by arguing that both virtuous and non-virtuous phenomena can only have conventional existence, since otherwise they would be causally independent (Westerhoff 2010b, 100–1). This would entail that auspicious phenomena were causally inert, and therefore could play no role in religious practice (Westerhoff 2010b, 101–2); likewise, suffering would be permanent, and therefore could not be removed (Westerhoff 2010b, 102–3). Given his defense of emptiness which I explicated in section 6.2 above, we can assume Śāntideva would endorse Nāgārjuna's reasoning. The choice then is between accepting that the conventional badness of suffering is

sufficient to explain why it needs to be removed, or to accept that suffering is not bad. Śāntideva's allusion to the universal agreement about the badness of suffering (BCA 8:103) shows that he takes the first option.

33 See chapter 1.3.3 and 3.3.3 above.

34 See Davis 2018 for a development of this concern in relation to Buddhist ethics.

35 See Davis 2013b for a development of this sort of possibility, arguing from a Yogācāra perspective. On the moral realism of Abhidharma moral psychology, see Keown 1992, 57–64.

36 Mark Siderits gives a particularly lucid presentation of the Madhyamaka position: "The middle path between realism and nihilism then turns out to be the position that all things contain elements of conceptual construction – and so are, while not real in the sense that the realist hankers after and the nihilist despairs of finding, real nonetheless. Chariots, houses, forests, trees, rivers, mountains, persons, psychophysical elements, atoms, quarks – all are real in the only way in which something could be real. Each has its own determinate nature by virtue of its functional role within some human practice. Each is of course empty – devoid of intrinsic nature, hence lacking in the reality of mind-independent reals. But since nothing could be real in that way, the appellation 'empty' attaches to everything there is" (Siderits 2003, 202).

37 See Candrakīrti 2004, 6:24–6 for the distinction between conventional truth and falsity.

38 For discussions of the validity of conventional truth from a Madhyamaka perspective, see Sweet 1979, 80–1, and Cowherds 2011. See Finnigan 2018 for a discussion of the relevance of Madhyamaka epistemology to the question of the badness of suffering. Tillemans 2010/11 emphasizes the importance of appeals to broad social consensus for Madhyamaka justifications of ethical claims (see pp. 358–9).

39 See Garfield 2014b, 281 and 312. See Goodman 2015 for a development of the idea that human vulnerability can act as the basis for Madhyamaka ethics.

40 See Tillemans 2011 for a fairly sympathetic reading of Madhyamaka that nevertheless raises this concern. See Garfield 2011 for a forceful defense of Candrakīrti on this issue. Both essays are included in Cowherds 2011, which includes numerous other essays relevant to concerns about epistemic authority and justification in relation to Madhyamaka metaphysics.

41 Notice the parallel with Aristotle, who begins the *Nicomachean Ethics* by commenting on the variety of positions about the nature of *eudaimonia*. See Aristotle 2009, 1.4: pp. 5–6.

42 See Tillemans 2010/11 for an analysis of Āryadeva and Candrakīrti's use of this strategy in the *400 Verses* (*Catuḥśataka*) and commentary, in their arguments against the four illusions, such as taking what is impermanent as permanent, taking what is painful as pleasurable and so on (p. 359). Tillemans describes the Madhyamaka method as "try[ing] to show that the

world's superficial attitudes on these matters are in conflict with its deep-seated intuitions – if the world reflected it would recognize the four illusions as indeed illusions" (p. 360). I take Śāntideva to be applying the same method in his claims that ordinary people are deluded as to the nature of suffering.

Chapter 7

1 Heim (2020, 47–8) also suggests that the *Guide*'s tenth chapter shows a deepened commitment to the well-being of others, enabled by mental development achieved through the trainings of the earlier chapters.
2 See chapter 2.3.1 above.
3 For discussion of this issue, see Basham 1981 and Clayton 2006. See Kajiyama 1989 for an explanation of the development of the idea of transferring (*pariṇāma*) karmic merit to others. Kajiyama helpfully distinguishes two senses in which merit can be transferred, both of which are found in Mahāyāna sources. It can be transferred from one individual to another, in terms of improving their next rebirth and so on; or it can be redirected, in the sense of transforming results in one's own future rebirth, from material prosperity to long life or an auspicious rebirth. Kajiyama calls the first of these "transfer of merits" and the second "transformation of merits." See Kajiyama 1989, 8–13. Śāntideva appears to reference the second sense in BCA 10:51, where the bodhisattva aspires to encounter the possibility of taking ordination in a future life. It is possible to read most of the rest of the chapter as performing transfer of karmic merit to other beings.
4 See Lele 2007 and 2013 for sophisticated treatments of the question of why Śāntideva sometimes depicts bodhisattvas as offering harmful gifts.
5 See chapter 2.2.1 above.
6 Śāntideva does not explicitly include the god or demi-god realms in his list of recipients of these offerings, perhaps because they are a fortunate rebirth where explicit suffering does not occur, and therefore provide a less effective object for the development of compassion.
7 See the introduction to this book, section six.
8 Manjushri is the bodhisattva who represents wisdom. Śāntideva sometimes refers to him by the alternate name "Mañjughoṣa" (BCA 10:14; 10:51). Avalokiteśvara is the bodhisattva who represents compassion.

Conclusion

1 Lele 2015 also emphasizes the importance of argumentation, for Śāntideva, in chapters preceding the wisdom chapter.

2 See also Wright 2009, 22–8 for an explanation of the relation between wisdom and generosity in Mahāyāna sources.
3 Good examples of studies of Yogācāra emphasizing the phenomenological quality of their thought in relation to subject object duality include Garfield 1997, Lusthaus 2002, Coseru 2012, and Li 2016 and 2022.
4 See my discussion of externalization in chapter 1.4.2 above.
5 See Aristotle 2009, 32 and 60–4.
6 See Harris 2017 for a broader treatment of this theme.

WORKS CITED

Abbreviations

BCA or *Guide*: *Guide to the Practices of Awakening* of Śāntideva. Edition: Vaidya, P. L. 1960. *Bodhicaryāvatāra of Śāntideva with the commentary Pañjikā of Prajñākaramati*. Edited by P. L. Vaidya. BuddhistSanskrit Texts, no. 12. Darbhanga: Mithila Institute of Post-Graduate Studies and Research in Sanskrit Learning.

MMK: *Root Verses on the Middle Way* (*Mūlamadhyamakakārikā*) of Nāgārjuna. Translation: 2013. *Nāgārjuna's Middle Way: Mūlamadhyamakakārikā*. Translated by Mark Siderits and Shoryu Katsura. Wisdom Publications.

SS or *Training Anthology*: *Śikṣāsamuccaya* of Śāntideva. Edition: Vaidya, P. L. 1961. *Śikṣāsamuccaya of Śāntideva*. Edited by P. L. Vaidya. Darbhanga: Mithila Institute of Post-Graduate Studies and Research in Sanskrit Learning.

References

Adam, Martin T. 2010. "No self, no free will, no problem: Implications of the *Anattalakkhaṇa Sutta* for a perennial philosophical issue." *Journal of the International Association of Buddhist Studies* 33(1–2): 239–65.

Annas, Julia. 1993. *The Morality of Happiness*. New York: Oxford University Press.

Annas, Julia. 2006. "Virtue Ethics." In *The Oxford Handbook of Ethical Theory*, edited by David Copp, 515–36. New York: Oxford University Press.

Arbel, Keren. 2015. "The Liberative Role of *Jhānic* Joy (*Pīti*) and Pleasure (*Sukha*) in the Early Buddhist Path to Awakening." *Buddhist Studies Review* 32(2):179–205.

Aristotle. 2009. *The Nicomachean Ethics*. Translated by David Ross and Lesley Brown. Oxford: Oxford University Press.

Banks, Ellison. 2003. *Dāna: Giving and Getting in Pali Buddhism*. Delhi: Motilal Banarsidass.

Barnes, William. 2020. "Is Anger ever Required? Ārya Śāntideva on Anger and its Antidotes." In *The Ethics of Anger*, edited by Court D. Lewis and Gregory L. Bock, 155–76. Lanham, MD: Lexington Press.

Barnhart, Michael. 2012. "Theory and Compassion in the Discussion of Buddhist Ethics." *Philosophy East and West* 62(1): 16–43.

Basham, A. L. 1981. "The evolution of the concept of the Bodhisattva." In *The Bodhisattva Doctrine in Buddhism*, edited by Leslie Kawamura. Waterloo, ON: Wilfred Laurier University Press.

Bell, Macalester. 2009. "Anger, Virtue, and Oppression." In *Feminist Ethics and Social and Political Philosophy: Theorizing the Non-Ideal*, edited by Lisa Tessman, 165–83. New York: Springer.
Bodhi, Bhikkhu, trans. 2000. *The Connected Discourses of the Buddha (Samyutta Nikāya)*. Somerville, MA: Wisdom Publications.
Bodhi, Bhikkhu. 2010. "Arahants, Bodhisattvas, and Buddhas." *Access to Insight* 22. http://www.accesstoinsight.org/lib/authors/bodhi/arahantsbodhisattvas.html.
Bodhi, Bhikkhu. 2011. "What Does Mindfulness Really Mean? A Canonical Perspective." *Contemporary Buddhism* 12(1): 19–39.
Bommarito, Nicolas. 2011. "Bile & Bodhisattvas: Śāntideva on Justified Anger." *Journal of Buddhist Ethics* 18: 357–81.
Bommarito, Nicolas. 2014. "Patience and Perspective." *Philosophy East and West* 64(2): 269–86.
Bommarito, Nicolas. 2018. *Inner Virtue*. Oxford: Oxford University Press.
Brassard, Francis. 2000. *The Concept of Bodhicitta in Śāntideva's Bodhicaryāvatāra*. Albany, NY: State University of New York Press.
Brekke, Torkel. 2002. *Religious motivation and the origins of Buddhism: A social-psychological exploration of the origins of a world religion.* London: RoutledgeCurzon.
Breyer, Daniel. 2013. "Freedom with a Buddhist Face." *Sophia* 52: 359–79.
Breyer, Daniel. 2015. "The Cessation of Suffering and Buddhist Axiology." *Journal of Buddhist Ethics* 22: 531–60.
Brons, Lajos. 2016. "Facing death from a safe distance: *Saṃvega* and moral psychology." *Journal of Buddhist Ethics* 23: 83–128.
Buddhaghosa. 1991. *The Path of Purification* (*Visuddhimagga*). Fifth Edition. Onalaska, WA: Pariyatti Publishing.
Burley, Mikel. 2017. "Conundrums of Buddhist Cosmology and Psychology." *Numen* 64(4): 343–70.
Candrakīrti. 2004. *Introduction to the Middle Way*. Translated by the Padmakara Translation Group. Boston, MA, and London: Shambhala.
Carpenter, Amber D. 2014. *Indian Buddhist Philosophy: Metaphysics as Ethics.* New York: Routledge.
Carpenter, Amber D. 2019. "Reason and Knowledge on the Path: A Protreptic Reading of the Guide." In *Readings of Śāntideva's Guide to Bodhisattva Practice*, edited by Jonathan Gold and Douglas Duckworth, 45–59. New York: Columbia University Press.
Chödrön, Pema. 2005. *No Time to Lose: A Timely Guide to the Way of the Bodhisattva*. Boulder, CO: Shambala.
Chuosavasdi, Thippapan. 2018. *Anger in Buddhist Philosophy: In Defense of Eliminativism*. PhD diss., University of York.
Clayton, Barbra R. 2006. *Moral Theory in Śāntideva's Śikṣāsamuccaya: Cultivating the Fruits of Virtue.* London and New York: Routledge.
Confucius. 2003. *Analects*. Translated by Edward Slingerland. Indianapolis: Hackett Publishing Company, Inc.

Conze, Edward. 1973. *The Perfection of Wisdom In Eight Thousand Lines & Its Verse Summary*. Bolinas, CA: Four Seasons Foundation.

Coseru, Christian. 2012. *Perceiving Reality: Consciousness, Intentionality, and Cognition in Buddhist Philosophy*. New York: Oxford University Press.

Cowherds. 2011. *Moonshadows: Conventional Truth in Buddhist Philosophy*. New York: Oxford University Press.

Cowherds 2015. *Moonpaths: Ethics and Emptiness*. New York: Oxford University Press.

Cozort, Daniel. 2013. "Suffering Made Sufferable: Śāntideva, Dzongkaba, and Modern Therapeutic Approaches to Suffering's Silver Lining." *Journal of Buddhist Ethics* 20: 355–75.

Crisp, Roger. 2021. "Well-Being." In *The Stanford Encyclopedia of Philosophy*, edited by Edward N. Zalta, Winter 2021 Edition. <https://plato.stanford.edu/archives/win2021/entries/well-being/>.

Dalai Lama XIV. 1994. *A Flash of Lightning in the Dark of Night: A Guide to the Bodhisattva's Way of Life*. Boston, MA, and London: Shambhala.

Dalai Lama XIV. 1997. *Healing Anger: The Power of Patience From a Buddhist Perspective*. Ithaca, NY: Snow Lion.

Davis, Gordon. 2013a. "Traces of Consequentialism and Non-Consequentialism in Bodhisattva Ethics." *Philosophy East and West* 63(2): 275–305.

Davis, Gordon. 2013b. "Moral Realism and Anti-Realism outside the West: A Meta-Ethical Turn in Buddhist Ethics." *Comparative Philosophy* 4(2): 24–53.

Davis, Gordon. 2018. "The Atipada Problem in Buddhist Meta-Ethics." *Journal of Buddhist Ethics* 25: 185–231.

Driver, Julia. 1998. "The Virtues and Human Nature." In *How One Should Live*, edited by Roger Crisp, 111–30. New York: Oxford University Press.

Dunne, John. 1996. "Thoughtless Buddha, Passionate Buddha." *Journal of the American Academy of Religion* 64(3): 525–56.

Edelglass, William. 2017. "Buddhism, Happiness and the Science of Meditation." In *Meditation, Buddhism, and Science*, edited by David L. McMahan and Erik Braun, 62–3. New York: Oxford University Press.

Engle, Artemus B. 2009. *The Inner Science of Buddhist Practice: Vasubandhu's Summary of the Five Heaps with Commentary by Sthiramati*. Ithaca, NY: Snow Lion.

Finnigan, Bronwyn. 2015. "Madhyamaka Buddhist Meta-Ethics: The Justificatory Grounds of Moral Judgments." *Philosophy East and West* 65(3): 765–85.

Finnigan, Bronwyn. 2018. "Madhyamaka Ethics." In *The Oxford Handbook of Buddhist Ethics*, edited by Daniel Cozort and James Mark Shields, 162–83. Oxford: Oxford University Press.

Finnigan, Bronwyn. 2019. "Śāntideva and the moral psychology of fear." In *Readings of Śāntideva's Guide to Bodhisattva Practice*, edited by Jonathan C. Gold and Douglas S. Duckworth, 221–34. New York: Columbia University Press.

Finnigan, Bronwyn. 2021. "The Paradox of Fear in Classical Indian Buddhism." *Journal of Indian Philosophy* 49: 913–29.
Finnigan, Bronwyn, and Tanaka, Koji. 2015. "Ethics for Madhyamakas." In *Moonpaths: Ethics and Emptiness* by The Cowherds, 221–31. New York: Oxford University Press.
Fiordallis, David. 2018. *Buddhist Spiritual Practices: Thinking with Pierre Hadot on Buddhism, Philosophy, and the Path.* Cazadero, CA: Mangalam Press.
Flanagan, Owen. 2011. *The Bodhisattva's Brain: Buddhism Naturalized.* Cambridge, MA: MIT Press.
Foot, Philippa. 2002. *Virtue and Vices and Other Essays in Moral Philosophy.* Oxford: Oxford University Press.
Framarin, Christopher. 2016. "Moral Saints, Hindu Sages, and the Good Life." *Comparative Philosophy* 7(1): 20–38.
Framarin, Christopher. 2017. "Renunciation, Pleasure, and the Good Life in the Samnyasa Upanisads." *Philosophy East and West* 67(1): 140–59.
Frankfurt, Harry. 1971. "Freedom of the Will and the Concept of a Person." *The Journal of Philosophy* 68(1): 5–20.
Frankfurt, Harry. 1977. "Identification and Externality." In *The Identities of Persons*, edited by Amelie Rorty, 58–68. Berkeley: University of California Press.
Ganeri, Jonardon. 2007. *The Concealed Art of the Soul: Theories of Self and Practices of Truth in Indian Ethics and Epistemology*. Oxford: Oxford University Press.
Garfield, Jay L. 1995. *Fundamental Wisdom of the Middle Way: Nāgārjuna's Mūlamadhyamakakārikā.* New York: Oxford University Press.
Garfield, Jay L. 1997. "Vasubandhu's Treatise on the Three Natures. Translated from the Tibetan Edition with a Commentary." *Asian Philosophy* 7(2): 133–54.
Garfield, Jay L. 2006. "Why did Bodhidharma go to the East? Buddhism's Struggle with the Mind in the World." *Sophia* 45(2): 61–80.
Garfield, Jay L. 2010. "What is it like to be a bodhisattva: Moral Phenomenology in Śāntideva's Bodhicaryāvatāra." *Journal of the International Association of Buddhist Studies* 33: 333–57.
Garfield, Jay L. 2011. "Taking Conventional Truth Seriously: Authority regarding Deceptive Reality." In *Moonshadows: Conventional Truth in Buddhist Philosohy* by The Cowherds, 23–38. New York: Oxford University Press.
Garfield, Jay L. 2012. "Mindfulness and Ethics: Attention, Virtue and Perfection." *Thai International Journal of Buddhist Studies* 3: 1–24.
Garfield, Jay L. 2014a. "Just Another Word for Nothing Left to Lose: Freedom, Agency and Ethics for Mādhyamikas." In *Free Will, Agency, and Selfhood in Indian Philosophy*, edited by Matthew R. Dasti and Edwin F. Bryant, 164–85. New York: Oxford University Press.
Garfield, Jay L. 2014b. *Engaging Buddhism: Why it Matters to Philosophy*. New York: Oxford University Press.

Garfield, Jay L. 2019a. "Seeing Sentient Beings: Śāntideva's Moral Phenomenology." In *Readings of Śāntideva's Guide to Bodhisattva Practice*, edited by Jonathan C. Gold and Douglas S. Duckworth, 192–208. New York: Columbia University Press.

Garfield, Jay L. 2019b. *The Concealed Influence of Custom. Hume's Treatise from the Inside Out*. New York: Oxford University Press.

Garfield, Jay L. 2021. *Buddhist Ethics: A Philosophical Exploration*. New York: Oxford University Press.

Garfield, Jay L., Stephen Jenkins, and Graham Priest. 2015. "The Śāntideva Passage." In *Moonpaths: Ethics and Emptiness* by The Cowherds, 55–76. New York: Oxford University Press.

Gethin, Rupert. 1997. "Cosmology and Meditation: From the Aggañña-Sutta to the Mahāyāna." *History of Religions* 36(3): 183–217.

Gethin, Rupert. 1998. *The Foundations of Buddhism*. Oxford: Oxford University Press.

Gethin, Rupert. 2001. *The Buddhist Path to Awakening*. Oxford: Oneworld Publications.

Giustarini, Giuliano. 2012. "The role of fear (*bhaya*) in the Nikayas and in the Abhidhamma." *Journal of Indian Philosophy* 40: 511–31.

Gold, Jonathan. 2018. "Freedom through Cumulative Moral Cultivation: Heroic Willpower (*Vīrya*)." *Journal of Buddhist Ethics* 25: 742–66.

Gold, Jonathan, and Douglas Duckworth, eds. 2019. *Readings of Śāntideva's Guide to Bodhisattva Practice*. New York: Columbia University Press.

Gómez, Luis O. 1973. "Emptiness and Moral Perfection." *Philosophy East and West* 23(3): 361–73.

Gómez, Luis O. 1995. "A Mahāyāna Liturgy." In *Buddhism in Practice*, edited by Donald S. Lopez, Jr. Princeton: Princeton University Press.

Gómez, Luis O. 1999. "The Way of the Translators: Three Recent Translations of Śāntideva's *Bodhicaryāvatāra*." *Buddhist Literature* 1: 262–354.

Goodman, Charles. 2002. "Resentment and Reality: Buddhism on Moral Responsibility." *American Philosophical Quarterly* 39(4): 359–72.

Goodman, Charles. 2008. "Consequentialism, Agent-Neutrality, and Mahayana Ethics." *Philosophy East and West* 58(1): 17–35.

Goodman, Charles. 2009. *Consequences of Compassion: An Interpretation and Defense of Buddhist Ethics*. Oxford: Oxford University Press.

Goodman, Charles. 2015. "From Madhyamaka to Consequentialism: A Roadmap." In *Moonpaths: Ethics and Emptiness* by The Cowherds. New York: Oxford University Press.

Goodman, Charles. 2016a. *The Training Anthology of Śāntideva: A Translation of the Śikṣā-samuccaya*. New York: Oxford University Press.

Goodman, Charles. 2016b. "Śāntideva." In *The Stanford Encyclopedia of Philosophy*, edited by Edward N. Zalta. <https://plato.stanford.edu/archives/fall2016/entries/shantideva/>.

Gowans, Christopher. 2014. *Buddhist Moral Philosophy: An Introduction*. New York: Routledge.

Gowans, Christopher. 2021. *Self-Cultivation Philosophies in Ancient India, Greece, and China*. New York: Oxford University Press.

Griffiths, Paul. 1994. *On Being Buddha: The Classical Doctrine of Buddhahood.* New York: SUNY Press.

Gunaratana, Henepola. 1980. *A Critical Analysis of the Jhānas in Theravāda Buddhist Meditation.* Buddhist Dharma Education Association Inc.

Gyatso, Janet. 2019. "Seeing from All Sides." In *Readings of Śāntideva's Guide to Bodhisattva Practice*, edited by Jonathan Gold and Douglas Duckworth, 99–113. New York: Columbia University Press.

Hanner, Oren. 2021. "In Search of Buddhist Virtue: A Case for a Pluralist-Gradualist Moral Philosophy." *Comparative Philosophy* 12(2): 58–78.

Harris, Stephen E. 2011. "Does Anātman Rationally Entail Altruism? On *Bodhicaryāvatāra* 8:101–103." *Journal of Buddhist Ethics* 18: 92–123.

Harris, Stephen E. 2014a. "Suffering and the Shape of Well-Being in Buddhist Ethics." *Asian Philosophy* 24(3): 242–59.

Harris, Stephen E. 2014b. *Demandingness, Self-Interest and Benevolence in Śāntideva's Introduction to the Practice of Awakening (Bodhicaryāvatāra).* PhD diss., University of New Mexico.

Harris, Stephen E. 2015a. "On the Classification of Śāntideva's Ethics in the *Bodhicaryāvatāra*." *Philosophy East and West* 65(1): 249–75.

Harris, Stephen E. 2015b. "Demandingness, Well-Being and the Bodhisattva Path." *Sophia* 54(2): 201–16.

Harris, Stephen E. 2017. "The Skillful Handling of Poison: *Bodhicitta* and the *Kleśas* in Śāntideva's *Bodhicaryāvatāra*." *Journal of Indian Philosophy* 45(2): 331–48.

Harris, Stephen E. 2018a. "A Nirvana that is Burning in Hell: Pain and Flourishing in Mahayana Buddhist Moral Thought." *Sophia* 57(2): 337–47.

Harris, Stephen E. 2018b. "Promising Across Lives to Save Non-Existent Beings: Identity, Rebirth and the Bodhisattva's Vow." *Philosophy East and West* 68(2): 386–407.

Harris, Stephen E. 2018c. "Altruism in the Charnel Ground: Śāntideva and Parfit on Anātman, Reductionism and Benevolence." In *Ethics without Self, Dharma without Atman: Western and Buddhist Philosophical Traditions in Dialogue*, edited by Gordon Davis, 219–34. New York: Springer.

Harris, Stephen E. 2021. "Śāntideva's Introduction to the Practices of Awakening (*Bodhicaryāvatāra*)." *Oxford Research Encyclopedias: Religion*. Oxford: Oxford University Press. https://oxfordre.com/religion/view/10.1093/acrefore/9780199340378.001.0001/acrefore-9780199340378-e-727.

Harris, Stephen E. 2022. "Śāntideva: Virtue on the Empty Path of the Bodhisattva." In *The Routledge Handbook of Indian Buddhist Philosophy*, edited by William Edelglass, Sara McClintock, and Pierre-Julien Harter, 511–27. New York: Routledge.

Harrison, Paul. 1987. "Who gets to ride in the Great Vehicle: Self-Image and Identity among the followers of the early Mahāyāna." *Journal of the International Association of Buddhist Studies* 10(1): 67–89.

Harrison, Paul, 2007, "The Case of the Vanishing Poet: New Light on Śāntideva and the Śikṣā-Samuccaya." In *Indica et Tibetica: Festschrift für Michael Hahn*, edited by Konrad. Klaus and Jens-Uwe Hartmann, 215–48. Zum 65. Vienna: Geburtstag von Freunden und Schülern überreicht.

Harrison, Paul. 2019. "Śāntideva: The Author and His Project." In *Readings of Śāntideva's Guide to Bodhisattva Practice*, edited by Jonathan Gold and Douglas Duckworth, 27–44. New York: Columbia University Press.

Harvey, Peter. 1995. *The Selfless Mind: Personality, Consciousness and Nirvāṇa in Early Buddhism*. New York: RoutledgeCurzon.

Harvey, Peter. 2000. *An Introduction to Buddhist Ethics*. Cambridge: Cambridge University Press.

Hayes, Richard P. 1996. "Ritual, Self-deception and Make-Believe: A Classical Buddhist Perspective." In *Self and Deception: A Cross-Cultural Philosophical Enquiry*, edited by Roger Ames and Wimal Dissanayake, 349–64. Albany, NY: State University of New York Press.

Heim, Maria. 2004. *Theories of the Gift in South Asia: Hindu, Buddhist and Jain Reflections on Dāna*. New York and Oxford: Routledge.

Heim, Maria. 2017. "Buddhaghosa on the Phenomenology of Love and Compassion." In *The Oxford Handbook of Indian Philosophy*, edited by Jonardon Ganeri, 171–89. New York: Oxford University Press.

Heim, Maria. 2020. *Buddhist Ethics*. Cambridge: Cambridge University Press.

Hirst, Jacqueline. 2005. *Śaṃkara's Advaita Vedānta: A Way of Teaching*. New York: Routledge.

Hume, David. 2007. *A Treatise of Human Nature*. Oxford: Oxford University Press.

Huntington, Erik. 2018. *Creating the Universe: Depictions of the Cosmos in Himalayan Buddhism*. Seattle: University of Washington Press.

Huntington, Erik. 2019. "Ritual Structure and Material Culture in the Guide to Bodhisattva Practice." In *Readings of Śāntideva's Guide to Bodhisattva Practice*, edited by Jonathan Gold and Douglas Duckworth, 132–45. New York: Columbia University Press.

Hursthouse, Rosalind. 1999. *On Virtue Ethics*. Oxford: Oxford University Press.

Irwin, Terence. 1995. *Plato's Ethics*. Oxford: Oxford University Press.

Jackson, Roger. 2019. "Taming Śāntideva: Tsongkhapa's Use of the *Bodhicaryāvatāra*." In *Readings of Śāntideva's Guide to Bodhisattva Practice*, edited by Jonathan Gold and Douglas Duckworth, 162–79. New York: Columbia University Press.

Jaini, Padmanabh S. 1992. "On the Ignorance of the Arhat." In *Paths to Liberation: The Mārga and Its Transformation in Buddhist Thought*, edited by Robert Buswell and Robert Gimello, 135–45. Honolulu: University of Hawai'i Press.

Jenkins, Stephen. 1999. *The Circle of Compassion: An interpretive study of Karuna in Indian Buddhist literature*. PhD diss., Harvard University.

Jenkins, Stephen. 2015a. "Waking into Compassion: the Three *Ālambana* of *Karuṇā*." In *Moonpaths: Ethics and Emptiness* by the Cowherds, 97–118. New York: Oxford University Press.

Jenkins, Stephen. 2015b. "Benefit of Self and Other: The Importance of Persons and their Self-Interest in Buddhist Ethics." *Dharma Drum Journal of Buddhist Studies* 16: 141–69.

Jenkins, Stephen. 2021. "Compassion blesses the compassionate." In *Buddhist Visions of the Good Life for All*, edited by Sallie King. London: Routledge.

Jinpa, Thupten. 2019. "*Bodhicaryāvatāra* and Tibetan Mind Training (*Lojong*)." In *Readings of Śāntideva's Guide to Bodhisattva Practice*, edited by Jonathan Gold and Douglas Duckworth, 146–61. New York: Columbia University Press.

Kagan, Shelly. 1998. "Rethinking Intrinsic Value." *The Journal of Ethics* 2(4): 277–97.

Kajiyama, Yuichi. 1989. "Transfer and Transformation of Merits in Relation to Emptiness." In *Studies in Buddhist Philosophy*, edited by Katsumi Mimaki, 1–20. Kyoto: Rinsen Book Co. Ltd.

Kapstein, Matthew. 2013. "Stoics and Bodhisattvas: Spiritual Exercise and Faith in Two Philosophical Traditions." In *Philosophy as a Way of Life: Ancients and Moderns – Essays in Honor of Pierre Hadot*, edited by Michael Chase, Stephen R. L. Clark, and Michael McGhee, 99–115. Chichester: Wiley-Blackwell.

Keown, Damien. 1992. *The Nature of Buddhist Ethics*. New York: Palgrave Macmillan.

Kierkegaard, Soren. 1983. *The Sickness Unto Death: A Christian Psychological Exposition for Upbuilding and Awakening*. Translated by Howard V. Hong and Edna H. Hong. Princeton: Princeton University Press.

Korsgaard, Christine. 1982. "Two Distinctions in Goodness." *The Philosophical Review* 92(2): 169–95.

Leighton, Taigen Dan. 2012. *Faces of Compassion: Classical Bodhisattva Archetypes and Their Modern Expression*. Boston, MA: Wisdom.

Lele, Amod Jayant. 2007. *Ethical Revaluation in the Thought of Śāntideva*. PhD diss., Harvard University.

Lele, Amod Jayant. 2013. "The Compassionate Gift of Vice: Śāntideva on Gifts, Altruism, and Poverty." *Journal of Buddhist Ethics* 20: 701–34.

Lele, Amod Jayant. 2015. "The Metaphysical Basis of Śāntideva's Ethics." *Journal of Buddhist Ethics* 22: 249–83.

Li, Jingjing. 2016. "Buddhist Phenomenology and the Problem of Essence." *Comparative Philosophy* 7(1): 59–89.

Li, Jingjing. 2022. *Comparing Husserl's Phenomenology and Chinese Yogacara in a Multicultural World*. New York and London: Bloomsbury.

Locke, Jessica. 2018. "Training the Mind and Transforming Your World: Moral Phenomenology in the Tibetan Buddhist *Lojong* Tradition." *Comparative and Continental Philosophy* 10(3): 251–63.

Lorde, Audrey. 1997. "The Uses of Anger." *Women's Studies Quarterly* 25(1/2): 278–85.
Lusthaus, Dan. 2002. *Buddhist Phenomenology: A Philosophical Investigation of Yogacara Buddhism and the Ch'eng Weishih Lun*. New York: Routledge.
Mackenzie, Matthew. 2018. "Buddhism and the Virtues." In *The Oxford Handbook of Virtue*, edited by Nancy E. Snow, 153–70. New York: Oxford University Press.
Mahoney, Richard. 2002. *Of the Progresse of the Bodhisattva: The Bodhisattvamārga in the Śikṣāsamuccaya*. MA thesis, University of Canterbury.
McRae, Emily. 2012. "Emotions, Ethics and Choice: Lessons from Tsongkhapa." *Journal of Buddhist Ethics* 19: 344–69.
McRae, Emily. 2015. "Metabolizing Anger: A Tantric Buddhist Solution to the Problem of Moral Anger." *Philosophy East and West* 65(2): 466–84.
Meadows, Carol. 1976. *Ārya-Śūra's Compendium of the Perfections: Translation and Analysis of the Pāramitāsamāsa*. PhD diss., Columbia University.
Mill, John Stuart. 1979. *Utilitarianism*. Indianapolis: Hackett Publishing Company.
Mrozik, Susanne. 2007. *Virtuous Bodies: The Physical Dimensions of Morality in Buddhist Ethics*. Oxford: Oxford University Press.
Nāgārjuna. 1998. *Nāgārjuna's Precious Garland: Buddhist Advice for Living and Liberation*. Translated by Jeffrey Hopkins. Ithaca, NY: Snow Lion.
Nāgārjuna. 2013. *Nāgārjuna's Middle Way: Mūlamadhyamakakārikā*. Translated by Mark Siderits and Shoryu Katsura. Boston, MA: Wisdom.
Ñānamoli and Bodhi, trans. 1995. *The Middle Length Discourses of the Buddha*. Boston, MA: Wisdom.
Nattier, Jan. 2003. *A Few Good Men: The Bodhisattva Path according to The Inquiry of Ugra (Ugraparipṛcchā)*. Honolulu: University of Hawai'i Press.
Nelson, Barbara. 2021. *Kṣānti in the bodhisattva path of Śāntideva*. PhD diss., University of Sydney. Revised edition.
Nussbaum, Martha C. 1994. *The Therapy of Desire: Theory and Practice in Hellenistic Ethics*. Princeton: Princeton University Press.
Nussbaum, Martha C. 2016. *Anger and Forgiveness: Resentment, Generosity, Justice*. New York: Oxford University Press.
Ohnuma, Reiko. 2006. *Head, Eyes, Flesh, Blood: Giving Away the Body in Indian Buddhist Literature*. New York: Columbia University Press.
Ohnuma, Reiko. 2019. "Bodies and Embodiment in the Bodhicaryāvatāra." In *Readings of Śāntideva's Guide to Bodhisattva Practice*, edited by Jonathan C. Gold and Douglas S. Duckworth, 114–31. New York: Columbia University Press.
Oldmeadow, Peter. 1994. *A Study of the Wisdom Chapter (Prajñāpāramitā Pariccheda) of the Bodhicaryāvatārapañjikā*. PhD diss., Australian National University.
Pelden, Kunzang. 2010. *The Nectar of Manjushri's Speech: A Detailed Commentary on Shantideva's Way of the Bodhisattva*. Translated by the Padmakara Translation Group. Boston, MA, and London: Shambhala.

Pettit, John. 1999. "Paul Williams: Altruism and Reality: Studies in the Philosophy of the Bodhicaryāvatāra." *Journal of Buddhist Ethics* 6: 120–37.
Powers, John. 2007. *Introduction to Tibetan Buddhism*. Revised edition. Ithaca, NY: Snow Lion.
Railton, Peter. 1984. "Alienation, Consequentialism, and the Demands of Morality." *Philosophy and Public Affairs* 13(2): 134–71.
Reeves, Gene, trans. 2008. *The Lotus Sutra*. Boston, MA: Wisdom.
Repetti, Rick. 2010. "Meditation and Mental Freedom: A Buddhist Theory of Free Will." *Journal of Buddhist Ethics* 17: 165–212.
Repetti, Rick. 2019. *Buddhism, Meditation, and Free Will: A Theory of Mental Freedom*. New York: Routledge.
Rhys Davids, T. W., trans. 1890. *The Questions of King Milinda*, 2 vols. The Sacred Books of the East; vols. 35–6. Oxford: Clarendon Press.
Ronkin, Noa. 2005. *Early Buddhist Metaphysics: The making of a philosophical tradition*. London and New York: RoutledgeCurzon.
Rotman, Andy. 2009. *Thus Have I Seen: Visualizing Faith in Early Indian Buddhism*. Oxford: Oxford University Press.
Saito, Akira. 1993. *A Study of Akṣayamati (=Śāntideva)'s Bodhisattvacaryāvatāra as Found in the Tibetan Manuscripts From Tun-Huang*. Project number 02801005, Faculty of Humanities, Miye University.
Saito, Akira. 1996. "Śāntideva in the History of Mādhyamika Philosophy." In *Buddhism in India and Abroad: An Integrating Influence in Vedic and Post-Vedic Perspective*, edited by Kalpakam Sankarnarayan, Motohiro Yoritomi, and Shubhada A. Joshi. Mumbai: Somaiya Publications Pvt. Ltd.
Saito, Akira. 2000. *A Study of the Dūn-Huáng Recension of the Bodhisattvacaryāvatāra*. Project Number 09610021, Faculty of Humanities, Miye University.
Samuels, Jeffrey. 1997. "The Bodhisattva Ideal in Theravāda Buddhist Theory and Practice: A Reevaluation of the Bodhisattva-Śrāvaka Opposition." *Philosophy East and West* 47(3): 399–415.
Śāntideva. 1970. *Entering the path of enlightenment: the Bodhicaryāvatāra of the Buddhist poet Śāntideva*. Translated by Marion L. Matics. New York: Macmillan.
Śāntideva. 1979. *A Guide to the Bodhisattva's way of life*. Translated by Stephen Batchelor. Dharmsala: Library of Tibetan Works & Archives.
Śāntideva. 1995. Reissued 2008. *The Bodhicaryāvatāra*. Translated by Kate Crosby and Andrew Skilton. Oxford: Oxford University Press.
Śāntideva. 1997. *A Guide to the Bodhisattva Way of Life (Bodhicaryāvatāra)*. Translated by Vesna and Alan Wallace. Ithaca, NY: Snow Lion.
Śāntideva. 2001. *The Bodhicharyāvatāra of Ārya Śāntideva with Commentary Pañjikā of Śri Prajñākaramatiī & Hindi Translation.* Edited and translated by Swāmī Dwārikādās Śāstrī. Varanasi: Bauddha Bharati.
Śāntideva. 2006. *The Way of the Bodhisattva: a translation of the Bodhicaryāvatāra*. Translated by the Padmakara Translation Group. Boston, MA: Shambhala.

Śāntideva. 2015. "How to Be a Bodhisattva: Introduction to the Practice of the Bodhisattva Path (The *Bodhicaryavatara*)." Translated by Luis Gomez in *The Norton Anthology of World Religions* vol. 1, edited by Donald S. Lopez (Buddhism editor), 1077–123. New York: W. W. Norton & Co:.

Śāntideva. 2016. *The Training Anthology of Śāntideva: A Translation of the Śikṣā-samuccaya*. Translated by Charles Goodman. New York: Oxford University Press.

Śāntideva. 2019. "Śāntideva's Bodhicaryāvatāra: A Translation." Translated by Ernst Steinkellner and Cynthia Peck-Kubaczek. In *Buddha-Mind – Christ Mind: A Christian Commentary on the Bodhicaryāvatāra*. Leuven: Peeters Publishers.

Schechtman, Marya. 2007. "Stories, Lives, and Basic Survival: A Refinement and Defense of the Narrative View." *Royal Institute of Philosophy Supplement* 60: 155–78.

Schmidt-Leukel, Perry. 2019. *Buddha-Mind – Christ Mind: A Christian Commentary on the Bodhicaryāvatāra*. Leuven: Peeters Publishers.

Segall, Seth Zuihō. 2020. *Buddhism and Human Flourishing: A Modern Western Perspective*. New York: Palgrave Macmillan.

Siderits, Mark. 2000. "The Reality of Altruism: Reconstructing Śāntideva." *Philosophy East & West* 50(3): 412–24.

Siderits, Mark. 2003. *Personal Identity and Buddhist Philosophy*. Burlington, VT: Ashgate.

Siderits, Mark. 2004. "Causation and Emptiness in early Madhyamaka." *Journal of Indian Philosophy* 32(4): 393–419.

Siderits, Mark. 2007. "Buddhist Reductionism and the Structure of Buddhist Ethics." In *Indian Ethics: Classical Traditions and Contemporary Challenges*, vol. 1, edited by P. Bilimoria, J. Prabhu, and R. Sharma, 283–96. Burlington, VT: Ashgate.

Silk, Jonathon. 2002. "What, If Anything, is Mahāyāna Buddhism? Problems of Definitions and Classifications. *Numen* 49: 355–405.

Simonds, Colin. 2021. "Buddhist Ethics as Moral Phenomenology: A Defense and Development of the Theory." *Journal of Buddhist Ethics* 28: 338–402.

Snow, Nancy. 2020. "Metaphysics, Virtue and *Eudaimonia* in Aristotle and Buddhism." In *Naturalism, Human Flourishing, and Asian Philosophy: Owen Flanagan and Beyond*, edited by Bongrae Seok, 74–91. New York: Routledge.

Sonam, Kunzang. 2019. *The Profound Reality of Interdependence*. Translated by Douglas Duckworth. Oxford: Oxford University Press.

Sumanacara, Ashin. 2019. "The Experience of *Dukkha* and *Domanassa* among Puthujjanas." *Journal of Buddhist Ethics* 26: 107–38.

Sweet, Michael J. 1977. *Śāntideva and the Mādhyamika: The Prajñāpāramitā-Pariccheda of the Bodhicaryāvatāra*. PhD diss., University of Wisconsin-Madison.

Sweet, Michael. 1979. "*Bodhicaryāvatāra* 9.2 as a Focus for Tibetan Interpretations of the Two Truths in the Prāsaṅgika Mādhyamika." *Journal of Indian Philosophy* 2(2): 79–89.

Thomson, Iain. 2013. "Death and Demise in *Being and Time*." In *The Cambridge Companion to Heidegger's Being and Time*, edited by Mark A. Wrathall, 260–90. New York: Cambridge University Press.

Thurman, Robert A. F., trans. [1976] 2003. *The Holy Teaching of Vimalakīrti: A Mahāyāna Scripture*. University Park: Pennsylvania State University Press.

Thurman, Robert A. F., ed. 2004. *The Universal Vehicle Discourse Literature (Mahāyānasūtrālaṃkāra)*. Translated by L. Jamspal, R. Clark, J. Wilson et al. New York: American Institute of Buddhist Studies.

Tillemans, Tom J. 2007. "Trying to be Fair to Madhyamika Buddhism." In *Expanding and Merging Horizons*, edited by Karin Preisedanz. Vienna: Austrian Academy of Sciences Press.

Tillemans, Tom J. 2008. "Reason, Irrationality and *Akrasia* (Weakness of the Will) in Buddhism: Reflections upon Śāntideva's Arguments with Himself." *Argumentation*. 22: 149–63.

Tillemans, Tom J. 2010/11. "Madhyamaka Buddhist Ethics." *Journal of the International Association of Buddhist Studies* 33(1–2): 353–72.

Tillemans, Tom J. 2011. "How Far Can a Mādhyamika Buddhist Reform Conventional Truth? Dismal Relativism, Fictionalism, Easy-Easy Truth, and the Alternatives." In *Moonshadows: Conventional Truth in Buddhist Philosophy* by The Cowherds, 151–66. New York: Oxford University Press.

Todd, Warren Lee. 2013. *The Ethics of Śaṅkara and Śāntideva. A Selfless Response to an Illusory World*. New York: Routledge.

Tsong-Kha-Pa. 2000. *The Great Treatise on the Stages of the Path to Enlightenment: Lam Rim Chen Mo*, vol 1. Translated by the Lamrim Chenmo Translation Committee. Ithaca, NY: Snow Lion.

Vaidya, P. L. 1960. *Bodhicaryāvatāra of Śāntideva with the commentary Pañjikā of Prajñākaramati*. Edited by P.L. Vaidya. BuddhistSanskrit Texts, no. 12. Darbhanga: The Mithila Institute of Post-Graduate Studies and Research in Sanskrit Learning.

Vaidya, P. L. 1961. *Śikṣāsamuccaya of Śāntideva*. Edited by P. L. Vaidya. Darbhanga: Mithila Institute of Post-Graduate Studies and Research in Sanskrit Learning.

Van Norden, Bryan. 2019. "Mencius." *Stanford Encyclopedia of Philosophy*, Fall 2019 Edition, edited by Edward N. Zalta. <https://plato.stanford.edu/archives/fall2019/entries/mencius/>.

Vasubandhu. 1988. *Abhidharmakośa*. Translated by La Vallee Poussin. English translation by Leo M. Pruden. Berkeley: Asian Humanities Press.

Vélez de Cea. 2010. "Value Pluralism in Early Buddhism." *Journal of the International Association of Buddhist Studies* 33: 211–37.

Vernezze, Peter. 2008. "Moderation or the Middle Way: Two Approaches to Anger." *Philosophy East and West* 58(1): 2–16.

Waldron, William S. 2003. *The Buddhist Unconscious: The ālaya-vijñāna in the context of Indian Buddhist Thought*. London and New York: RoutledgeCurzon.

Wallace, Vesna, and Alan Wallace. 1997. Introduction to *A Guide to the Bodhisattva Way of Life* (*Bodhicaryāvatāra*) by Śāntideva, 11–13. Oxford: Oxford University Press.
Walshe, Maurice, trans. 1995. *The Long Discourses of the Buddha (Dīgha Nikāya*). Boston, MA: Wisdom.
Wangchuk, Dorji. 2007. *The Resolve to Become a Buddha: A Study of the Bodhicitta Concept in Indo-Tibetan Buddhism.* International Institute for Buddhist Studies of the International College for Postgraduate Buddhist Studies.
Westerhoff, Jan. 2009. *Madhyamaka: A Philosophical Introduction*. Oxford: Oxford University Press.
Westerhoff, Jan. 2010a. *Twelve Examples of Illusion*. Oxford: Oxford University Press.
Westerhoff, Jan. 2010b. *The Dispeller of Disputes: Nagarjuna's Vigrahavyāvartanī*. New York: Oxford University Press.
Westerhoff, Jan. 2018. *The Golden Age of Indian Buddhist Philosophy*. Oxford: Oxford University Press.
Wetlesen, Jon. 2002. "Did Śāntideva Destroy the Bodhisattva Path?" *Journal of Buddhist Ethics* 9: 34–88.
Whitehill, James. 1994. "Buddhist Ethics in Western Context: The Virtues Approach." *The Journal of Buddhist Ethics* 1: 1–22.
Williams, Paul. 1998. *Altruism and Reality: Studies in the Philosophy of the Bodhicaryāvatāra*. Richmond: Curzon.
Williams, Paul. 2009. *Mahāyāna Buddhism: The Doctrinal Foundations*. 2nd edition. New York: Routledge.
Williams, Paul. 2010. "Is Buddhist Ethics Virtue Ethics." In *Destroying Mara Forever: Buddhist Ethics Essays in Honor of Damien Keown*, edited by John Powers and Charles Prebish, 113–40. Ithaca, NY: Snow Lion.
Williams, Paul, with Anthony Tribe. 2000. *Buddhist Thought: A Complete Introduction to the Indian Tradition*. New York: Routledge.
Wright, Dale. 2009. *The Six Perfections: Buddhism and the Cultivation of Character*. Oxford: Oxford University Press.

INDEX

www.ingramcontent.com/pod-product-compliance
Ingram Content Group UK Ltd.
Pitfield, Milton Keynes, MK11 3LW, UK
UKHW020732280225
455688UK00012B/621

9 781350 379534